KT-488-608

atching The Daisies

Lessons on the Importance of Slow

Brigid P. Gallagher

978-0-9935923-6-2

Copyright © 2017 Brigid P. Gallagher

All rights reserved. No part of this book may be reproduced, stored in a retrieval system, or transmitted by any means, electronic, mechanical, photocopying, recording or otherwise without written permission from the author. Published in Ireland by Orla Kelly Publishing.

The ideas and suggestions in this book are not intended as a substitute for the medical advice of a trained professional. All matters regarding your health require medical supervision. Consult your physician about any condition that may require diagnosis or medical attention. The author disclaims any liability arising directly or indirectly from the use of this book.

The conversations in the book all come from the author's recollections, and are not written to represent word for word transcripts. The author has retold them in a way that evokes the feeling and meaning of what was said, and in all instances the essence of the dialogue is correct.

A must read for anyone who loved Eat, Pray, Love

A very enjoyable biography from Brigid, who experienced childhood tragedy in the loss of her young mother and went on to become one of the first champions of alternative healing in Scotland.

Her story takes you through her childhood in Kippen to the smorgasbord of natural therapies and healings in which she trained, through to her own serious health struggles with fibromyalgia and rheumatoid arthritis. She finds healing in many travels and immerses herself in her love of gardening where she learns the joys of slow and "watching the daisies".

Like "Eat, Pray, Love" Brigid's is a spiritual journey, the insights from each chapter were lovely. I recommend this book to anyone who has struggled through poor health. The book carries a message of hope as Brigid perseveres with her search for both spiritual and physical healing.

Amazon Customer

Sowing Seeds

As someone who has chronic health challenges, I embarked upon this journey with Brigid, seeing parallels in my own life, and found her approach refreshing and full of useful insights. Her love of gardening permeates her work and sows seeds to germinate in the minds of others who are also searching for answers.

Amazon Customer

Gentle, positive and wise

I read this book very quickly. I kept wanting to pick it up again. This memoir of a varied and interesting life is enriched by the author's expertise in complementary health and her openness to spirituality in its many forms.

One of the most resonant aspects for me was the impact of physical ill health and the all too familiar difficulties with diagnosis and treatment. I have lived with autoimmune disease for almost 10 years and I found the book to be affirming, informative and hopeful; whilst remaining realistic about the reality and challenges of these circumstances. Its overall message of the value in a slower pace of life emerges gradually and convincingly.

This memoir left me feeling more positive about the future and inspired by the possibility of a different, more fulfilling way of life.

Amazon Customer

An inspiring read with evocative descriptions of the author's journeys...

An inspiring read with evocative descriptions of the author's journeys. Lots of learning points and suggestions. It shows that you can overcome all sorts of problems by slowing down, taking stock and following your heart.

Amazon Customer

Brigid does a great job in capturing her journey of health challenges...

Brigid does a great job in capturing her journey of health challenges and bringing spirituality to life to help a person move through difficult times.

Divya Parekh

Author of "The Entrepreneur's Garden: The Nine essential relationships to Cultivate Your Wildly Successful Business"

A wonderful insightful book!

A wonderful book! I forced myself to put it down a couple of times because I didn't want to stop travelling vicariously with the author. Gallagher has written a memoir that takes to many beautiful countries but also on her journey of family loss, health and commitment to learning. Her gifts as a healer and gardener add to the beauty of the book.

Alexis Rose

Author of "Untangled: A Story of Resilience, Courage and Triumph"

Brigid is fortunate enough to have a kind of sixth sense and...
Brigid P. Gallagher's "Watching the Daisies" is not only an armchair travellers dream, it is also a mine of information for anyone suffering from symptoms of fibromyalgia, fatigue, aches and pains, and irritable bowel problems in particular. Brigid is also fortunate enough to have a kind of sixth sense and can tell if people are ill or healthy by the colours around them. She is also an expert on natural medicines and horticulture...
Stevie Turner
Author of "Waiting in the Wings"

A thrilling and informative memoir
What a great story! An alternative treatment pioneer who perseveres through countless personal and medical challenges to learn and help many. This book is extremely well written and you won't be able to put it down. It is a charming read and makes you feel that you are everywhere Brigid travels from the UK to Majorca, Spain and much more.

It is also a primer on alternative healing techniques from reflexology to crystal therapy to aromatherapy to colour therapy to auras.

You will learn about the author's battles with various medical conditions from dental abscesses to depression to fibromyalgia and a lot about the history of alternative practices such as Bach Flower Essences and Electro-Crystal Healing.

One of my favourite parts of the book was the description of essential oil treatment and the fact that" chemical constituents of oils" travel up the olfactory nerve to the limbic system of the brain and so can affect "memory and emotion." I thus learned scientifically why and how this type of therapy actually works.

All in all, this is a wonderful read that will teach you a lot about yourself and personal stamina and alternative treatments. Don't miss it.
James D. Okun M.D.
Author of "The History of New Innovations in Modern Medicine: New Thought and the Threat to Traditional Medicine."

"Dedicated to all my loved ones-both in this life and the next."

"Adopt the speed of nature; her secret is patience."

Ralph Waldo Emerson

Contents

Prologue

Rainbows over Belfast – August 2012

"To watch us dance is to hear our hearts speak."
Hopi Indian saying

I am standing in front of the mirror in my bedroom at The Europa Hotel, applying a sparkly aubergine eye shadow, similar to Biba's Metallic Grandma of my youth. My coral lip gloss matches my cheesecloth top. I layer up with my cool dude black leather jacket and finish the look with a scarf in shades of pink, coral and turquoise.

Showers are forecast, so I put my new maroon coloured mac in my handbag, just in case. There is now no room for my camera. I will live to regret this!

The evening is mellower now after the afternoon's downpours, as I walk towards Custom House Square, the venue for The Voice of Sir Tom Jones, legendary singer and sex bomb, ably supported by Belfast's own Brian Kennedy. I am already excited at the prospect of dancing outdoors among legions of loyal fans, many of them of a certain age like myself.

Tickets state that the gates open at 6pm, so I decide seven is a good time to arrive. My intuition serves me well, as I enter a small queue and await a handbag search by an efficient female PSNI officer. I continue past a series of white tents into a delightful square flanked by modern flats and the elegant neoclassical architecture of The Custom House.

A small row of dedicated fans have already gathered in front of the stage, clinging to silver metallic barriers for dear life. I'm hoping to find a space along the railing, but no such joy.

I stand behind two elderly ladies, one blonde and dressed in white, the other brunette with a stay-away aura. They're not for shifting. Neither is the girl to my right with titian hair and matching lips and eye shadow on pale skin that makes her look like Morticia from *The Addams Family*. She too demonstrates dogged determination as she extends her elbows as wide as possible across the barrier, resting her limp head atop the cool metal. Her boyfriend stands close by in loving admiration, despite his partner's space cadet demeanour; it must be love!

I attend to my own unloving thoughts, sending out a sea of pink light to my stoic companions.

The stage lights encircle Brian Kennedy, as he steps onto the stage dressed in formal black. A smiling, attractive blonde lady dressed in white stands beside me; she grabs my left arm high as Brian belts out "You Raise Me Up".

He continues to warm the cockles of our hearts wiggling his cute, shapely behind to a series of tunes, before leaving the stage to loud applause.

Seconds later, a series of efficient roadies dressed in sombre shades of black, grey and olive clear the stage for Sir Tom, before tuning guitars, taping song order sheets to the floor and laying out six cool glasses of water for our septuagenarian hero.

The two ladies in front, precision-apply shades of pink and red to their lips without the aid of a mirror. A pale grey mist of dry ice clouds covers the stage as Tom emerges to rapturous applause. He is dressed in dark grey from head to toe, topped by a silver beard and cropped curls, a more sophisticated look than his dyed days of the past. He now looks classy, mature and perhaps wise.

My new friend in white grabs my arm again as we dance joyfully to a series of hits including my favourite, "Mama Told Me Not to Come". A young girl behind me captures the moment for posterity on her iPhone. Tom is perhaps only 10 feet away and I miss my camera. He is radiating pure gold now as he gets into the groove of his spiritual destiny—to heal with his golden voice. He is embraced by the rainbow of stage lights above—magenta, crimson, green and pink—dancing to the words of each song.

"The Green, Green Grass of Home" brings more applause from his emerald audience as silver droplets of rain begin to fall. My maroon mac comes out of its pocket, as others don see-through ponchos in olive green emblazoned with JAMESON or clear white models inscribed with ABSOLUT.

Three young girls behind me bring out a brown, ribbed

cardboard banner with WE LOVE YOU TOM! on one side and CAN WE COME BACKSTAGE? IT'S COLD OUTSIDE! on the other.

Sensible women turn to folly, as knickers in every colour of the rainbow are launched towards the stage in the hope of catching their hero's attention. Tom doesn't blink an eyelid, as lace *sex bombs* continue to ricochet in shades of cerise, turquoise and red. I move sideways, making way for more lady *soldiers* to catch a better aim.

He removes his jacket and sings "You Can Leave Your Hat On", donning a silver silk scarf in the process, to match his grey ensemble, before waving his hips in his own charismatic way, while each word is sung tongue in cheek, with that inimitable twinkle in his eye.

Sadly, the performance ends, and although every muscle and joint in my body aches as I hobble back to my cosy hotel room, I am floating on an orange cloud of joy.

Dear reader, you may now wonder why my body was aching; you will find your answers if you read the remainder of my memoir!

I will though enlighten you over my fascination for colour.

I sense rainbows around everything, for I have been blessed with the gift of clairvoyance or clear seeing.

Insights from Rainbows over Belfast

- No matter how difficult your journey has been, you will find blessings on every corner.

Busy as a Bee

The Kippen Girls

"It takes a whole village to rear a child."

Nigerian proverb

I was born on March 8, 1955 at exactly 9pm. The moon was full in Virgo—the sign of the virgin, all very grounded and sensible—while the sun rose in the more sensitive, intuitive and dreamy sign of Pisces. I am therefore my own unique mix of the realms of Heaven and Earth!

My parents had met in their native Donegal, a county with breathtaking scenery including long stretches of windswept beaches, native peat bogs, majestic mountains and an abundance of freshwater lakes filled with fat trout that are a mecca for fishermen.

Mum was another Brigid, born in a townland known as Mullaghderg Mountain. She was the oldest daughter in a family of eleven and became a nurse, as did two of her four sisters.

Dad hailed from the nearby village of Mullaghduff and was christened Michael Gallagher. He was known locally as Mhicí Mhicí Eoin—a traditional way of naming— after his father, another Mhicí, and his grandfather, Eoin.

Dad and his handsome horse Prince transported turf, groceries and other utilities around the Rosses area of Donegal. Life was tough.

Sadly, unemployment has always been high in the northwest of Ireland, and emigration was the norm for many young people.

In the early 1950s, my parents were forced into emigration to Scotland, and Prince was sold. I believe Dad must have been heartbroken selling his beloved horse, for he never spoke of Prince to us children. Indeed, I never once saw him ride a horse.

I only heard Prince's story in recent years, when I was researching my ancestors. Dad's sister, Auntie Peggy had kept a treasured photograph of Prince pulling a wooden cart, with Dad's arm embracing his beloved equine friend. I copied and restored this precious image, and it is now framed among my cherished collection of family photographs. I like to think that Dad and Prince would be delighted.

On March 1, 1954, my parents married and moved to Callander, a pretty Perthshire town known as "The Gateway to the Highlands". I was born in a castle called Airthrey Castle, then a maternity hospital located near Bridge of Allan, Stirlingshire.

In 1956, we settled in the quaint village of Kippen, around ten miles from our previous home. Kippen was set on a hillside, with scenic views over a flat area of land known as the Carse, also home to the meandering River Forth. The Grampian Mountains could be seen in the distance. Our new home had a stunning backdrop, the steep Gargunnock and Fintry Hills, which have a similar topography to Sligo's Benbulbin.

The main street provided villagers, with three grocer's shops, a dressmaker's, a post office, two garages and a hotel called The Cross Keys. We lived on Fore Road, home to the Church of Scotland, an antique shop and another hotel—The Crown. Our house was called Beech Cottage and was situated right next to the village hall.

Kippen was a popular tourist destination, not least because it was home to the world's largest vine, housed in four greenhouses. The vineyard sadly closed in 1964, but I can still remember visiting the spot, located at the far end of the Main Street.

In Scotland, Dad found a new form of employment, on farms, creating clay tiled drains for waterlogged fields. He worked long hours to provide for his growing family. Margaret arrived thirteen months after me, and two years later the twins Marie and Ann, were born. Ann was such an unexpected surprise, that her first cot was a drawer!

My earliest memory is of feeling unwell, getting up from my bed in tears, and meandering through to the living room to complain to Mum and Dad.

Mum told me, "You always looked *green* as a baby!"

The doctor said my tonsils were unhealthy, so they were removed well before my second birthday. I can still recall being in a high sided cot in the children's ward of the local hospital. Sadly, the other children did not want to play with me, perhaps they felt I was too young and cramped their style. I know ice cream was used as part of a gentle diet after tonsillectomies. This may be why I acquired a life-long love of it!

I have always considered myself Irish, although I grew up in Scotland. Donegal was definitely in my blood, and Mum took us back there every summer but one, to holiday in her childhood home. In fact, the only summer we did not travel to Ireland, was when the twins were babies. Instead, Mum took us children to the seaside resort of Portobello— near Edinburgh—for a week by the beach. Dad continued to work.

We always travelled to Donegal on the Burns and Laird Line's Derry Boat, which sailed down the River Clyde from Glasgow, to the port of Derry in Northern Ireland. Buoyed with holiday excitement, we delighted in the adventure of sailing to Ireland in a private cabin, sleeping in bunk beds, and peering out of the porthole to view the Irish Sea.

The reason we had a cabin was that passengers without cabins suffered a very uncomfortable night sleeping on any available seat, and more often the floor, among a multitude of drunken Irishmen, excited at the prospect of going home. The air was usually putrid with vomit and the smell of diesel fumes. Thankfully, I have always had good *sea legs*, and I was never seasick. A taxi driver from the local village of Annagry, called Anthony McGinley or Anthony Dora (after his mother—don't ask me about the logic), collected us for the final part of the trip to Donegal. He was a natural comedian and amused us all by pressing his nose to sound the car horn.

"Press your nose, please press your nose," we children cried out in unison!

The car horn would then sound, causing all bystanders to turn and stare at the passing taxi. We could never fathom out how Anthony's *miracle* was executed, but it certainly helped shorten the journey!

Several hours later, we alighted at Mullaghderg Mountain, about three miles from the village of Kincasslagh. Our maternal grandfather's home was located around two miles by track from the main road. It enjoyed stunning views across Mullaghderg Lake and beyond to the Atlantic Ocean. *Grandja* had added a two-storey extension to the original family home, on his return from working in the oilfields of Bayonne, New Jersey, making the house quite *grand*, compared with many others in the Rosses.

Mullaghderg Mountain was far away from shops, but most people were very self-sufficient in 1960s rural Ireland. Grandja grew many of his own vegetables and reared chickens and cows, while the Temple Crone Co-op delivered other essential groceries once a week in the *Cope* van.

I usually slept in an outside barn bedroom above the cow byre, with two of my aunts who filled my head with lots of esoteric stories of fairies, banshees and ghosts. My first holiday walk always included a visit to two fairy dells, hidden among rocks and overgrown with vegetation. They had an otherworldly atmosphere.

Other less esoteric holiday activities included playing outside, visiting neighbours for a chat, and swimming in the lake—in all weathers. I loved the feel of the cool fresh water on my skin, and I could happily have swum for ever…

On Sundays, we walked around three miles each way, to mass in Kincasslagh Parish. We donned old shoes to hike to the main road, hid them among long grass or bushes, and then changed into pristine white shoes for the remainder of the *marathon* on a tarred road. A small shop, at the gates to the church, provided us all with a delicious treat after mass—a choc ice. Thus replenished, we walked the long road back home.

I was eight years old when Grandja died. My memories of his final summer include queuing at his bedside, before getting a goodnight sweetie, usually a Smartie.

He would then say, "Omnia, saecula saeculorum." A literal translation being, "Forever and ever."

I cherish a photograph of him standing over me as though he is *my minder*; I like to think he does watch over me from Heaven. When he passed over, he was reunited with my grandmother, who had died of breast cancer, aged forty, when her youngest child Bernadette, was only four months old. Mum had only been eighteen.

Dad's family were victims of a similar tragedy; his father died when Dad was only five, the youngest in a family of eleven. Uncle Owenie was still only a teenager, when he took on his father's old job as a council worker, to provide for his widowed mother and the younger members of the family. The two oldest children, Brigid and Mary had already emigrated to New York, to find a better quality of life—a poignant tragedy that still continues for *Irish children* today.

Our summer holiday always included several visits to our paternal granny, nicknamed Granny Mullaghdoo. She dressed in black, like many of her widowed peers, and her hair was tied back in a bun. Her youngest daughter, my Auntie Peggy, stayed at home taking care of her mother, until her death in 1969, at the age of eighty-six.

Dad continued to work in Scotland for the first month of our holidays, only taking two weeks' vacation for himself. Every August he travelled with the car to Donegal, where we usually created a homecoming variety concert in his honour. Of course we all had to dress up for the occasion, clad in old clothes from a dressing-up box, complete with high heels, and assorted gaudy jewellery. We loved to sing and learned lots of traditional Irish ballads for our repertoire.

Dad's favourite tune was "The Homes of Donegal". He would often say to us, "Come on, girls, please sing my favourite song."

We did not need a lot of encouragement and would launch into the song.

I feel very tearful now, for it brings back so many poignant memories.

I hated leaving Donegal at the end of the summer holidays, and I was often despondent for weeks. I missed the people, the scenery and the *magic*. However, I was incredibly lucky to attend a great village school back in Kippen, with about one hundred pupils, three female teachers, and the headmaster—a Mr Siddle. As classes were small, we were always given lots of individual attention.

Miss Murray was the kind infant teacher, who taught us basic writing and arithmetic skills, known as *sums*. We created imaginary shops in her classroom, using empty tea packets, jam jars and tins. We would then take turns at playing shopkeeper or housewife, learning how to do basic mental arithmetic in the process.

Every morning we had a chance to stand in front of the blackboard and tell our classmates any exciting news. One momentous morning stands out in my memories, when I told my classmates, "Our cat Sooty had four kittens yesterday. We christened them John, Paul, George and Ringo, after the Beatles. Poor Ringo died…"

Tears and sighs followed for Ringo.

Sooty's remaining offspring soon found new homes, and she went off to the vet to be neutered. We returned from school one day with *twenty questions*, about the stitches on her tummy and her shaved fur. I didn't understand their significance for many years to come!

Sooty was a very docile pussycat, and we often took her to the village shops in a doll's pram, where she would lie quietly, smiling at us from under the pram hood. Passers-by would peer inside and see a contented, coal black cat instead of a doll!

When we reached the age of six, Mum taught us all the catechism, to prepare us for our First Holy Communion.

The parish priest would then *test our faith* asking, "Who made you?"

And, "What is the difference between a mortal and a venial sin?"

I could not tell you the *correct answer* now!

Dad often worked on Sundays, but Mum always ensured we attended mass in St Mary's Parish, Stirling, taking us all on the bus—quite an undertaking. She also instilled in us a dedication to Our Lady, The Virgin Mary. We created a special altar for her each May, atop a small table, covered with a lace tablecloth. We then adorned the table with Our Lady's statue, candles and spring flowers.

We learned an enormous amount about Jesus and the Bible, at Kippen Primary School, and I loved the story of Moses, the Prodigal Son, Lot and his wife…

After leaving the infants' room, it was a shock to discover my second teacher was less approachable. She was called Mrs Dippy (really) and was forever saying, "Shoosh, shoosh."

Miss Millar, our next teacher, had a stern exterior, but was really a big softie at heart. Her lessons included basic geometry and how to work with fractions. We also learned how to write with old-fashioned ink pens, dipped into inkwells on our desks. Everyone's writing looked much the same, for we had to copy each letter from charts on the wall. This was termed *real writing* but it did not encourage individuality or indeed creativity.

Once a week we had music lessons from a visiting teacher, Mr McKillop. He taught us how to read music, and we created a school choir. There was an annual Burns Festival in the village, and we competed against other local schools, for a variety of prizes in singing and poetry recitation. I longed to compete in the solo singing, but sadly missed out to a better singer called Marion Brown.

In my other worldly imagination, however, I was on stage singing:

"Ca' the yowes tae the knowes,
Ca' them whar the heather grows,
Ca' them where the burnie rows,
My bonie dearie..."

We had a great visiting art teacher who encouraged us to be more creative individuals. I loved painting and drawing, and I delighted in getting an art set from Santa one Christmas!

However, there was one subject I dreaded, and that was PE or physical education. We had to wear shorts and T-shirts, and jump over a wooden horse or climb along narrow benches. In good weather we played *Rounders* (similar to baseball) or sports such as high jump, long jump or running. I was pretty poor on all counts, despite my tall, slender frame. I loved swimming though and enjoyed visiting a local pool to perfect my technique. Mullaghderg Lake had thankfully given me a good start in the swimming stakes.

In the headmaster's class, we were all encouraged to write poetry and short stories, which I enjoyed. However, I hated learning grammar, as we had to answer lots of tedious questions with lengthy sentences. Ugh! I loved reading though, as it flew me away to other *imaginary worlds*.

Drama was another great *Piscean* love of mine. Mum's friend Mrs McGregor had created a drama club in the village hall, and we produced a number of pantomimes under her guidance. Although I was quite shy, I just loved being on the stage, and I was chosen to play Snow White in our performance of *Snow White and Rose Red*. Sadly, I did not get past rehearsals, for Mrs McGregor who was a heavy smoker, died suddenly from lung cancer. Although, I was really disappointed at not getting to play the lead role, I missed Mrs McGregor more, for she had been a very kindly mentor, and so full of *joie de vivre*.

I did, however, continue to *perform* in other ways. The White Heather Club was a popular television show with the comic singer Andy Stewart as host. The White Heather Club Dancers would dance as a backdrop to his songs, and we would imitate them, stripping down to our petticoats to dance up and down the living room while Andy sang the song "Donald Where's Yer Troosers"!

Oh to be a *fly on the wall!*

Mum took us to Glasgow to see Andy Stewart live in a Glasgow theatre once, and I also have fond memories of seeing other Scottish singers on the Glasgow stage, including The Alexander Brothers and Calum Kennedy.

Singing, drama, art and swimming, were not my only *passions*. I loved sewing, knitting and cooking—skills my mother had in spades. She passed these gifts to all of us in various combinations. Indeed, we could all cook and bake well, filling our kitchen and tummies with scones, buns, cakes, fudge…

Mary Berry would have been impressed!

Mum was also very stylish, wearing beautiful clothes she had often made on her Singer sewing machine, which sat in a corner of the living room. She looked like a movie star, dressed in her favourite long black dress which had a fitted bodice, a net petticoat, and a coral fabric rose highlighting her slender waistline. If she and

Dad were going to a dance in the village hall, she would come into our bedrooms to show us her dress and do a twirl.

Dad was a very handsome partner, with his dark wavy hair, his bright eyes and gentle smile. I always sensed that he and Mum were still very much in love, as they were always radiant in each other's company.

Aged twelve, it was time to attend St Modan's Secondary School, located ten miles away in St Ninians, on the outskirts of Stirling. This was a huge wrench for me as all my school friends from Kippen were going to the Protestant secondary school, ten miles in the opposite direction, in the town of Balfron. I so wished we could have all gone to the same school, and I had to start making a whole new group of friends.

It was a major logistical operation to get to St Modan's, for the *Kippen bus* arrived in central Stirling with only twenty minutes to spare, before the school bell. Unfortunately, there was often a shortage of spaces on connecting buses, and I generally arrived late. The school rector added to my *nightmare*, as he invariably waited by the school gates, chastising latecomers.

I still hate being late for anything, and I blame this paranoia on the *horror* of the school bus!

Sadly, Mum's health deteriorated after she lost two baby girls in the late stages of pregnancy. In a few short years, she also suffered a deep vein thrombosis followed by two strokes. The first stroke was devastating enough, when she lost the power in one hand—which she later regained—but the second stroke was even more shocking as she temporarily lost the power of speech. I do not know how she coped, for she was in my mind incredibly positive, and invariably smiling and laughing.

She was regularly confined to bed by the time I reached my teens. She also spent time in hospital in Glasgow, where they carried out extensive investigations. We travelled to Glasgow with Dad, remaining seated in the car outside. Antiquated rules prevented children from visiting hospitals, although I know seeing her four girls would have been a great tonic. My sisters Ann and Marie wrote her little letters while she was in hospital, enclosing some of Sooty's fur for solace.

Dad occasionally took us to Kippen graveyard, to visit the unmarked graves of our dear baby sisters. I realise now that grief was a regular visitor to our little family. Mum had lost a second baby after attending her brother Francie's funeral in Donegal, after he had tragically drowned aged just seventeen.

We were now proficient in housework, and the house was kept spick and span although we were still only fourteen, thirteen and eleven respectively. We created rotas for each household chore, including washing dishes, cooking meals and bringing in coal.

On Valentine's Day 1970, Mum said she felt unwell. Dad was working, so she quietly went to her bed until he returned. Dad then immediately phoned our GP Dr Scott, who ordered an ambulance. The sound of the ambulance bells ringing and the paramedics rushing in our front door did not shock me away from my love affair with *the box*, for I sat enchanted by the film *Houseboat* starring the beautiful Sophia Loren and her suitor, the handsome Cary Grant.

Sadly, my last glimpse of Mum came as she was carried through the front door on a stretcher.

She smiled weakly, saying, "I'll see you all tomorrow."

I smiled back at her and then continued to watch the film. If only I could turn back the clock!

Mum died the following morning. She was all alone, for the hospital had sent Dad home.

Dr Scott called later that day to offer his condolences. As always, he had such a kind and gentle manner. He told us Mum's heart had been badly damaged by the strokes, and there was nothing they could do to prolong her life.

She was only forty-two years of age.

I was only recently given a copy of her obituary, which read:

"The whole community has been greatly shocked to learn of the death of Mrs Michael Gallagher, Beech Cottage. Mrs Gallagher who was 42 years of age, died in Stirling Royal Infirmary in the early hours of Sunday. She had not enjoyed good health for some time but no one looked for her too early end. A native of Donegal, Mrs Gallagher and her husband and young family came to Kippen some fifteen years ago. Of an essentially bright and happy disposition, she quickly endeared herself in the village. She was a keen member of the W.R.I. and was also a most generous supporter of every good cause. The sympathy of the entire community goes out in overflowing measure to her husband and four young daughters in their irreparable loss. Fellow Girl Guides would specially express their sympathy."

It is a particularly poignant reminder of the shock of her death, which still haunts me today.

I had always wanted to travel in an aeroplane, but my first experience of air travel was filled with grief, as we accompanied Mum's remains to her homeland. I felt in a daze, and everything appeared surreal, as I climbed the steps into what seemed like a *giant* aeroplane. When we alighted at Belfast Airport, we travelled onwards by road to our Aunt Anna's home in Mullaghduff, for my first experience of an Irish wake.

Lots of strangers called to the wake house to offer their condolences; men sat on wooden benches smoking and chatting, as though oblivious to our grief, while the women quietly made tea and sandwiches in the kitchen. I sat there feeling angry when visitors avoided talking to us children.

Someone asked me, "Who made your lovely Aran jumper?"

I replied, "Mum."

She had knitted and sewed most of our clothes.

The day of the funeral remains a complete blank. I cannot remember it at all. Mum was laid to rest in Our Lady Star of the Sea cemetery in the village of Annagry. A few feet away lay the remains of her dear sister-in-law Kathleen, who tragically predeceased her by seventeen months, at the tender age of twenty-eight.

One conversation still sticks in my mind though, as a series of new mourners visited us back in Kippen.

I was asked, "Do you know the facts of life?"

Indeed, none of us children knew much on this topic. I recall being teased as a fourteen year old in front of my classmates, as I was asked a similar question by a brazen girl called Carol.

"Do you know about the birds and the bees?" she asked.

I replied, "They are a group on *Opportunity Knocks*."

Opportunity Knocks was a forerunner to *The X Factor*. Boy was I innocent!

Although we were all truly devastated at losing Mum, we never spoke about our feelings, and we never spoke about Mum. In true stoic fashion, we kept our feelings of sadness unexpressed and mourned inwardly. There was no outward sign of Dad's grief either; he was simply trying to continue with life, as best he could, still working long hours in damp field drains, although he now suffered severe pain from arthritis in his hips and spine. He cried at night, when he thought we were asleep; I felt very helpless and wished we could all talk about Mum and her death.

Many of our relatives helped us in practical ways. Dad's sister Auntie Madge invited my sister Margaret and I to stay with her in Edinburgh, while Marie and Ann visited Mum's sister, Auntie Ottie (short for Bernadette) and her husband, Uncle Joe. These short breaks felt like exciting adventures, filled with trips to the seaside at nearby Portobello, viewing the floral clock in Princes Street gardens or admiring Edinburgh Castle atop its craggy hill.

The residents of Kippen were also incredibly caring. A knock on the door would announce the arrival of a chicken from the local minister and his family, or a huge treat of a tray of Coca-Cola, from Dr Scott and his family. Our parish priest was also a regular visitor. Somehow we felt we needed to entertain him, and we would launch into our latest singing repertoire!

We carried on baking every Saturday, as a way of honouring Mum's memory. My own specialities were scones cooked on a traditional girdle, coffee and walnut sponge or chocolate cake topped with chocolate butter icing and chocolate drops. Yum! I still bake regularly as a form of therapy.

To this day, I love to hear stories about Mum from my aunties. She had such an incredible zest for life, and I remember her eyes were often crinkled from laughter. She will always have a special place in my heart.

I also feel very blessed to have had such a wonderful Dad. He was a real gentleman and did his very best for us all, in his own quiet, unassuming way.

My sisters and I continued to enjoy being members of 1st Kippen Girl Guides, a fabulous organisation that encourages girls worldwide, to learn a variety of practical skills. They also nurture teamwork. The minister's daughter Lorna was our guide leader, and she received an invitation shortly after Mum's death, for two girls to represent Kippen at a week-long international guide camp, near the shores of Loch Fyne.

Would Margaret and I like to go? she enquired.

"Yes," we replied in unison.

Kitted out with new skirts, shoes and spotless uniforms we left home midsummer, to travel to the town of Inveraray, by train. The camp was HUGE and covered several very large fields, falling down to a river that fed the loch. There were four other girls representing Stirlingshire, and we all shared a tent.

On arrival, we put up our heavy canvas tent, attaching the guy ropes with sturdy pegs, hammered well into the ground; the sides could be rolled up if the weather permitted. We laid waterproof groundsheets on the grass and unrolled our sleeping bags, before gathering wood, to create a frame to store our rucksacks above the damp ground. We collected more wood for our campfire and formed a rota for keeping the toilets pristine. Toilets or latrines as they were called in *Girl Guide speak*, were hand-dug pits that we squatted over, our modesty preserved by a small canvas tent. Toilet roll holders were fashioned from a Y-shaped stick impaled in the ground!

The week progressed well, and we enjoyed an exciting programme of activities. The Scottish weather was *inclement*, and it rained almost continuously. However, I found great pleasure in two new pursuits, hill climbing and canoeing, in the rain!

Back in our team tent, we created more entertainment, telling stories and laughing well into the night—great grief therapy. One of our Stirlingshire colleagues seemed to think she was a *beauty queen* and suggested we all have a lovely legs competition. We dutifully rolled up our nightdresses and stood in line to be judged. Finally, the much anticipated results were announced. I was deemed first, Margaret second and BQ was awarded a lowly third. I have to say my pins are somewhat less shapely now, but my self-esteem was greatly boosted by this momentous event!

Towards the end of the week, the nearby river had swollen to capacity and was ready to burst its banks. In the interests of safety, we were all evacuated to Inveraray Masonic Hall. Dad travelled by car to collect us, and we regaled him with tales of camping in the wilds of Loch Fyne. I did not, however, tell him of my legs' award!

We continued to enjoy the wide range of activities the Girl Guides promoted, earning badges for cooking, sewing, camping… Indeed, we Gallagher sisters probably set a record, as we all eventually received the highest award in guiding—The Queen's Guide Award.

Dad continued to take us back to Donegal every summer for our annual holiday. However, we never returned to Mullaghderg Mountain, staying instead with his family in Mullaghduff. We no longer swam in Mullaghderg Lake, but enjoyed a new *pond*—the mighty Atlantic Ocean. There were two beautiful, long, sandy beaches within a mile of Dad's childhood home, and we refined our swimming skills in the sea, oblivious to the freezing waters!

Back home in Kippen, we often built a roaring coal fire in the living room; there was no such thing as central heating in the early seventies. The fire had an added advantage in helping to dry the washing if it was wet outside, a logistical nightmare with four teenage girls in the house. Indeed, it was always a fight to see who could get their clothes washed first in the twin tub washing machine and onto the solitary clothes horse!

On Sunday nights we all looked forward to a bit of *dance therapy*, when DJ Alan Freeman played "Pick of The Pops". The fire would still be blazing as we danced wildly to Slades' "Coz I Luv You", Neil Diamond's "Sweet Caroline" or Rod Stewart's "Maggie May". If we got too hot, we simply opened the back door for a quick breath of fresh air, and then returned to the living room for another session of our version of "Bikram (hot) yoga"!

Dad wisely left us alone to dance, while he went to Stirling for an evening of bingo. He would then return home with fish suppers, negating the positive effects of all our healthy exercise!

I had sailed through my primary education, winning the prize for runner-up dux of Kippen Primary School. At St Modan's, I achieved top marks in maths in first and second year, scoring 93% and 90% respectively. Unfortunately, my marks dropped in third year, after Mum's death, to 77%. A maths teacher, Miss O'Sullivan known as Maggie Tarzan or Tarzan, felt it her duty to call me out in front of my classmates, ridiculing my *poor* results, although I was still top in my year. I wonder now did she know what a terrible time I had endured.

Thankfully, there were a number of supportive teachers in school who were more understanding of my family's predicament. I had set my heart on becoming a doctor, and the lady supervisor—a Miss MacNamee—was a great support. She encouraged me to apply for medical school, after I had passed five Scottish exams known as Highers.

In sixth year, we were short of teachers for Sixth Year Studies, the equivalent of A levels, and had to stay at school after four o'clock, several times a week. Fridays generally had a more relaxed timetable; thus, I often stayed at home. My form master turned a blind eye. Instead of relaxing or catching up on homework, I cleaned the house: hoovering, dusting, and washing clothes, bed linen and towels.

I also loved moving furniture or painting the walls in a more *exciting hue.* Dad never ever chastised me, although he often returned home to discover the bathroom, kitchen or living room looked different. I reckon I was honing these new skills for my future career in colour healing, space clearing and intuitive feng shui!

Around this time, Dad started to go out more often and returned home late. The late nights were soon explained when he introduced us to a lovely lady called Sheila. She soon became a very kind mentor, with a great understanding of teenage girls and their issues.

Sheila suggested we get another pet for company; thus we bought a handsome dog called Lauder. He was a rough collie, the same breed as the famous *film star*, Lassie. Lauder was a pedigree and an ex show dog; thus, he was extremely well behaved and a true *gentleman*. Walking Lauder round the village always brought admiring glances, and we often stopped to give neighbours a chance to pet him. Happily, he and Sooty seemed to get along well.

I think Lauder was a huge support in healing our grief, for he and Sooty always gave us bucket loads of unconditional love.

My sixth year exams loomed and I had a conditional acceptance for Glasgow University to study medicine. My preliminary exam results were excellent, and I had again excelled in maths and physics. Indeed, I had more than 20 per cent more marks than any other student in my year for the joint subjects of computing and numerical analysis.

I sat four Sixth Year Studies papers in physics, chemistry, calculus and geometry and finally my favourite—computing and numerical analysis. On the day of the final exam, I returned a calculator called a Facit to school (most of the class had taken one home to brush up on their skills). Unfortunately, one unknown student did not bring their *Facit* back, and somehow I was the one person left without a calculator.

My mind was filled with angst, and I could not concentrate at all well; I had to defer answering questions that used a calculator. Our teacher, Dennis Canavan went to neighbouring Stirling High School for a replacement and returned perhaps half an hour later, with two calculators, neither of which worked properly.

My paper was a disaster. I was so distressed that I ran out of the room at the end of the exam, saying nothing to my teacher.

I gained three Sixth Year Studies passes and a D grade in computing and numerical analysis. I did not think to appeal my results in view of the circumstances. I was thus not accepted to study for a degree in medicine and reluctantly settled for my second choice of dentistry, at Glasgow University.

In hindsight, I realise a career in medicine was just not meant to be, for I was destined to study natural medicines instead.

Dad never, ever said anything about being disappointed in my results.

However, one of my aunts later took it upon herself to say, "Your father felt you could have done better."

These insensitive comments certainly contributed to my growing feelings of not being good enough, initiated by my teacher Maggie Tarzan.

However, I did make the most of the intervening long summer holiday and applied for a temporary job. I found a placement as a kitchen maid in the Waverley Hotel, Callander, where I enjoyed shared accommodation with a girl who was a waitress. My first wage was £15 per week, an absolute fortune to me. All our meals were free, and I was thus able to save most of my wages.

My duties included washing the pots and pans, preparing salads and fish, and cleaning the kitchen floors. The restaurant was always busy and high teas were incredibly popular. They consisted of fish, chicken or salad with chips, tea and bread followed by an array of home-baked cakes and scones. Every diner left with a laden stomach!

By the end of the season, I had saved quite a bit of money and travelled to Glasgow for a mammoth shopping trip. I went to my favourite shop—Bus Stop—and bought two lovely dresses in 1940's and 50's style, plus a cream skirt suit. I added several pairs of chic shoes from the equally exciting Chelsea Cobbler, plus a pair of denim dungarees, and several T-shirts and cardigans.

My new wardrobe gave me a great confidence boost for my *grand entrance* into university life. I was further boosted by a very nice friend from St Modan's, who was studying English, and stayed with a family near Glasgow's Botanic Gardens, while I stayed in the nearby university halls of residence. We supported one another on our new adventure, and I was very glad of her friendship.

My new bedroom was rather small and furnished in a somewhat minimalist style. I soon put my artistic skills to good use and brightened one large wall with pictures of female models wearing the latest fashions, in a giant colourful collage. It certainly made the room more appealing and perhaps a little homely.

Weekdays were hectic with lectures, tutorials and practical classes in biology and chemistry. We studied every evening, which left little time for a social life. However, one handsome first year medical student caught my eye, and he became my imaginary boyfriend; I never spoke to him though for I remained quite shy!

I did make several other new friends, including a fellow dental student called Gina, who remains a friend to this day. We bonded over our mutual love of fashion, food and music. I remain envious of Gina's lovely curly red hair; I always wanted red hair instead of my own boring dark brown, which is sadly now turning grey!

Despite these new alliances, I returned home as often as possible, for I missed my family.

Sheila suggested that Dad take us girls on our first holiday abroad, and thus we spent Christmas 1973, on the sunny island of Majorca.

The holiday was a BIG adventure and included staying up late, going out to local discos and tasting new Spanish dishes. We all admired the beautiful beaches, mountains and secluded villages, and I still treasure a family photograph taken at one of Palma's famous nightspots.

Finally, I admitted that my heart was just not in dentistry, and I made the decision to leave university after one year. I know Dad must have been incredibly disappointed, but he never expressed any such feelings to me. In hindsight, he probably did not want to add to my angst.

Before my departure from Glasgow University, I had one final outing at the Men's University Union, to see a new Irish band called Thin Lizzy. The band had just had a hit single with the now famous anthem, "Whiskey in the Jar". My feet were simply *on fire* that night, and I became a lifelong fan of Phil Lynott and the band.

Back home in Kippen, I found a temporary job in the Cross Keys Hotel as a barmaid. I loved dressing up in my new fashionable attire, to chat to the friendly locals, and pour a pint or two. The price of a pint of lager in 1974 was just 17 pence, while Guinness was more costly at 22 pence!

The hotel had a gourmet restaurant, mentioned in Egon Ronay's famous guide, where my sisters had all found Saturday jobs, while I was away at university. In my absence, they had the added pleasure of serving several of the famous Monty Python team, who were filming *Monty Python and the Holy Grail* in the nearby Fintry and Gargunnock Hills.

Ann and Marie were asked to a party for them in the Cross Keys. Amazingly they replied, "No," for they were too tired and simply wanted to go home to their beds!

If I had been asked I would most surely have accepted. My vivid imagination transported me to a fun Monty Python party, where I listen to the iconic Python songs, "The Lumberjack Song" and "Always Look on the Bright Side of Life"!

Mum would certainly have wanted us to laugh and smile and dance and sing, just as she had done throughout her short life. She would certainly have enjoyed a *Python Party*!

Dad decided we should move to Scotland's capital. He always wanted the very best for us and Edinburgh would surely provide great employment opportunities. Auntie Madge and I accompanied him on a house hunt, and we soon discovered a nice detached house in Fairmilehead, on the edge of the city. A backdrop of the Pentland Hills and nearby rolling countryside, made sure our new surroundings were not too dissimilar from Kippen.

Thus began a new stage of our lives...

Insights from the Kippen Girls

- Live every moment as though it were your last

- Never underestimate the healing power of music, dancing, baking, friends and pets!

A Capital City - early 1975

"We are all visitors to this time, this place. We are all just passing through. Our purpose here is to observe, to learn, to grow, to love... and then we return home."
Australian Aboriginal proverb

Dad was different; he was happier and more relaxed after having had a hip replacement. However, he was determined to carry on working after his convalescence.

Very dapper now, he was buying new suits, shirts and ties, all signs of a womanly influence. He had a new hobby too, eating out, and we delighted in accompanying him and Sheila for culinary treats. One of our regular eateries was a beautiful country house called Pow Fowlis, near the village of Airth. Although the whole menu was quite exquisite, my favourite part of the meal was always the dessert. The sweet trolley was laden with Pavlova, chocolate mousse, crème caramel...

Sheila continued to be a very timely mentor for me. She was a great listener, and I confided in her over a number of *women's issues*, which I could not easily discuss with Dad. I was very glad of her support.

I needed to find work, but I had absolutely no idea what I wanted to do. I visited a job agency in the city centre, where the recruitment consultant studied my qualifications, before commenting, "You are very good at maths. Why don't we send you to an insurance office, for an interview?"

That was how I ended up working for Scottish Provident Life Assurance Company for nigh on thirteen years!

My first post was in the Actuarial Department, where I spent each day calculating surrender values, paid-up values and estimated maturity values for clients, all anxious to know how their monthly insurance premiums were accumulating. I found the work exciting at first and enjoyed making lots of friends among my new workmates. We had a lively girl in our room who used to organise girly meetings in the toilets, when everyone was feeling bored and in need of a break. She was the department's anarchist!

I was glad to have a steady income of my own and my first salary of £1485 per annum was a princely sum to me. Shopping for new clothes became a passion, and I often spent my lunch hours strolling along the *magical* shops of Princes Street, Hanover Street, and George Street. Jenner's department store was right across the road from the SPI, and *delicious* shoes often enticed me inside, most notably when there were generous reductions in January and July.

Our new home was also getting a makeover, and Ann, Marie and I soon brought the rooms up to date. Dad had bought a new brown striped, living room suite, while I took delight in creating matching Laura Ashley curtains. Lauder and Sooty enjoyed the comforts of a twinned, long haired, brown, fluffy fireside rug!

Our dining room was soon adorned with more handmade curtains and a lovely, dark wooden table and chairs. A bookcase Mum had chosen lined one of the walls, filled with the *Encyclopaedia Britannica* and other educational tomes.

Next on our transformation list was the kitchen, which was duly painted in earthy green and brown hues. Looking back now it was somewhat depressing. In my artistic defence, these were the fashionable colours of the 1970s!

Margaret had married and was a new mum; she stayed behind in Stirling, but we still saw her on a regular basis.

Sadly, Dad's brother, Uncle Owenie, died on September 20, 1975, many years after a road accident, in which he had lost the power in his legs. He was only sixty-four, and Dad missed him terribly.

Bad news often comes in twos, and his dear sister, Auntie Nellie, succumbed to lung cancer on November 20. She too had suffered many tragedies in her life, losing all five of her children to an unknown disease, and her husband Patrick to pneumonia. Auntie Nellie loved all children and always remembered our birthdays and Christmas. We treasured her parcels, which often included Donegal's famous *Crolly* dolls.

The sudden loss of both his siblings must have affected Dad deeply, but again he remained stoic, and life continued as normal.

Around this time, I began to suffer a new health complaint of abscesses in my teeth, and I became a frequent visitor to the dentist, and the dental hospital in Edinburgh's Chamber Street, which treated emergencies.

If you have ever had a dental abscess, you will know how painful it can be. They are quite excruciating and are often accompanied by an embarrassing swelling in the face. Every time an abscess formed, I had the offending tooth extracted, and a course of antibiotics was prescribed. Unfortunately, abscesses continued to plague me for a number of years to come.

Music, however, helped to soothe the pain, and I travelled to Glasgow to visit my new friend Gina, who was still a dental student, and we delighted in seeing Paul McCartney and Wings, at the Apollo Theatre. It was a hugely exciting evening for me, and I swiftly became a music buff.

Thin Lizzy were next in town—Leith Town Hall to be precise— and I just had to go. The audience was tiny, and Ann and I danced like dervishes to our new Irish music heroes (Marie was now a student studying Russian and French at Salford University, near Manchester). Ann and I began to collect the band's albums: *Shades of a Blue Orphanage, Vagabonds of the Western World, Nightlife, Fighting...*

Marie, Ann and I continued to return to Donegal every summer with Dad, but Donegal was alive in Edinburgh too—in the Irish Club. It was located in Pilrig Street, just off Leith Walk, and was filled with other emigrants from Donegal and Mayo. Dad loved to play "Whist" there on a Friday night, and we girls usually joined him and Auntie Madge, for Sunday music nights, in the lounge bar downstairs. Auntie Madge was very sociable, and a lively night of banter was assured in her company. Dad was a great dancer, and I loved to dance an old-time waltz with him for we just glided round the floor. *Strictly Come Dancing* eat your heart out!

The club always organised functions for St Patrick's Day, when we danced and chatted all night with our new Irish friends. It was a chance to dress up too; the *Kippen Girls* as we were nick named, were now regular *followers of fashion.*

Approaching my twenty-first birthday, I wanted to organise a party. I rented a room in central Edinburgh, complete with a DJ and a buffet, before inviting a number of friends and relatives, for a night filled with birthday felicitations. I wore a red pencil skirt with a matching jacket and Chelsea Cobbler shoes. My new outfit gave me much needed courage for mingling among the crowds, for I remained quite shy and did not enjoy being the centre of attention.

I had a very generous gift from Auntie Ottie and Uncle Joe—a holiday to Athens! Thus, in the summer of 1976, Ann, Auntie Ottie and I travelled to Greece. Our days soon filled with trips to the beach, crammed into local buses with friendly natives. We discovered the Greek delicacies of thick yoghurt and natural honey, moussaka (a combination of spiced meat with aubergine, topped with a white sauce), souvlaki (meat and vegetables cooked on a skewer) served with an accompaniment of tzatziki (a yoghurt and cucumber dressing). Our hunger satisfied, we danced the night away in the roof top discotheques, of the district of Plaka. Our energy was boundless!

I met a tall, blonde Yugoslavian *hunk*, and we dated regularly for the remainder of the holiday. He wanted to write to me on my return home, but I was not yet ready for a serious relationship. I still felt a great need for independence.

Sadly, Sheila and Dad stopped dating, but she remained a great friend, and we carried on visiting restaurants around central Scotland. As a result, I became a more adventurous cook, creating my versions of chicken liver pate, French onion soup, coq au vin, boeuf bourguignon, Pavlova, chocolate mousse...

My musical heroes, Thin Lizzy returned to Edinburgh once more, this time to a sold-out concert at the Usher Hall. I was overjoyed that they were on their way to stardom. I also returned to the Apollo, to see a new band called Roxy Music, with lead singer Bryan Ferry. He was incredibly stylish and *cool.* Roxy Music albums were soon added to my growing music collection: *Stranded, Country Life, Siren, Viva*…Playing the band's records at home, we danced mimicking Bryan's backing singers, in super *cool* fashion of course!

Dad was going to be fifty, on Boxing Day 1976, so we organised a surprise party for him, filled with friends and relatives, good music and a home-cooked buffet. He seemed to enjoy the night. However, many years later, I discovered that he had been celebrating his fifty-first birthday; he had never said a word.

On questioning, he declared, "I did not want to burst the party bubble, for you had all worked so hard."

I felt a fool for not knowing his year of birth. I never forgot it again.

The gloss had gone from my work in Scottish Provident, and music was my much needed escape. New bands entered my radar: Steve Gibbons and his band singing "Tulane", Graham Parker and the Rumour with "Hey Lord, please don't let me be misunderstood", the Boomtown Rats and "I don't like Mondays", Blondie, Kate Bush, Queen…

Edinburgh was also a great place to spot *celebrities*, especially during the Edinburgh Festival. I watched the very dishy actor Robert Powell walk along Princes Street. Sadly, he was married to Babs, one of the Pans People dancers from *Top of the Pops!*

One day I spotted Cliff Richard walking along Rose Street. I just **had** to follow him. He went into a shoe shop and then a health food store, where I hid in the shadows like a member of MI5. I returned to regale my office friends with Cliff's every detail!

Ann and I often went dancing in central Edinburgh, at weekends. The evenings were interspersed with slow numbers like 10cc's "I'm Not in Love" or the Moody Blues "Nights in White Satin", and we were both soon dating. My first regular boyfriend was a handsome, dark haired Iranian student. Together we enjoyed fun outings to the beach, and a number of nights at the disco. However, I called time on our relationship after a few months, as I felt the relationship had run its course.

Travel abroad joined my list of passions, and in the ensuing years, I discovered the joys of the streets of Paris with my three sisters, the Greek island of Mykonos with a friend, Tenerife and the Algarve with Ann. I also made regular trips to Holland, where Marie was now living. However, I never missed my two summer weeks in Donegal, this was always considered an essential vacation.

Scottish Provident produced a bright, shiny *carrot*—a cheap mortgage at an interest rate of 4%, way below the national average. I so wanted to own my own home and to decorate the interior in a palette that was truly mine. My wish was fulfilled shortly after my twenty-fifth birthday, when I held the keys to a semi-detached, three-bedroom house in Baberton Mains Brae, on the edge of the city. It had a good sized front and back garden, filled with roses, shrubs and herbaceous perennials.

I became focussed on yet another *interior design mission,* filling my new home with a lovely new settee and armchairs covered in Sanderson floral fabric, white fitted wardrobes, and fresh and colourful soft furnishings. It was *heaven!*

Dear Lauder and Sooty had sadly gone to their own *heaven,* and we now had another rough collie, called Shane who had a somewhat mischievous personality. You could tell he was planning some naughtiness by the look on his face, and he just loved to chase the girls!

A job vacancy arose in the Underwriting Department at the *SPI,* more in keeping with my previous medical ambitions. I applied and was duly promoted. My mornings were now incredibly hectic, filled with checking new proposals for life assurance. If a prospective client had a lengthy medical history, I had to create a synopsis of their most critical illnesses, plus any medical investigations. The company's medical examiner called daily to assess these cases. An extra premium was subsequently added to proposals considered as high risks of early mortality. I enjoyed the challenge of this new job and was glad to have a better income.

Ann and I had previously considered moving to Ireland, as we hated leaving Donegal every summer. However, our hopes had been dashed when we discovered most employers looked for native

Irish speakers. Not to be outdone, we decided to visit Donegal more often, and we holidayed in all seasons, delighting in evenings by roaring fires in Bonner's or Neddie's Bar, Mullaghduff or winter walks on wild Atlantic beaches.

In the summer of 1980, I returned to Donegal as usual, for my much needed summer holiday, and unexpectedly met my first serious boyfriend—an Irishman. He was incredibly good fun and took me right out of my shy shell. Our relationship continued, on and off, for several years.

However, my teeth continued to present problems, and the abscesses continued; I think I suffered around ten in total. I came to work one day in severe pain from the latest offending tooth, doped up on DF118 tablets. I had to go home in a taxi and go straight to bed. I was relieved that everyone had seen my swollen face, as *skiving* was common among bored employees!

Recurrent laryngitis joined my list of symptoms. One night I went to bingo with Dad and Auntie Madge, circled the winning number and was unable to call out, "House!"

I was both frustrated and disappointed not to get my prize.

I also started to suffer from a host of problems in the week before my period, including swollen ankles, skin sensitivity, weight gain, mood swings, chocolate cravings and depression. My GP referred me to a clinic at the Royal Infirmary, and I was prescribed a drug called Duphaston. However, it brought little relief. Researching possible alternatives, I discovered the benefits of evening primrose oil, which did help a little.

On reflection now, I think some of my symptoms were due to a lack of natural daylight, as there were no windows in the office where I worked. In winter, I rarely saw daylight, and SAD or Seasonal Affective Disorder was not yet widely recognised.

A happy event soon lifted my ailing spirits—I passed my driving test. Dear Dad was so thrilled he bought me a new car—a Nissan Sunny Coupe—a rather sporty metallic red, model. I felt incredibly blessed. Ann and I had relied on buses to travel, and we set out on a series of exploratory expeditions around central Scotland. Our next holiday was therefore, a *grand tour* of Ireland.

Taking the ferry to Larne, we stayed north of Dublin for a night, and then travelled to Navan staying with our cousin Brian and his lovely wife Mary. Next on our itinerary was the seaside town of Bray, the delights of the Dingle peninsula, followed by a stop near Durty Nelly's Pub next to Bunratty Castle, where some Irishmen invited us to accompany them to the Ballybunion Bachelor Festival. We declined their invite, as they obviously had lecherous intentions!

Our holiday ended in our beloved Donegal, yet the lengthy drive had not fazed me. Indeed, I seemed to thrive on the experience. Long distance driving holds no appeal for me nowadays; I find driving for more than an hour a challenge, as it drains my energy.

Back at work I was promoted again, to supervisor of the Policy Endorsements section. I was now team leader, to a bunch of girls who were a delight, both in and out of work, for we often partied together, at the end of the week. Our regular after work haunts included the Café Royal and a nearby pub called the Abbotsford. My social life was always great in their company; every night out was filled with laughter.

On St Patrick's Day 1983, Thin Lizzy played at the Playhouse Theatre; I had now seen the band live six times in all. Sadly, it was to be the last time I swooned at Phil Lynott, for he died prematurely in 1986.

The music world mourned a *shining star*.

I went to a lot of great concerts in 1983: Eric Clapton, Spandau Ballet, Robert Palmer and The Police. I was compiling my own list of great guitar legends. I gave star ratings to those I had seen live: Eric Clapton, Phil Lynott, Brian May from Queen, and Robert Cray. I still hoped to witness the legendary skills of Mark Knopfler, from the band Dire Straits.

In February 1984, I enjoyed seeing the talented Tina Turner, on her Private Dancer Tour. Bryan Adams was her support act. Imagine our delight, when Ann and I spotted Bryan in the bar next door to the Playhouse, before the show—we were star struck for days! Of course Bryan went on to delight millions with his iconic songs.

One of his songs was particularly poignant. It was called "Straight From The Heart". The words mirrored my own love life, for my Irish romance had come to an abrupt end. We were simply not meant to be, and my mood began to plummet. I became quite reclusive and stopped going out at weekends.

By the end of 1984, Ann had bought her own home on Gorgie Road, nearer to the city centre. So, I decided to move nearer the centre too. My search area was Shandon, as it was not far from Ann. I quickly found a three-bedroom, terraced house that looked a good buy. However, a structural survey highlighted several potential problems. I felt quite despondent.

However, they say, "What is meant for you won't pass you by." And it didn't.

Quite by chance, I found a much better, three-bed terraced house in nearby Alderbank Terrace, which had a huge floored attic, lots of period features, and a fixed price of £35,000. It was known as a colony dwelling, one of many houses built between 1850 and 1910, for artisans and skilled working class families. They were built by philanthropic organisations such as the Edinburgh Cooperative Building Company Limited. I knew it was *destined* to be mine.

I sold my home in Baberton Mains Brae and moved house in early 1985. Dad took one of the double bedrooms and helped me decorate every room in colourful new hues. I remember the hall and stairs were painted a pale green called *eau de nil*, the living room in a shade of coral called *guava,* and my bedroom in pale lilac. I put my sewing talents to good use once again and made all my own curtains, to match the house's period features. The living room had exquisite cornices, an antique fireplace and a fabulous bay window. I created a *dream* window seat, covered in pale blue silk, enhanced by Sanderson floral curtains.

I used some of the profits from the sale of my previous home, to buy some vintage furniture, including a dresser, a coffee table, a wardrobe and a chest of drawers. I hired a sanding machine, smoothed the wood grain, and then waxed my new period gems.

I felt incredibly proud of my new abode and organised a

housewarming cum birthday party, to celebrate. On March 8, 1985, I turned thirty to a fun, fancy dress party with more than one hundred guests. I dressed as a clown, accompanied by a priest, a nun, a spider...We had a truly memorable night, dancing in the attic, chatting in my designer living room and kitchen, and generally having FUN. The party was a talking point back in the SPI for many weeks afterwards!

Dad decided to try living in Donegal for a time, and possibly retire. He had two hip replacements now, but he still suffered a lot of pain from arthritis in his other joints. I felt incredibly lonely when he left. The new house soon lots its sheen, as I quickly fell from my party *high*. I descended into the grips of a major depression.

Stupidly, I put on a happy mask for work, but on returning home, I would eat my evening meal then climb into bed. This routine continued for several months. Eventually, I found the courage to go to my GP, who prescribed an antidepressant called Bolvidon. I felt better for a time, but the medication soon lost its effectiveness, and the dosage was increased.

What did I do meantime? I decided to jump from an aeroplane, quite literally!

Ann and I went to Auchterarder Parachute Club, for a weekend's training, to raise some funds for the Sick Children's Hospital in Edinburgh—a very worthy cause. Enclosed in harnesses, we practised our impending jump, from a tall platform inside the aerodrome. The focus of our training was learning how to land safely. It felt quite nerve-racking on the first day but by day's end, we were proficient jumpers!

On the second day, we sat a theoretical and a practical examination, which we both passed. However, safety regulations meant we needed to wait for the wind to die down, to less than ten miles per hour. We waited, and waited, and waited...

It was the summer of Live Aid. On July 13, an audience estimated at 1.9 billion, watched two concerts of the world's greatest music legends live on television, broadcast from Wembley Stadium in London, and John F. Kennedy Stadium in Philadelphia. It was party time around the world. One of my SPI friends decided to have a garden party on the day of this memorable, musical event.

We enjoyed many of my favourite bands:
The Boomtown Rats sang, "I Don't Like Mondays",
Ultravox sang, "Vienna",
Spandau Ballet sang, "True",
Bryan Ferry sang, "Slave to Love" and "Jealous Guy",
Paul Young sang, "Every Time You Go Away",
U2 sang, "Sunday Bloody Sunday"
Dire Straits sang, "Sultans of Swing",
Queen sang, "We Will Rock You",
Bryan Adams sang, "Cuts Like a Knife",
And Simple Minds sang, "I Promised You a Miracle".

A miracle happened, and the event raised 40 to 50 million, for starving people in Africa.

Meanwhile, Ann and I returned to Auchterarder several times over the summer, sitting patiently for countless hours, waiting for the correct wind speed. It never came. Finally, Ann gave up on her parachuting dream, but I decided to give it just **one** more attempt—I think it was in October.

I returned to the aerodrome and waited inside for good jumping conditions. Lo and behold, the wind speed dropped, and before I could change my mind, I was in a small aircraft wearing my parachute, and the door was opened. I jumped. I just loved the whole experience, floating gently down to earth, like a dandelion clock. Yet it was over in minutes. Back on *terra firma*, I rolled onto my side, as per instructions. Boosted by my adventure, I floated home on a cloud of euphoria. I raised over £100 for my cause.

However, the black dog of depression soon returned to haunt me. What happened next was some much needed divine intervention…

I had visited The College of Parapsychology, several times to hear evidence of survival after death, from noted Edinburgh mediums including Nita Saunders and Mary Duffy. The evenings were incredibly interesting, as each medium would pick a member of the audience, describing in detail a loved one who had died. They then provided names and other snippets of information that no one else could have known. The deceased's loved ones often melted into tears, on hearing proof of an afterlife.

One evening I was chosen from the audience by visiting medium Mary Duffy.

She said, Can I speak to the dark haired girl in the third row?"

"Yes."

"You are unhappy in your current job."

"Yes."

"You are going to be a teacher of unusual subjects."

I thought this a bit odd but still replied, "Yes."

"There are lots of book shelves around you filled with books."

"Yes…"

Searching for more answers to my unhappy condition, I booked a private sitting with another well-known male medium. He immediately tuned into my depressed state and told me I needed healing, more than a message from the afterlife. He recommended that I go to a local Spiritualist Church, as it provided spiritual healing.

I followed his wise advice, and I tentatively visited the church the following weekend. I enjoyed the service and a demonstration of mediumship, followed by a very welcome cup of tea. Healing sessions took place afterwards, for anyone in need.

I felt somewhat apprehensive, as I sat in a queue not quite knowing what to expect, before it was my turn to receive healing. I then sat down in front of a young blonde haired girl, who smiled and asked me what ailed me.

I replied, "I am suffering from depression."

She reassured me and explained that she would be moving her hands slowly around me, several inches from my physical body. On her instructions, I closed my eyes and surprisingly began to relax. The girl's hands seemed to radiate extreme heat now, although she had not even touched me, and I felt a growing sense of calm. My first healing session ended maybe ten or fifteen minutes later, but it felt like mere minutes.

I thanked the girl and described the sensations I had felt from her hands, "Your hands were on fire," I said. "Your healing energy has given me an amazing sense of peace."

"It was not me," she replied, smiling. "I am only a channel for healing energy."

I was puzzled by this description, but did not dwell on it.

I went home and slept really well, dreaming of an ANGEL who told me, "I have come to help you heal."

I know it truly was an angel, for it was an incredibly vivid dream. I awoke with a new sense of wellness and threw my antidepressants down the toilet!

Coincidently, a new Scottish band Eurythmics had also entered my rock radar. Lead singer, Annie Lennox, had a truly mesmerising voice and sang "There Must Be An Angel," which really resonated with me and my *journey*.

I was experiencing a momentous inner shift, and within a few weeks I noticed an advert for Westbank Healing Centre, in *Here's Health* magazine. It was situated in the village of Strathmiglo, in Fife. A day workshop on reflexology and massage was scheduled soon, and I was compelled to book a place. I was now following my heart, as per Eurythmics' song.

The morning filled me with excitement, as I watched a demonstration on the ancient art of reflexology. I learned that each foot represents a side of our body, and its internal organs. The top of each foot, our toes, represents the head, including the teeth and sinuses. I learned that pressing on the toes can help relieve headaches, sinus congestion and toothache. Pressing the lower parts of the feet, around the heel, could perhaps ease back problems.

We now had a chance to both give and receive a treatment. I found it quite relaxing to practise as well as to receive. Some parts of my own feet felt sore to the touch, a bit like sharp glass or a nail being pressed on my foot. Ouch! However, it was *soo* relaxing, just like my first experience of spiritual healing.

The group were extremely friendly, and we enjoyed a lovely vegetarian lunch together, before the afternoon's joy—learning how to do a basic back massage. I delighted in more pampering and drove home to Edinburgh filled with a growing excitement.

My experience at Westbank and the spiritual healing propelled me through an exciting new *doorway*. Within months, I was learning as much as I could about natural medicines from magazines, and classes in the Edinburgh area. I enrolled with the National Federation of Spiritual Healers, an organisation that trains students in the art of channelling healing energy, and I became a probationer healer.

I enrolled in a weekly class in astrology, a subject that had always fascinated me. I soon learned that Pisceans are incredibly sensitive and have a very active imagination. Tell me about it! They are also very intuitive and tend to make good health care professionals.

I also learned that I was born on the night of a full moon, in the sign of Virgo, which made me very practical, liking order and fine detail. Yes, I am incredibly tidy and love ordered cupboards and shelves! Happily, these Virgo traits have a grounding effect on my more *otherworldly* Piscean tendencies. I also discovered that the sign on the horizon when I was born was Libra, giving me my love of fashion, colour and interior design.

I immersed myself in yet more new learning, on the subject of nutritional medicine, when I discovered a great health food store in the village of Corstorphine. I refined my diet and started to take nutritional supplements to boost my wellbeing. My PMS symptoms receded into my dark and distant past. My friends and family sighed with relief!

In early 1986, a series of new coincidences led me to discover the ancient art of crystal healing, and I travelled by train to Lytham St Anne's near Blackpool, for a weekend under the tutorage of Geoffrey Keyte.

The first day began with a brief introduction of crystals and their healing qualities, which appeared to be linked to their colour. There were giant pieces of amethyst, quartz crystal, rose quartz, citrine, topaz… in the room, and they all enchanted me with their brilliant lustre. I was intrigued.

Geoffrey led us in a guided visualisation, another new experience for me, "Close your eyes, and imagine you are taking a walk through a beautiful meadow, filled with flowers in a myriad of colours..."

I quickly relaxed and travelled off to *other worlds*. I opened my eyes afterwards and everyone looked *different*. They were surrounded by a shimmering glow of colour. What had happened? Upon discussion of our experiences, I blurted out my tale, "I can see a shimmer around everyone," I said.

"You are seeing everyone's aura," Geoffrey explained. "The aura is a sea of energy that surrounds everyone. It can be seen as colours depicting our thoughts, moods and feelings. It is constantly changing throughout the day. In time you will learn what each colour means."

WOW!

This was to be my first of many experiences of clairvoyance.

The weekend continued, crammed with more new learning. We began to practise crystal healing, using a variety of crystals, which we laid on points called chakras (energy centres located within the aura). My head was bursting with excitement by Sunday evening, as I took the train home. I just had to put my name down for further crystal healing courses.

I was now attending the Spiritualist Church every Sunday and after a welcome cup of tea, I always returned downstairs for some spiritual healing.

Dad and Ann often accompanied me to these meetings. A very talented medium often *took the platform*, as we called it, to demonstrate survival after death. She was clairaudient or clear hearing, and would pick a person from the audience who would be asked to reply "yes" or "no" as she gave a rapid fire list of information, about deceased loved ones.

Sometimes I received a message from Grandja or Granny Mullaghdoo, delighting in their wisdom.

One night, Dad received one from Mum.

The medium opened with, "I have a lady here who died very

suddenly from a heart complaint."

"Yes," Dad replied.

"She says you gave her a two stranded string of pearls."

"Yes."

"She also says, remember my red dancing shoes."

"Yes."

"You loved to dance together."

"Yes."

More information followed; every bit was accurate and very precise. No one could have known these very personal details; it was irrefutable proof of Mum's spirit's survival after death. Our eyes filled with tears, for we got so much comfort from that message.

I felt compelled to learn more about mediumship and healing, so I put my name on a waiting list, to train with the church's spiritual development circle. It would be several months before a place became available.

Meanwhile, I heard of yet another training course, this time in colour healing, with a well-known author and colour therapist, called Theo Gimbel, who lived near Stroud, in Gloucestershire. Again the long journey did not faze me, and I travelled to Theo's weekend courses three times in all. I learned more about colour and its healing qualities, of the aura and the energy centres known as *chakras*, of the colour wheel…

I continued with my studies in astrology, alongside my courses in natural medicines, and I learned that I was experiencing my first Saturn return, where the planet Saturn returns to the point it was at birth. Saturn is the planet of learning from past experiences, and I soon realised that Saturn's influence was teaching me to follow my heart now and not my head!

Geoffrey Keyte was organising the first professional training in crystal healing in the UK. It was to be based in London and starting in early 1987. I reserved a place, and I began to commute to London overnight by bus, gaining more new knowledge on crystals and their healing qualities. It was such a joy to study.

Finally, I saw Mark Knopfler and Dire Straits in Edinburgh's

Playhouse. However, the *jury was still out*, on who was the world's greatest guitar legend! Sadly, I never saw Donegal's Rory Gallagher, for he had an early demise.

Rock concerts were no longer a priority for me.

I was now a member of the development circle at the Spiritualist Church, joining a group of perhaps sixteen others, to learn clairvoyance, clairaudience and spiritual healing skills.

Once a week, we sat in a circle, with curtains drawn and lights extinguished.

"Close your eyes and relax," our teacher began, as we entered into a silent meditation.

Later, she took each class member's hand in turn and asked them to channel any thoughts that might jump into their mind.

She told us, "Forget what others might think, and stay true to your spiritual guidance. Just repeat it as it is given to you..."

I felt sensations like spiders' webs on my skin, or a slight breeze blowing around me, and I soon learned that this was a sign that a spirit guide was near, helping me to relay a short message, for someone in the group.

"I have a man here who passed away with cancer. He was extremely tall and had dark hair and a beard..."

It was reassuring if the message was understood.

The weeks progressed, and I now had the impulse to open my eyes during meditation. I could see outlines rather like luminous shadows, around the others in the room, while their faces seemed to mould into different features. I believe this was a manifestation of their guardian angels and spirit guides. I now realised that I was both clairvoyant and clairaudient—hidden gifts I had never expected. My main priority had always been to learn to channel spiritual healing.

I soon became part of a group of trainee healers within the church, under the guidance of more senior members, and I joined them in channelling healing after the Sunday service. I was also attending training days with the National Federation of Spiritual Healers, and I had a new mission, to find a full-time training course in natural medicines, somewhere in the UK. Yet I did not even know if such a course existed!

In early 1987, *Here's Health* magazine came to my aid once more, when I spotted an advert for Raworth College, located near Dorking in Surrey. The college was offering a new one-year full-time course in the study of anatomy, physiology and massage, aromatherapy, counselling skills, reflexology, nutritional therapy...

I just knew it was my *destiny* to study there. I made an immediate enquiry; I was invited for an interview, and I travelled south once more. I was accepted as a student, although I had no idea how I was going to pay for my studies. I managed to save a fair bit of money, by living more frugally and relinquishing my old frivolous pastimes. Dad made my new dream come true, when he made up the difference.

Finally, in the summer of 1987, I handed in my notice to Scottish Provident, for a new career path awaited me.

Insights from a Capital City

- Never leave the ground without a parachute!

- There is more on this earth than our physical reality

- Healing opens unexpected new doors with *endless* possibilities.

Back to School – summer 1987

"Educating the mind without educating the heart is no education at all."

Aristotle

Dad was now spending a lot of time in Donegal, as he had finally retired!

I decided to join him for a few weeks quiet respite, before travelling onwards to college in Surrey. Although I was still sad from leaving all my friends in the SPI, I enjoyed catching up with Dad's news, cooking nice meals, walking to the beach, and visiting LOTS of relatives. New babies had arrived, and I delighted in meeting them.

In October 1986, Marie had given birth to her first baby, another Brigid, and the whole family had enjoyed visiting her in Holland, at Christmas. Witnessing all these new arrivals added to the yearning inside me to be a mother myself some day. Perhaps I would never meet a lifelong partner, and I would simply run out of time.

Dad often spent sunshine holidays with Marie and her family, who were almost self-sufficient, growing their own vegetables, and rearing chickens and ducks.

Dad would spend most of his time outside, riding their tractor, and helping in the garden, returning home, bronzed and radiating good health, commenting, "The sunshine really helped my sore bones."

Ann soon joined us in Donegal, and I looked forward to a few evenings out in the Rosses.

One evening we decided to visit Danny Minnie's pub in the neighbouring village of Annagry, where good *craic* was assured. My friend Helen and my cousin Ann accompanied us on our social outing; I was the designated driver.

The bar was packed, and we delighted in seeing new faces.

Seated at the bar was a familiar figure—was that my old maths teacher Dennis Canavan?

Ann thought it might be, so she decided to investigate on her next trip to the bar. "Are you Dennis Canavan?" she enquired.

He replied in the affirmative, and they chatted animatedly about our old school. Dennis had left teaching for a career in politics and was now a Labour party MP for the constituency of Falkirk West. We had heard on the grapevine that he had holidayed in Donegal on occasion, but this was the first time we had seen him in fourteen years. He joined us at our table.

My first question was, "Do you remember me?"

And he did.

He had ventured out alone, so we invited him to join us at Dodge Disco. He followed us in his car, to the metropolis of Gweedore. Still somewhat independent, in keeping with my oldest sibling status, I was first in the queue at Dodge and paid my own entrance fee. Dennis followed and paid for the remainder of the company!

The disco was somewhat quieter than we had hoped, but we had a few lively dances nonetheless. The evening ended, and Dennis invited me to join him for a meal, the following evening. I accepted, looking forward to reminiscing on my old school days.

We met up in a small thatch roofed restaurant back in Gweedore. The food was delicious, and we chatted animatedly about life at St Modan's and the intervening years. I learned that Dennis now had four children, three boys and a girl—Mark, Dennis John, Paul and Ruth. Sadly, he and his wife had separated.

Quite unexpectedly, that meal became our first date, and more dates followed. Dennis left Donegal a few days later, but promised to keep in touch. Meantime, I enjoyed the remainder of the summer with my family, for we would soon be separated by the long distance to Surrey.

I arrived back in Edinburgh, relaxed, refreshed, and eager to start my new studies. Dad decided to return to Scotland and stay in my home, to keep it maintained and secure; I was glad of his enduring support.

I was sad leaving my family and friends, as I embarked on the lengthy car journey south. However, Ann promised to visit soon. Dennis spent several days in London each week for his work in the House of Commons, so I planned a stop with him, before travelling onwards to Surrey.

The trip did not go as planned, for my car was somewhat sick. I was filled with despair when it chugged into a town north of London, coughing as though it were on its last gasp. Thankfully, it was an hour or so before teatime, so I managed to find a garage that was open. I cannot recall the exact diagnosis, except that it got a temporary fix. My Nissan Sunny coupe eventually limped into the capital city, well behind schedule. I was so very glad to see a welcome face and enjoyed a lovely dinner with Dennis, at a restaurant that would soon become a firm favourite.

The car was repaired the following day, and I journeyed onwards to Surrey.

Raworth College was set amidst beautiful, mature gardens with lots of ancient trees. The original college was also the home of its founders, Maria Raworth and Norma Williamson. It was a huge mansion, split into their living accommodation and our teaching rooms. I was very fortunate to rent a much coveted room in Norma's home, which I would be sharing with a lovely girl from Northern Ireland, who was embarking on the full year course like me. We soon bonded over our love of all things esoteric.

Our studies would span three ten-week blocks, interspersed with mid-term breaks, and longer holidays at Christmas and Easter. The timetable appeared both exciting and challenging. Our first term of study included anatomy and physiology, alongside aromatherapy, reflexology and massage. Thankfully, I had a basic knowledge of the human body from my studies at university. However, there was still an awful lot to learn.

We were gifted with great teachers; Robert Tisserand, an aromatherapy pioneer was one of our tutors. Happily, he had a very kind, gentle personality—very different from some of my previous teachers!

Robert had published a bestselling book *The Art of Aromatherapy*, which gave a scientific overview of a topic often associated with spa treatments and skin care products. Aromatherapy is not a new science though; the Egyptians are believed to have used a mix of essential oils known as *kyphe* for therapeutic purposes. I learned that the first known work on aromatherapy was in the first century, by Dioscorides.

In 1910, a French chemist called René-Maurice Gattefossé, burned his hand in a laboratory explosion. He later developed gas gangrene, which led to him experimenting with the therapeutic uses of lavender essential oil. In 1937, Monsieur Gattefossé published the book *Aromathérapie: Les Hormones Végétales*.

In more recent years, a French surgeon Dr Jean Valnet used essential oils as antiseptics, on wounded soldiers during World War Two.

Essential oils are extracted from plants, flowers, woods and resins by methods known as distillation or expression. We learned that they are very potent chemicals and are therefore normally diluted in carrier oils such as almond oil, grapeseed oil, avocado oil or jojoba oil, for aromatherapy massage. It is believed that the chemical constituents in the oils travel via the olfactory nerve to the limbic system of the brain, which affects memory and emotion. The constituents also have a physical effect on the body and may help a number of health conditions.

We each purchased a wooden box filled with around twenty-five different heavenly scented essential oils. Our studies included learning the Latin names of each oil, its properties and main chemical components. It was quite a challenge!

Aromatherapy was also offered as a single module, studied over one ten-week term; thus, we were joined by a much larger group of students, who came to study more briefly. They were a great bunch of girls; there were no male students in our classes. There was, however, a sports medicine class running alongside the Natural Medicines Diploma course and it had a mix of both sexes. We did not share class time though, only meeting in the coffee room at break time.

I have rarely since experienced so many great pampering treatments. I enjoyed practical sessions in Swedish massage, aromatherapy and reflexology, where I alternated between being *therapist* and *client*. Swedish massage is a very gentle form of massage, and a delight to give as well as to receive. I also learned some basic acupressure techniques that involved gently releasing blocked CHI, or energy from a series of points on acupuncture meridians, known as pressure points. My favourite acupressure sequence was called a head and neck release. During or after this treatment, I often felt pressure release from the top of my head, akin to releasing the valve on a pressure cooker. It was very much needed as our studies were now very intense.

Thankfully, I passed all my first term exams with good grades and enjoyed a relaxing Christmas break back home in Edinburgh. I had also received my very first diploma in natural medicines, when I completed my training in crystal healing in early December 1987. I was now qualified in aromatherapy, reflexology, massage and crystal healing.

The second term of studies introduced us to the benefits of nutritional medicine and the therapeutic uses of diet, vitamin and mineral supplements. We did further training in massage including facial massage, and we were introduced to counselling skills, including client centred therapy based on the work of Carl Rogers.

Nutritional medicine continued to fascinate me, and I took great interest in poring over the ingredients of *multitudes* of nutritional supplements. I now realised that RDAs or recommended daily allowances were often significantly less than the suggested therapeutic dosages, for disease.

On many levels, I have never felt so ALIVE before or since, but my physical body was grumbling. I was developing severe pains in all of my joints, most notably in my hands and feet. I felt afraid that I might be developing rheumatoid arthritis. In class, we discussed our own medical histories, and I recounted stories of my tonsillectomy, dental abscesses, recurrent laryngitis and joint pains.

"You have a lowered immune system, and you would probably

benefit from some immune enhancing supplements," my tutor suggested.

He then added, "You might also have some food sensitivities."

Thus, I experimented even more with my diet, reducing my intake of specific food groups until I found one culprit—dairy products. I eliminated cow's milk, butter, cheese and cream for a number of weeks, and the joint pains disappeared—as if by magic.

If only it were so simple!

I spent any free time I could muster, commuting to see Dennis in London, and yet I still found the energy for more studies! Once a week, I travelled to a Spiritualist Church in Surrey, to continue my training in colour healing. I also attended a weekend course with a local colour therapist called Bernadette Cleary. Colour and its healing qualities truly fascinated me, so my next step was to join IACT, the International Association of Colour Therapists and attend their AGM in London.

The meeting room was filled with people, and several speakers were giving talks on the theory of colour healing. I was particularly interested in seeing Vicky Wall, a blind colour therapist, who had written a great book, on her Aura Soma colour healing bottles. Vicky's bottles were filled with two layers of jewel coloured liquid. The top layer was oil based, allowing it to float over the water-based lower layer, which created endless colour combinations that dazzled the senses.

Vicky stood up and called on members of the audience, to open Aura Soma colour *pomander* bottles, to demonstrate a simple form of colour healing. I watched in awe as LOTS of people around me opened small plastic bottles, poured liquid into their palms, rubbed their hands together, then waved their hands up and down, a few inches from their bodies. I later learned the pomanders used colour, aromatherapy oils and crystals to promote healing of the aura.

I was *enchanted* once again.

The next speaker was a very handsome Scandinavian colour therapist. He had erected a plain white screen, to the front of the room, and then placed a projector complete with a clear prism in the middle of the room. He asked for volunteers and they duly lined up, to sit in turn on a chair, in front of the projector screen.

I watched on expectantly, as the light from the projector shone through the prism, lighting up the face of each seated volunteer. What amazed me was that as the light changed colour, the volunteer's facial expressions changed too. They soaked up each colour, but in each and every demonstration, one particular colour created a dramatic change. It was a different colour for each volunteer, according to their individual needs. To me it was the most profound demonstration of the day, and yet it was the simplest.

My final term at Raworth passed in an *instant*, filled with more studies on nutritional medicine including the therapeutic use of Dr Bach flower essences, and more advanced massage techniques.

Dr Edward Bach recognised that his patients' attitude played a vital role in their recovery from illness. Both a conventional doctor and a homeopath, he died in 1936 leaving a legacy of thirty-eight specific flower remedies, plus one combination remedy called Rescue Remedy, all created from native flowers, trees and shrubs. The one exception is called Rock Water, prepared from a natural healing spring.

Today, Rescue Remedy in particular is well known around the globe. The other thirty-eight remedies remain less well known, but are equally beneficial.

In the summer of 1988, I emerged from Raworth College, with a much needed boost to my self-esteem—the award for the natural medicines therapist of the year. I felt elated that I had finally found my niche in life, and I had gained recognition for all my hard work. I returned home with my prize of £100—a fortune to me. I treated my family and Dennis to dinner, my way of saying "thank you", for all of their support.

Dennis suggested a holiday to the Algarve, accompanied by his youngest son Paul, and a friend. It was much needed after my studies. Paul was a lovely, quiet boy with an innocent nature. As we soaked up the Mediterranean sun, I noticed a large mole on his arm. Paul's sister Ruth commented on the mole on our return, perhaps it was growing larger?

Medical advice was sought and a terrible diagnosis delivered. Paul had malignant melanoma, an aggressive form of skin cancer. The mole was excised and further treatment followed. The family enjoyed a holiday together in Donegal, and Paul walked with us to Mullaghderg Mountain, admiring the stunning scenery. He seemed to be doing well. The families' hopes rose, but were sadly and cruelly dashed. Paul died peacefully in early 1989. He was only sixteen.

Everyone was devastated.

The lovely girl I had shared a room with at Raworth College, had lost her mother suddenly, before the end of our studies. We had kept in touch, and she told me of the work of Swiss psychiatrist, Dr Elizabeth Kubler Ross on grief, death and dying. I read Elizabeth's book *On Death and Dying* trying to make some kind of sense of what was happening around me. It also helped me understand my own history of depression and lowered immunity following Mum's death.

Meanwhile, Dad had weighty worries of his own, and he wanted me to intervene in a family situation. I felt torn trying to help everyone, and I sought help from a counsellor who listened and encouraged me to put my own needs first. I was caught in what I now know to be the role of the *rescuer*, not at all healthy for my own mental health. It would be many more years before I finally relinquished this title!

In 1988, there were very few qualified natural medicine practitioners in Scotland.

However, I had attracted a lovely mentor at a natural medicine's exhibition. Her name was Dr Muriel Mackay. Muriel was a naturopath, living and working from her home in central Edinburgh. She had been practising her craft long before I qualified, and she wanted to take me under her wing.

Muriel introduced me to others in the natural medicines community in Edinburgh and gave me support as and when I needed it. She was an incredibly generous spirit, and I was glad to count her as a friend.

I soon met a small group of qualified aromatherapists,

who shared a determination to prioritise our own wellbeing. We exchanged treatments on a regular basis, for I did not want to slip back into old unhealthy habits or indeed the black dog of depression.

Around this time, I booked a private consultation with Darlinda, a respected astrologer who had a weekly column in a well-known Scottish newspaper. She was incredibly kind and had a lovely personality.

She told me, "You have many lessons to learn about the flow of money. You do, however, have the chart of a millionaire."

I am still waiting for the *golden cheque* but I have indeed had many, many lessons about the flow of money!

I now focussed my energies on creating a healthy, healing practice. I was anxious to create both a comfortable and a professional environment, so I invested in a good quality massage couch, new towels, a desk and soft, safari type, canvas chairs. One of my larger bedrooms became my therapy room, while a single bedroom became an office, cum reception area.

I was now ready to accept my first clients. Marketing was low in my skills group, so I travelled south once more to a workshop run by a chiropractor and his wife, on simple advertising and marketing strategies. It was incredibly valuable.

Within a few months I built up a good client base, and word of mouth was soon my strongest source of new business. I was thriving. I created a logo for a business leaflet depicting a pair of hands opening outwards, as though in healing position. The paper was in soft green, embellished with my professional credentials, the therapies I offered, and health conditions that might be improved with my therapeutic skills.

I offered a free initial consultation for each new client, where I spent around one hour with them, recording their medical history, current symptoms, medication, diet and habits. I then gave them a reflexology treatment, recording tender areas on the feet that depicted areas of the body that were out of balance. All of this information gave me a good idea of the client's overall health, and I could discern what might be done to help them. I encouraged all my clients to be proactive in their health care and did not promote the idea that I was their healer. Instead, I suggested I was only a catalyst for the body to heal itself.

During consultations, I was often prompted to ask unusual questions which elicited further valuable information on the root causes of my clients' disease. I knew this happened because of my intuitive training at the Spiritualist Church.

One of my clients admitted to feeling incredibly angry with her husband, after her first treatment in reflexology for migraines. I intuited that she had marriage difficulties. In her own time, she opened up, telling me of her husband's infidelities. The headaches had been a manifestation of her anger, which she now felt ready to release and perhaps heal.

Another client had been diagnosed with ME, and his voice sounded incredibly slurred as though he had just had a stroke. I felt strongly that he would benefit from colonic hydrotherapy, and I recommended a practitioner to him. A few weeks later he telephoned me to say "thank you," in a voice I did not recognise. His speech was now clear and he felt so much better. I had lost a client, but he had regained his life.

I kept clear records for everyone, as part of my professional code of conduct. I also ensured that each client was in receipt of their GP's approval. Natural medicines was still in its infancy, and I wanted to create a healthy relationship with the medical profession.

My tax records were immaculate too; I was equally conscientious with my finances.

One day I received a letter to visit HM Revenue office. I gathered all my financial records and duly awaited my appointment. I was eventually shown into a large room with a HUGE wooden central desk and a stern-looking tax inspector. He was quick to explain the reason for my visit, producing one of my leaflets from across his mighty desk. One sentence was highlighted with a luminous marker. "Brigid Gallagher has been practising Colour Healing for several years".

He enquired as to my income from this part of my profession.

"There was no income," I replied. "I gave colour healing voluntarily, at the Spiritualist Church."

He smiled now.

"I thought you called me in to explain the tax system to me, now that I am self-employed," I added.

"I will get you help for that now," a more mellow tax inspector offered!

He was true to his word, calling in another revenue officer, to sift through the reams of papers I had brought with me. I left HM Revenue confident in filling in my tax returns, but perplexed as to who wished me such ill. I never did discover the name of the informer. They must be an incredibly unhappy person to have been so malicious.

My client base continued to thrive, and I found I attracted cycles of people with similar symptoms. I initially saw many ladies who suffered severe PMS symptoms as I had done in the past, then clients followed with arthritis in its many forms including osteoarthritis, rheumatoid arthritis, ankylosing spondylitis, psoriatic arthritis, systemic lupus erythematosus or SLE for short...

I also met many more people with post viral fatigue or ME, who often had to give up work and could not afford treatments; they were invariably depressed. I gave them my support in the form of notes on possible self-help tools. I felt sorry I could not offer them more assistance.

On a brighter note, clients with many other conditions improved very quickly. Many migraine sufferers responded well to reflexology and remained pain free. PMS symptoms and menopausal hot flushes were often quick to disappear; thus, I attracted many more clients.

I was a fan of an author called Deepak Chopra, who had trained in conventional medicine, but had become interested in the ancient Indian healing traditions of Ayurveda. Ayurveda divides people into three body types or doshas—kapha, vata and pitta. Some people could be described as being combinations of body types. Everyone is seen as an individual, and unique in their disease patterns. I learned that two people with the same condition could be given quite different prescriptions, under the principles of Ayurveda.

This knowledge tied in with my own learning, for I found that the principles I had learned *by the book* did not always hold true. For example, in aromatherapy, lavender essential oil is described as promoting relaxation; I found this did not always happen. I myself found it often energised me, and some of my clients had similar experiences. This new knowledge, combined with my intuitive skills, helped me create better treatment plans for each individual.

I was soon drawn to speak to a larger audience and wrote to one of Edinburgh's many WRI groups. I spoke to my first Women's Rural Institute, on the subject of aromatherapy and was soon inundated for requests from similar organisations around the city.

I began facilitating my own weekend workshops from home, in reflexology, aromatherapy and crystal healing. I *soo* enjoyed these days, and it was a delight to see others benefit from these therapies. Indeed, many of my students eventually became qualified natural medicine therapists.

I also promoted my business at lots of natural medicine exhibitions in both Edinburgh and Glasgow. I loved talking to the public, and I seemed to thrive on my new stage. I felt that my old drama teacher Mrs McGregor was guiding me!

The joint pains I had suffered at Raworth did not return, but I started to suffer from chest infections on a regular basis, and I developed pleurisy, just before a planned holiday to Donegal. My GP was somewhat surprised at my X-ray results, as I looked quite healthy. To this day I often look healthy, even if I am in fact feeling poorly!

However, the pleurisy episode was a stern warning to me, and I realised that I needed to slow down and see fewer clients. I gradually reduced my working hours and began to attend yoga classes with Ann. The class was filled with many ladies much more senior than me, but they looked wonderful and they were incredibly agile.

Our yoga teacher had two dogs who always sat at the back of

the room. The class always ended with a meditation, during which the dogs often fell asleep and serenaded us with their snoring! Yoga continued to play a significant role in my self-healing routine, for many years to come.

The Salisbury Centre was an Edinburgh spiritual and healing centre, providing a plethora of courses in exciting New Age topics. The emblem for the centre was the Celtic trine, symbolic of the unifying link between mind, body and soul. One of its founders had been a doctor called Winifred Rushforth, who had travelled to India early in her career as a surgeon. She returned to Edinburgh with a passionate interest in women's health and family therapy and eventually became an esteemed Jungian psychoanalyst. I would love to have met her, but Winifred passed away in 1983. Prince Charles was one of her many admirers.

She left a wonderful legacy, and Ann and I decided to enrol in one of the Salisbury Centre's evening classes—in dream analysis.

Each week, we would recount a recent dream and share it with the group, before taking turns on a possible interpretation. There could be two or perhaps three different interpretations offered by members of the group. The dreamer usually found one interpretation felt just right.

The knowledge I gained from this class has been incredibly valuable. I have several recurring dreams, one of which follows:

I am travelling on holiday and my luggage is immense. It includes several large suitcases and smaller bags; I am struggling to carry it all.

This dream regularly appears when my subconscious is alerting me to deal with accumulating baggage. Thankfully, the amount of luggage I am now trying to carry is much more compact!

Eventually, I too became a tutor at the Salisbury Centre, facilitating workshops in a variety of healing modalities.

Edinburgh continued to be a truly exciting place for New Age wisdom and learning, and I soon discovered a new inspirational venue that promoted workshops by well-known authors including Lilla Bek, who had written *What Colour Are You?*, *To the Light*, and

The Seven levels of Healing.

She was an exciting speaker and well ahead of her time. Her workshop included lots of information on colour healing, chanting which I had started to learn in yoga classes, numerology, the science of numbers and much, much more. The weekend was incredibly inspiring and FUN.

I managed to book a private appointment in numerology with Lilla, and she told me, "You have LOTS of exciting work to do yet."

"You are a very professional therapist, and I would love to have the time for an appointment with you myself. However, my time is limited, and I need to return home tonight."

Her final words were, "The best years of your life will come later, probably in your sixties."

I contemplated my future, but did I really need to wait so very long to blossom?

At Lilla's workshop I spoke to several people who had travelled to India, to visit a man called Sai Baba, who is believed to be an avatar or manifestation of God. They told me that Sai Baba *miraculously* produced a sacred ash called *vibhuti*, which can even appear around his photographs. I learned he could also manifest rings, precious stones and other items *out of the ether*, for his followers known as devotees. I subsequently unearthed several books on Sai Baba's life story, written by *devotees* who had witnessed these *miracles of manifestation*.

Sai Baba began to appear in my dreams. He had an unusual appearance, dressed in long orange robes topped by a shock of dark frizzy hair that stood out wildly from his head. I knew deep inside, that someday I would travel to India to see him.

I continued to attend weekly classes in the Spiritualist Church until 1989, when they sadly ended due to our teacher's personal commitments. Ann and I serendipitously met another interesting lady, who was a National Federation of Spiritual Healers tutor. We enrolled in an evening class with her, and although Ann eventually left the class, I continued to attend weekly classes for the next four years!

She was a fabulous tutor, who made learning exciting. Every week was varied, but always included healing sessions on each other and some form of psychic development. Our new tutor was a very gifted medium, and I became enchanted at the sight of the faces of her spirit guides around her when she spoke.

One night I was washing my face before bedtime, and looked into my bathroom mirror. I was shocked to see my face was overlaid by a dirty one, with a wolf's head worn as a head dress. The face kept changing between a male and a female form, the images lasting for several minutes in total. I definitely had to investigate further.

I had always been drawn to Native American wisdom and I owned several books on the subject, including author Jamie Samm's and David Carson's *Medicine Cards*. In time, I discovered that Native American shamans sometimes wear wolves' heads in sacred ceremony. A medicine man or woman is given this title through respect for their healing powers.

Native American workshops were rare in Scotland, but imagine my surprise when a short time later, a Native American shaman advertised a workshop. Again, I felt *destined* to go.

I enjoyed several of his workshops, where he shared many teachings on Native American wisdom; he demonstrated the art of smudging, where dried herbs are lit in a small container, often an abalone shell, and the resulting smoke is fanned around the body to cleanse any heavy or sticky energy in the aura; he used sacred feathers to fan the smoke.

The most dramatic part of his teachings was a ritual called the Fire Dance.

Our teacher prepared for the ceremony, dressed in Native American costume. In the centre of the room, lay a cloth, on which he placed his healing tools, including his bowl of sacred herbs, his sacred feathers and a large clear quartz crystal. Then he lit a pair of tall white candles.

The energy in the room felt *electric* as we began to dance, in a large circle, while he remained in the centre, taking each of us one by one, to kneel before the flames of the candles. He anointed our foreheads with the *energy of the fire*, before we returned to the edge of the group and continued our dance. The ceremony continued for several hours, yet like the energy of the fire, I remained energised, rather than tired.

Yet more amazing people continued to cross my path, including Dr Patch Adams. Patch was giving a talk at a natural medicine's exhibition, on the use of laughter as a powerful healing tool. Sadly, I did not hear him speak, for I was manning a stand to promote my work, and I could not get someone to cover for me to attend his talk. Patch did, however, walk past me dressed in a colourful outfit; he appeared to be very tall and somewhat charismatic. I remember he sported a large, zany moustache similar to the musician Frank Zappa!

Robin Williams portrays Patch in one of my favourite films *Patch Adams*; it is both funny and poignant in equal measures.

In 1990, I sold my home in Alderbank Terrace and moved to Bannockburn to be with Dennis. I continued to work part time in Edinburgh, commuting to see my clients at a new natural medicine's clinic.

I began to facilitate classes in Stirlingshire, mainly with community groups including mental health and disability projects. I felt I could empower more people with self-help techniques, and thus facilitating classes, eventually became the main focus of my work.

My birthday on March 8 each year was always busy with workshops, for I discovered I had been born on International Women's Day. How apt!

My friend Muriel was impressed by a therapy called electro-crystal healing, pioneered by scientist Harry Oldfield. Harry had created a healing device using pulsed high frequency electromagnetic energy, to stimulate crystals at specific frequencies that aided in the rebalancing of individual chakras. The device could be placed on the chakras or other significant points on the body, to promote healing and balancing of the aura and physical body. Intrigued, I embarked on Harry's training and travelled south to London once again. I obtained my Electro-Crystal Healing diploma in December 1990.

Harry had also developed polycontrast interference photography, known as PIP, a system that portrays a coloured image of the human energy field via a computer screen. My aura was shown on PIP, as part of my electro-crystal training. I decided to do a colour healing meditation, while being filmed. The results were amazing. My aura showed a sea of colour around my body, but as I began to meditate the colours around me changed dramatically, mimicking the colours I was visualising—simple proof that meditation can transform the aura. I took a copy of the PIP *DVD* home with me to share with my students.

Dennis and I embarked on a new hobby back in Bannockburn—horse riding—and I formed a friendship with Minty, a lovely, white horse of medium height, with a placid disposition. I learned how to trot, canter and gallop at weekly classes and outside hacks. I preferred to trot or canter, and learn dressage skills in the riding school's indoor ring. However, Dennis loved to ride outside, the faster the better!

It was a beautiful day, perfect for a hack over the nearby Sheriffmuir Hills. Minty was on another hack, and I tentatively straddled a different horse. Horses tune into their riders, and I was nervous. However, not wanting to let anyone down, I set out with the group. We had a lovely ride into the hills, and I began to relax. However, everyone wanted to canter on the last long stretch, so I stayed to the rear of the group, not wanting to ride too fast on an unfamiliar horse. If only I had had the courage to say no!

The inevitable happened, and I fell off my horse, my head just missing a stone. I lay shocked and dazed on the ground, as the other members of our party came to my aid. I cautiously managed to remount my horse, but I returned home and went straight to bed. The right side of my head felt rather strange for several days. In hindsight, I should have gone straight to the Accident and Emergency Department of our local hospital.

I did return for our weekly riding sessions, but I refused to canter over open hills again!

I had lost my riding nerve, and it never returned; I eventually gave up horse riding, after yet another fall in the indoor ring. However, just like Dad I continue to love horses, but remain content to pat them instead of riding.

While my work as a therapist often took me into esoteric realms, I determined to keep my feet very firmly on the ground. I began to redesign our new garden, digging and planting a myriad of colourful blooms. I found gardening immensely therapeutic, and I was soon hooked. Our garden blossomed, and I invariably had a new horticultural project on the go.

However, my thirst for new knowledge continued....

Radionics is a very precise form of distance healing that uses the principle of dowsing or divining using a pendulum. Most people are more familiar with water divining which uses the same principles. A water diviner uses a pendulum to ascertain the location of underground water, and can even tell the water quality, quantity and depth needed to drill a well!

In radionics, a witness—usually a snippet of hair—is used to dowse the health and well-being of a client, including possible causes of any disease. The practitioner then uses a radionic instrument, sometimes known as a radionic box, to transmit treatments to the client from a distance. Radionic treatments are often carried out on animals such as racehorses, to heal injuries or trauma. It has also been used to prevent pests or diseases on crops—another truly fascinating subject. I had been receiving treatment from a radionics practitioner who lived in the south of England, with much success, so I was familiar with some of its theories and practice.

I began my radionic training in 1992, travelling back to the south of England. I became fascinated by dowsing and practised my techniques on LOTS of willing volunteers. I quickly became even more proficient at assessing chakras, the mental, emotional and physical health of the aura, and causes of disharmony and disease.

One of these *culprits* is known as *geopathic stress*, a title given to unhealthy energies emanating from the Earth, from stagnant underground water, traumatic events that have happened in the past, negativity from previous tenants, electrical pylons…

One of my clients, who had severe arthritis, doubted my dowsing skills when I told him of several possible allergens in his diet. Unfortunately, whiskey was one of them! He eventually took my advice on board, and his pain and inflammation reduced dramatically.

In September 1992, I became a healer member of the NFSH after a long apprenticeship. I was incredibly thrilled. I could now see coloured lights entering the room with my clients, and I knew from experience that they heralded their guardian angels or spirit helpers.

I must point out that professional conduct does not permit healers or therapists to give clairvoyant readings to clients. However, I found that my clairvoyant skills were of immense help in aiding my clients' self-healing for I was often guided to ask them key questions regarding their lifestyle or particular stress issues. It was then easier to co-create a way forward.

In 1993, I approached the Open Studies Department at Stirling University to facilitate classes in natural medicines. I had prepared a number of outlines for classes in aromatherapy and colour healing, plus a general evening class called "Simple Steps to Self-Healing." It included a medley of my healing tools.

I was most surprised, when I was accepted to facilitate several daytime classes, plus an evening class in "Simple Steps to Self-Healing", over a ten-week term. I was quite overcome, because the venue for my classes was Airthrey Castle—the place of my birth. It was now part of Stirling University's adult education facilities!

All my classes filled to capacity, and a waiting list developed for some subjects after several terms. "Simple Steps to Self-Healing" eventually grew into a twenty-week course, and I continued as a tutor for the Open Studies Department until 1999.

Mary Duffy's prediction had been incredibly accurate, I was now teaching unusual subjects and I was surrounded by books!

On June 18, 1993, it was cloudy, and showers of rain had

fallen on and off, all morning. A traditional Scottish piper played under a nearby sequoia tree, as Dad walked me out the front door, around the side entrance, and onto the lawn. I wore a dark green silk Monsoon dress, with a strapless bodice, a ballerina skirt, and a matching bolero jacket.

Dennis waited for me before our new arbour, which stood amidst a border of my favourite cottage flowers. We were married by our dear friend Father Jim, in front of a small group of family and friends. Thankfully, the clouds miraculously disappeared, and the remainder of the day was bathed in glorious sunshine. We were thus able to enjoy a fabulous al fresco meal, prepared for us by a local hotelier. The bridal waltz took place on the lawn, accompanied by dear Paul's beloved long haired cat called Nelson, (after Nelson Mandela) who somehow sneaked into the photographs. He did not want to be left out!

Later in the evening, additional guests arrived, thinking they were coming to a simple garden party! They split into groups, some enjoying the balmy evening outside, others mingling in the kitchen, while our living room became the venue for a singsong. I sang "The Old Woman from Wexford", and many other singers followed.

Although it had been organised in just three short weeks, to tie in with Father Jim's visit, our wedding celebrations were a big success and very joyful. In the past, I had witnessed a number of friends getting incredibly stressed over their wedding arrangements; three weeks of preparation had been long enough for me!

The press were initially oblivious to our marriage. However, a few days later, it made the front page news of *The Sun* newspaper. They had little to write, but it was fun to view the headlines!

Insights from Back to School

- Learning **never** stops

- Follow your heart, and you will have no regrets

- Weddings need not take forever to plan!

Life Can Turn on a Sixpence – July 1993

"Out of difficulties, grow miracles."

Jean de la Bruyerè

One sunny, Friday morning in late July, I embarked on a road journey to Dumfries, where I had an appointment for a one-to-one tutorial in radionics. The roads were incredibly busy, and traffic was nose to tail. I was perhaps ten miles from home when I glimpsed a lorry on a slip road. Alarmingly, the driver did not appear to be slowing down to enter the dual carriageway. He brazenly sneaked in front of me and left me no room to manoeuvre. I had no option but to brake.

A transit van travelling behind me rammed into the rear of my smaller Ford Fiesta, and I was shunted along the motorway like a dodgem car in a fair.

BUMP, BUMP, BUMP!

I was lifted high into the air in my car seat. If I had not been wearing a seatbelt, I would have been catapulted through the windscreen!

Several drivers stopped to help me, while I waited for the police to arrive on the scene. Police statements were taken, and my car was surprisingly considered roadworthy enough to drive home, even though the rear window was smashed, and the car's body was severely traumatised, like me. No ambulance was called.

Still in shock, I drove myself to the hospital in Stirling. The examining doctor in the Accident and Emergency Department told me I had a whiplash injury. I was given a collar and sent home.

The garage declared, "Your car needs a complete new body."

It was eventually repaired.

Luckily, I had a good friend who was a chiropractor. He kindly gave me several free treatments to relieve my injuries. Despite his help, my neck never made a full recovery, and I have difficulty in moving it fully, to this day.

On October 9, 1993, a legendary leader *lit up* a crowd of

around 10,000 people, in George Square, Glasgow. Dennis and I stood among them, as a gentle rain fell. We watched Nelson Mandela stand tall on a stage, beaming benevolence with his customary, charismatic smile. He gave a memorable, moving speech, but it is his dancing that stays in the *camera of my memories*. He had such a great sense of rhythm and boy could he dance!

That day remains one of my most treasured memories. Sadly, one of life's worst experiences soon followed.

It was late October 1993, and Dennis was abroad. I was relaxing at home, in a nice, hot bath when a small foetus appeared in the water, the size of a thumbnail. I had not even known I was pregnant, as my periods had continued as normal—our baby was perhaps eight weeks in gestation.

I was extremely upset, and I cried alone for a number of days. My dreams of motherhood were receding, for I was now thirty-eight years old.

I felt absolutely devastated, and I never became pregnant again.

I mentally christened our baby Brigid, for a succession of Brigids, including Mum and both my grandmothers. I talk to my daughter on a regular basis, for her spirit still endures. I often imagine her as a grown woman who is most probably a teacher as I am now, and her father was in the past. She has long brown hair and watery Piscean like eyes like mine.

Sadly, I buried much of my grief in my work and my radionic studies, a pattern that was not at all healthy.

Part of my studies was to write an essay on the work of noted theosophical author Alice Bailey, called *Esoteric Healing*. It was a thick tome and very difficult to develop into a good essay. I could not get any clarity to write.

I decided to embark on a liquid fast, to still my *monkey mind*. The fast quickly cleared my muddled brain; the essay flowed and was completed with ease. I could not believe it. I was delighted when I received an excellent mark for my work. I have kept my essay for posterity!

Looking forward to gaining my diploma in radionics, I reached the half way stage in my training known as a licentiateship. Eighteen months of further study stretched ahead, before I could get my full diploma.

I travelled south, for my oral assessment. However, I felt incredibly sad, and I could not reason why. Still, I entered the examination room, feeling reasonably calm, and I answered an array of complex questions, to the best of my ability.

We had a guest lecturer at the weekend, a doctor called Christine Page who had written a book *The Frontiers of Health*. It was filled with information on the aura, chakras and possible causes of disease, quite different from conventional medical thinking.

She talked for a while and then guided us in a creative visualisation.

"Close your eyes and concentrate on your breathing," she began. "Imagine you are going for a lovely walk. Take note of your clothes and surroundings."

In my visualisation, I was wearing a summer dress, a sunhat and stout sandals.

"You are carrying a bag filled with tools for your journey. Check inside to see what you are carrying."

I opened my bag, surprised to see a hammer, a saw, nails and a power saw!

"Release any belongings you no longer need to carry."

I ditched the power saw. It was way too heavy.

"Up ahead is a T-junction, with a choice of paths. Look ahead to see where each one goes."

I had a choice of an easy route through a flower filled meadow, or a steep climb over a mountain.

"Make your choice of path."

Yes, I chose the flower filled meadow.

"You will soon meet someone who has a gift for you."

I then met my mother, who gave me a big hug. It was an AWESOME experience.

"Open your eyes now and feel your feet on the ground."

I was back in the room again.

I processed the visualisation and its message, on my journey home. I was incredibly thankful for my mum's continuing support from the afterlife. I knew she was telling me to stop and review where I was going. The tool bag's contents seemed to represent all the therapies I had already studied, and the power saw appeared to be radionics!

A short time later I ended my radionic studies.

To this day, I do not regret this part of my natural medicines' training, for it fine tuned my dowsing skills, I learned a huge amount about the human aura, and I gained much more insight into the many more subtle causes of human disease. I became a licentiate in radionics in March 1994.

I still feel immensely proud of my achievement but for me *the gold* was in the *journey*.

****

Sadly, our dear feline friend Nelson joined Paul in heaven, after being run over by a car. I felt incredibly lonely without him.

My friend Cathy came to the rescue.

"Our cat is having kittens, would you like one?" she gently asked.

I could not refuse her offer. Cathy lives near Colchester, so another long journey by train was needed to collect my new offspring.

I decided to book a healing workshop to coincide with my travel. Paul Lambillion is a fun healer, medium and teacher whom I first met at the College of Parapsychology, in Edinburgh. He would be facilitating a weekend in Bury St Edmunds, not too far from Colchester. I booked a place on Paul's course and promised Cathy I would pick up my new kitten on the return journey.

It was love at first sight.

My delightful, tabby kitten was christened Toby. He had a very lively disposition and soon lifted my spirits, after the trauma and sadness of the past year. We travelled home by train, and Toby was *inundated* with admirers.

They cried, "Oh what a lovely boy."

And, "Can I rub him?"

While Toby replied, "Miaow" from his little basket.

I was a very proud new *mum*.

He quickly settled into his new home and delighted in exploring our surroundings. He would often keep me company as I worked in the garden or relaxed in the evening by the open fire. He loved a good cuddle, and so did I.

Dad had moved back to Edinburgh, as he had missed us all too much in Donegal. I visited him once a week, when we caught up with our news, and he often cooked me a nice dinner—roast chicken, peas and potatoes were a favourite. He remained a very quiet, private, gentleman who loved his garden, his family and an odd night out at bingo or dancing. However, his health was deteriorating and he had recently suffered a lot of pain in his leg. Perhaps he needed a further hip replacement? An X-ray was therefore arranged.

He telephoned me in great distress.

"The doctor has just called," he said, sounding very emotional.

What was wrong? I wondered.

Devastating news followed.

"He says I have terminal cancer. The X-ray has found it in my bones."

I could not comprehend this news. He was on his own, when the doctor delivered this verdict, and how could he know the cancer was terminal from an X-ray?

"Can you come now?" Dad continued.

He was in tears, and so was I. He was just sixty-eight years old, and I did not want him to die.

Somehow I gathered all my inner strength and managed to drive to Edinburgh. When I arrived Ann was with him, but I discovered she did not know of his prognosis. In fact, I learned that Dad had sent her out to the shops, and she had missed the doctor's visit!

I now had to share the terrible news with her, and we cried together downstairs, out of sight.

I was filled with anguish when I first saw him, and I did not know what to say. All I could do was give him a hug and listen to the story of the doctor's visit.

"Can you phone Marie and Margaret?" he asked, after a while. So we did. They were the hardest phone calls of my life.

Margaret still lived in Scotland and could travel easily, but Marie and her family were a *million miles away* in Holland. I knew she would love to have been by Dad's side, right there and then. Distance apart, we were all shocked and devastated by the doctor's unexpected diagnosis.

Dad was to be admitted to hospital the following day, for further tests. I drove everyone in Dad's estate car. We were all struck dumb with nerves, so I switched on one of his favourite Daniel O'Donnell tapes. It was a melancholy song, and I quickly turned it off again.

Silence filled the car.

Tests soon revealed a more positive prognosis. Dad had non-Hodgkin's lymphoma, which could possibly be treated with chemotherapy, but first he needed surgery to repair a break in one of his cancer ridden leg bones. He was eventually able to return home, with the aid of morphine and other medication. Sadly, he had become impatient and short tempered—not the man we knew and loved.

I reduced my work schedule and worked part time. I usually spent two days and nights with him each week in Edinburgh, before the next person on our care rota took over. Dad still loved eating out, and we sometimes managed wee trips to his favourite restaurants. It was tough though knowing that each trip might be our last.

On December 25, 1994, we gathered for Christmas. Marie and her family travelled from Holland, and we tried our best to create a joyful atmosphere. Dad got a present of a DVD, *Mrs Doubtfire,* starring Robin Williams. It is both hilarious and poignant. We laughed and cried together watching the film. I still think of Dad every time I watch it.

Amidst his illness our lives continued, though in a more sombre fashion. On March 8, 1995, I would be forty. A birthday party was out of the question, as Dad was now very sick, and we feared he would slip away very soon. I gathered with a small group of friends for a day trip to a spa, followed by a lovely Indian meal.

Remarkably, Dad picked up a little, and the rollercoaster continued.

I was scheduled to facilitate a four-day summer school on colour healing and I did not want to let the students down, so the course went ahead as planned. It helped me to heal my own wounds and eventually became the basis of something bigger.

I felt there was a great need in Scotland, for a training course in spiritual healing that included counselling skills and care of the dying. I decided to set up a two-year course that would be recognised by the BCMA or British Complementary Medicine Association, allowing students to avail of public liability insurance on completion. Gaining accreditation was a lengthy process. However, it helped me to focus on the future.

Dad was now very emaciated and no longer recognisable as the handsome man of just a year ago. However, he was still determined to stay with us; he simply did not want to die.

If you have witnessed a loved one with cancer in their bones, you will know that it is incredibly difficult to control the all consuming pain. Despite Dad's longing to stay alive, I prayed that he would soon have a peaceful release.

He now had a large assortment of religious medals pinned to his pyjamas and wore a relic called a green scapular around his neck. We recited the rosary with him at bedtime and his faith in a loving God endured until the end. He spent his final weeks in hospital, where he experienced visions of an old donkey friend and other members of his deceased family. Around five days before he died, he slipped into unconsciousness. We then took turns sitting by his bedside, reassuring him and praying.

He died in the early hours of October 17, 1995, fourteen months after his initial diagnosis. Sheer determination had kept him alive, way beyond all medical expectations. Although I had spent the previous afternoon at his bedside, I was home in Bannockburn when he passed away.

Margaret, Ann and I pulled together to arrange his funeral and register his death, while Marie made arrangements to travel back from her home in Holland. Later in the day, I returned to Bannockburn and tried to get some sleep.

I slept little.

The following morning, I entered our living room and there was Dad! He appeared healthy and happy, quite different from recent days. Although he uttered no words, I felt glad to have proof of his spirit's survival after death. I remain thankful that he had chosen to say goodbye to me, in his own quiet way.

He had given us very precise instructions for his funeral. He wanted to be buried with Mum in Annagry's Our Lady Star of the Sea cemetery, and he also wanted a funeral meal for family and friends, at Daniel O'Donnell's hotel—The Viking House.

A few days after his passing, we made the sad journey back to Donegal with his remains, arriving at Donegal Airport to a guard of honour by Naomh Mhuire Football Club. A beautiful meal awaited us in Mullaghduff, while HUGE numbers of people came to pay their respects and showed us such kindness.

On the day of his funeral I was overcome by the poignant singing in the church, and the lowering of his coffin as we each held a chord.

I felt God had let me down, and I now had questions needing answers:

How could he allow this? Why did he take Mum, Paul, my baby and now Dad? It felt so very unfair, and I questioned my faith. I stopped attending mass for a number of years to come.

I had suffered umpteen chest infections, in the past year. I also felt extremely tired; I was literally on my knees. I reduced my workload to a bare minimum, to regain some strength, but I began to suffer from knife-like pains in my right side. They were excruciating. I immediately went to my GP, who arranged an ultrasound test. He felt I might have gallstones. The ultrasound confirmed his diagnosis, and an operation was suggested. However, I wanted to try an alternative to surgery. Perhaps acupuncture would help?

Happily, it did. I had no more pain after two or three treatments, and I postponed my op. However, I continued to have regular acupuncture treatments.

I was in the throes of grief, so ably described by Elizabeth Kubler Ross in her book *On Death and Dying*. Acupuncture helped bring a huge amount of anger to the surface, considered to be one of several stages in the grief process. I knew I was angry at God, but I was also angry at myself, and I was angry at Dennis.

I was forced to face a glaring reality. I was not in great shape, and neither was my marriage.

Serendipitously, I was invited to attend a workshop on dealing with grief, using Native American ritual. It was specifically tailored for health care professionals and was led by a Native American doctor, specialising in the treatment and care of AIDS patients. He talked of his own upbringing where grief is shared by the whole tribe and dealt with in a loving way.

Ritual is considered an important part of healing.

Our group shared in a poignant ceremony, as we walked forward in turn, lighting a candle(s) and naming our deceased loved ones. I included my little baby in my long list. It was an incredibly healing experience.

However, I was also facing my own mortality.

While Dad was sick, a maternal aunt had been hospitalised with a heart attack; she was only fifty. The doctor's questions led to the uncovering of a genetic weakness within my mother's family, predisposing them to blood clots and strokes. It was called Factor V Leiden. They suggested that all family members and their children have their blood checked.

I tested positive, as did several other members of my immediate family. Prophylactic medication in the form of anticoagulants was recommended for surgery, or for travelling long distances. Forewarned is forearmed, and I was glad I could prevent an early demise.

Mum had not been so lucky.

Around this time, I acquired my NFSH training skills certificate, which enabled me to train others to a professional level, in spiritual healing. Soon after, the BCMA gave their seal of approval to my *new baby*, and the Scottish School of Holistic Healing was born!

I promoted the school, and students enrolled, all keen to share in learning the principles and practice of spiritual healing. Once the course began, I facilitated all of the first three weekends, but handed over to a skilled tutor in counselling skills for the next part of the course. It gave me a new purpose in life.

However, I intuitively felt there were more new beginnings ahead for me...

In the spring of 1996, I was passing through a Victorian arcade in the centre of Stirling, which I had walked through many times since childhood. A shop unit was lying empty and *called me* to enquire about its lease.

A vision developed of a shop in the downstairs room, selling books, tapes, crystals, aromatherapy oils... Upstairs, a large room could become the venue for classes including the Scottish School of Holistic Healing. There was an additional upstairs room that looked ideal for a therapy room, which I could use to see my clients. Perhaps it could become a source of additional income, if other therapists joined the practice?

My solicitor negotiated a lease, and I christened the prospective healing centre and shop *Healthworks*. The project lifted me out of my grief and despair, and also helped me move forward with my life.

I sensed the building needed a thorough energy cleanse, so I called on the skills of Dr Patrick MacManaway, who was both a conventional doctor and a skilled healer, specialising in healing buildings and geopathic stress. Patrick used smudging as one of his healing tools.

He and I prepared for a healing ceremony on the building, noting a series of smoke detectors in each ceiling.

I asked the caretaker of the arcade, "Is it safe to burn sacred herbs?"

He replied, "Those are heat detectors, it won't be a problem."

Patrick lit the herbs and moved through the downstairs, fanning the smoke into each corner of the room. We then moved upstairs, and he continued the ritual.

Suddenly, the fire alarm began to SCREAM. We stopped in our tracks and went downstairs.

The caretaker announced, "Everyone needs to leave. The fire brigade are on their way!"

Later, Patrick and I stood at the foot of the stairs, subdued like naughty children, as a series of handsome firemen raced upstairs to investigate. We were soon questioned, "What was the source of the smoke?"

We replied in unison, "We were only burning herbs. In our defence, we were told that those were heat detectors."

The firemen smiled and eventually went home to recount the "Tale of Two Naive New Age Healers".

Although, it did make a funny story, the reality is that fire can kill. I take my hat off to all the brave firemen and women who are committed to saving lives, day in and day out.

It took way longer than anticipated to transform the building, but we opened in time for Christmas 1996. Healthworks' logo became a sun surrounded by a rainbow, taken from an image that had been created at the four-day colour healing workshop.

The large room upstairs was now completely transformed and included silk cushions for seating, in all the colours of the rainbow. They were soon put to good use, as I invited a number of tutors to facilitate weekly classes in chi gung, yoga, belly dancing, and meditation.

We soon had lots of lovely people sharing the building, who all passed word of Stirling's new healing venture.

Our weekend workshop programme included my own Scottish School of Holistic Healing, sound medicine using Tibetan singing bowls, colour healing, angel healing and an array of other enchanting topics with notable New Age teachers including Frank Perry, Paul Lambillion and Ruth White.

The adjoining room upstairs was now a therapy room, and

a selection of skilled therapists joined me at the clinic. We had a massage therapist, a homeopath, a shiatsu therapist and a multi skilled therapist who had once been my radionics tutor.

Business boomed, and my business plan was soon exceeded.

I worked in the shop several days per week. If business was quiet, I read book catalogues, in the hope of finding the right blend of books for my customers. I soon discovered a fabulous new book called *Creating Sacred Space with Feng Shui* by Karen Kingston. It was captivating, and I felt compelled to learn more about the ancient Chinese art of feng shui and Karen's new brainchild called *space clearing*.

I enrolled on a weekend workshop with Karen in London.

I already knew that she lived part of the year in Bali, an Indonesian island steeped in the traditions of creating sacred space in the home. The Balinese physically cleanse their homes daily, sweeping debris, polishing and so on. I learned that they also create daily healing rituals: smudging with sacred herbs and incense, making offerings on sacred altars to their Gods, and using sound energy from sacred bells. The bells polish the energy or chi, promoting better health and wellbeing. It seemed that the Balinese people were a very happy, enlightened race.

Karen advocated the use of salt for clearing heavy energies from the past. Scattering salt into the corners of a room created a lightness that I soon utilised in my own home and at Healthworks.

She also taught us how to create a space clearing ritual which could include:

- Setting down salt in each room in sequence
- Smudging with sacred herbs or incense
- Clapping our hands systematically into the corners of rooms, to break up stuck or stagnant chi
- Polishing the chi using Balinese bells
- Sprinkling Holy water in a final blessing.

I compared space clearing to a traditional spring clean, when we change beds, clean and polish rooms, move furniture, recycle belongings we no longer need, and throw open windows to allow fresh air to circulate.

Salt and smudging were cleaning the energy or chi. Clapping was moving the energy, rather like moving the furniture in a room. The Balinese bells and holy water were creating a lovely polish on the room's energy.

The most interesting thing about space clearing is what happens after a ritual. It ALWAYS precedes CHANGE.

- People release belongings they no longer need
- They also release objects with sad memories
- Homes then feel *lighter*
- Inhabitants feel healthier
- Relationships improve
- Money flows more easily
- Abundant new beginnings just happen

I felt compelled to buy my first Balinese space clearing bell from Karen. It had a unique sound, and I was soon using it for my own space clearing rituals.

I enrolled on more training and eventually bought a second more refined bell, called a priests' bell. It had an even more exquisite, somewhat heavenly sound. Ringing my new bells at home and at work, helped refine the energies in both buildings. They became more peaceful, as did I.

Two Indian ladies called into Healthworks one day and said, "The energy in your shop is like a temple."

I was very touched.

****

Dawn was approaching as I left Dennis asleep in our rustic hotel room.

Outside it was still warm, as I settled down to watch the sunrise. The rays of the sun appeared quietly at first, illuminating the trees around me. It was incredibly peaceful, and I felt glad to be alive. Within ten minutes the scene had changed into a mesmerising spectacle of muted colours, and the trees had filled with sound. The land before me had also transformed, and I could see the sun start to climb in the distance, illuminating the mighty Masai Mara.

I realised I was not alone. The trees were filled with monkeys, chattering now, and the garden had several other human inhabitants, all sitting quietly waiting for a new African dawn. I felt at one with Nature, and with God.

My trip to Kenya brought a sad realisation—my marriage was ending.

I eventually found the courage to leave Dennis in March 1997, knowing I would not return. I filled my car with very few possessions.

My sister Margaret kindly offered me refuge in her home, and I will always be thankful for her support. I stayed with her for a number of months.

In the aftermath of my marriage break up, I often played a sad tape of the uilleann pipes by Davy Spillane. It helped me release my tears. A strange synchronicity brought me several new clients, all in the throes of marriage endings. Professional conduct prevented me from disclosing my own heartache.

I continued to cry daily for six months, and then I suddenly woke up to LIFE again.

I definitely needed a holiday, but where to go?

A television advert soon caught my attention, and Egypt called me!

Insights from Life Can Turn on a Sixpence

- This too shall pass.

Egypt – summer 1997

"Travelling is learning."

Kenyan Proverb

I knew very little about Egypt or its history before my trip, but I learned a HUGE amount in the space of two weeks!

I flew to Luxor and travelled by road to Aswan, for a week long cruise on the River Nile. It would be my very first *solo* holiday abroad, and I was a little apprehensive. I entered my cabin, to view a haven of luxury, with a large double bed and an en-suite bathroom, all reminiscent of a five star hotel. There was a large viewing window, through which I could watch sailing boats called feluccas, against a desert backdrop. I was immediately enchanted!

I delighted in making new acquaintances at dinner, and I bonded with two English couples and an Egyptian family, who had two little girls aged nine and ten.

I learned that the Aswan Dam had been built to provide electricity for rural areas of Egypt, creating a huge man made lake called Lake Nasser. The Temple of Philae was rescued from the waters and restored on high ground by UNESCO in 1960. It was the site of our first evening tour and a Sound and Light spectacle.

We travelled in small boats to the temple's new home, where we watched beams of coloured light illuminate the temple, as the following story unfolded: Isis, The Great Mother goddess also known as the Goddess of Magic, wed her husband, Osiris, the God of the Afterlife. However, Osiris was murdered by his brother Set, and then dismembered, but was restored again by Isis to conceive their son Horus!

Philae is believed to be one of the burial sites of Osiris. The temple at Philae also contained a temple dedicated to Hathor the Cow Goddess, who was the Goddess of Music, Dance and Fertility.

On our arrival back in Aswan, a small group of traders gathered round our small ferryboat. They were selling traditional handmade necklaces that looked quite exquisite.

A man's voice called to me from the other side of the boat, "Don't buy anything from them, you can buy cheaper elsewhere."

I bought several necklaces, there and then—no one was going to bully me!

The cruise commenced, and we were advised to rise very early to avoid the intense heat. We were also told it was best to avoid iced drinks to prevent stomach cramps. I heeded the advice and had no belly problems at all.

Our first stop was Kom Ombo and a temple complex dedicated to Sobek the Crocodile God, also God of Fertility, and Horus the Falcon God, God of Sun, War and Protection.

The site was impressive, with high temple walls that were incredibly well preserved and covered in hieroglyphics. I learned many new words like Hypostyle Hall and soaked up the tour guide's every word on Egyptology!

We sailed on to Edfu, site of the most well preserved temple in Egypt, dedicated to Horus, and then continued our Nile cruise through two locks, based at Esna before arriving back in Luxor.

Luxor, was the site of the Temple at Karnak, which was constructed over the periods of the Middle Kingdom to the Ptolemaic times, the lifetimes of thirty pharaohs! It is considered the largest religious site in the world and is part of the ancient city of Thebes. The site was HUGE and really warranted several days to tour in great depth.

The Valley of the Kings, on the West bank of the Nile is believed to originate from the sixteenth to the eleventh centuries BC—again very hard to comprehend. The bodies of the pharaohs are buried here, in a series of tombs, along the valley. We were able to visit one tomb and descended down steep stairs to witness painted scenes of the Underworld, where the spirits of the deceased are transported to eternal life.

I was concerned about exposure to moulds inside the tomb, as I had experienced a severe allergic reaction after visiting Maeshowe, an ancient chambered tomb on the island of Orkney. Maeshowe was older and considered to originate from 2800BC. The rear wall of the central chamber is illuminated by the rising sun at the winter solstice.

Happily, I was unaffected by moulds, in the Valley of the Kings.

The Valley of the Queens held the tombs of the pharaohs' wives and families, but it was the temple dedicated to Hatshepsut—the only female pharaoh—that was the most dramatic. Hatshepsut had reigned from 1473 to 1458 BC. Her temple was built into giant cliff sides and held three colonnaded terraces, with its main axis aligned to the winter solstice sunrise, just like Maeshowe.

I wondered how people on Orkney and people in Egypt built tombs with such similarities 1400 years apart.

Our final visit was to a temple dedicated to the goddess Hathor, at Dendera. A ceiling covered in astrological symbols was the most memorable of the sights I witnessed, and we were even able to view the surrounding vista, standing on the temple's roof!

I relaxed in a luxurious hotel in Luxor, for the second week of my holiday, and enjoyed several trips to a local village with my new friends from the cruise ship. We were given a guided tour by a resident, who showed us a tile making factory, a house under construction, the village mosque, roses grown for the market, and introduced us to a family living in a modest house who invited us inside for a cup of tea! I felt very humbled, for this family obviously had little money, yet they were only too happy to welcome strangers.

I also befriended two young boys who worked in the local shops, and they invited me to a wedding. I declined the full wedding invite, but delighted in accompanying them to see the bride. She wore a beautiful lace dress and lots of stunning jewellery. I wished her well for the future.

I was relaxing in my hotel room watching a film, when a sad news announcement was made, "Princess Diana has been killed in a car crash in Paris."

Like millions of others around the world, I cried for Diana, and I cried yet again for my own losses. There is nothing quite so healing as letting go of tears. I felt much better for another mighty release!

Before I left Egypt, I was gifted with a significant dream:

I was back in the temple at Dendera. In the dream, I was a young girl entering the temple as an initiate. A priestess led the girl and a group of other initiates into the great hall, which was illuminated by torches. She produced a heart shaped box that was encrusted with turquoise and lapis lazuli. It was quite beautiful.

"Please take a card from the box, it will signify your major life lesson," she announced to the group. "Tell no one what you have read, as it will only be shared with our mother goddess, Hathor."

One by one, the girls in my dream took a card, read its message and returned it to the box.

I took mine. It read: "First, learn to love thy self."

I then realised that every girl in my dream had received the same message!

I returned to Scotland both revitalised and more confident. My trip to Egypt became the first of many solo trips worldwide.

I could not impose on Margaret and her family for ever; thus, I began to house hunt for a more permanent home. My dream was to live in the countryside, and a little village called Thornhill had enchanted me. It was a few miles from my childhood home in Kippen. However, there were no houses for sale, but I waited....

Meanwhile, the students who had embarked on the two-year training course with the Scottish School of Holistic Healing were nearing the end of their studies. They had spent more time with me, expanding their knowledge of the chakras, the aura, particular diseases they might encounter...

They had also enjoyed a very interesting two-day class with Dr Patrick MacManaway on the topic of geopathic stress. I had christened Patrick *Geo Patrick* in honour of our escapade with the smoke detectors!

Patrick showed the students how to dowse for *ley lines* and other energy lines running through the Earth. Sometimes several lines of energy cross, creating special energies that are wonderful for wellbeing. We found several good healing hotspots in Healthworks.

The final weekend of training was scheduled with a very skilled practitioner on the topic of "The Care of the Dying". My own grief was still somewhat raw so I did not attend.

A party followed for the graduating students—a fine reason to celebrate. The students gave me a beautiful brooch, made from rose quartz, embraced in silver and embellished with amethysts and haematite. I treasure it still.

One of the many books I read around this time was Julia Cameron's *The Artist's Way*. Julia suggested a series of writing and other creative exercises designed to unblock potential in artists, writers, sculptors, film producers, therapists…

She also stressed the importance of making creative dates with ourselves, called Artist Dates.

Harriet Buchan is still remembered for the role she played in the Scottish detective drama *Taggart*. She played actor Mark McManus's wife Jean, who was wheelchair bound on screen. In reality, Harriet was once a music teacher, and is now a very skilled voice and sound workshop facilitator.

Harriet had come to Stirling to facilitate a workshop for me, before Healthworks had opened its doors. Our group had enjoyed two days of singing, chanting and playing a host of musical instruments, including Tibetan singing bowls, crystal bowls, rain sticks, drums…

Thus, I decided to travel to Glasgow for a one-to-one consultation with Harriet, as part of my *Artist Dates*. One consultation led to another, and I continued to work with Harriet for nigh on a year.

During our sessions, I could see Harriet's aura light up—it was filled with golden energy, which depicts wisdom. I felt very blessed to have Harriet's help, and I *blossomed*. I had rarely sung since the death of my mum, and my singing voice grew stronger. My inner confidence soared as I relinquished the role of *rescuer*, which I had played throughout most of my life. I was now putting my own needs to the top of my list.

On one of my reconnaissance missions to Thornhill, I discovered Garlands Cottage, a semi-detached cottage that had been lying empty since its previous owner had died. It was in dire need of modernisation. The garden was huge, and it too needed lots of TLC. I was ready for a new makeover challenge.

The house purchase went ahead, and I moved home in early 1998; Toby rejoined me. He had stayed with Dennis until I could find a safe feline home. Like most cats he showed his displeasure at being left behind for so long, when he sat with his back to me for several days. However, he soon relented and was looking for hugs!

Workshops and classes were *flowing* back at Healthworks, and I loved creating an eclectic programme, on an array of topics. I was now a regular guest on local radio, and I even appeared on television. I travelled to Dundee for a magazine programme, to talk about crystal healing. It was a very joyful experience!

Vicky Patterson was a Scottish space clearer mentioned in Denise Linn's book *Sacred Space*. Denise held Vicky in high regard; thus, I invited her to facilitate a workshop.

She was a delightful character and very practical in her approach to her work. She recommended several sacred herbs for smudging—white sage for purification of mind, body and spirit, sweetgrass to invoke more feminine energy, cedarwood for protection and cleansing a new home...

Vicky suggested drumming to break up stagnant energy or chi, which helps inhabitants move forward with their lives. I felt a drum would create a strong, healthy barrier between my aura and any nasty energy that could sometimes be encountered in buildings with a harrowing past.

It was time to create my own drum.

Vicky's husband Graham Walkinshaw, facilitated drum making workshops and agreed to come to Healthworks. He was wise, grounded and intuitive like Vicky. On the morning of the workshop, Graham smudged his aura with sacred herbs, just outside the front door, to avoid the smoke detectors!

The day unfolded in ceremonial fashion, as we gave thanks for our deer skin and the spirit of the deer. We then placed our chosen deerskin over a round, wooden frame, before lacing it, to form a taut drum. The fact that my drum was created from the skin of a deer was highly significant for me.

In Dad's last few weeks of life, I had travelled to Kippen to see a massage therapist, who helped soothe my sad, tired body. On my drive back to Bannockburn, a young deer had crossed the road in front of my car. It had travelled so fast, that I could not avoid hitting it. Distraught, I stopped to help. The young deer was now quivering at the edge of the road. I felt helpless, as I cradled it as best I could. A kind driver stopped and went to find a vet.

Unfortunately, a gamekeeper from the nearby estate arrived before the vet and said, "The kindest thing to do is to put it down."

I gave the gentle deer one last hug and walked towards my car. One sharp shot rang out, and I dissolved into tears for the deer, and for my dear gentle Dad. The pain felt absolutely unbearable.

Native traditions consider the spirit of the deer is that of gentleness, and the power to heal our wounds.

My drum was completed, and I bought two separate drum beaters from Graham. One was soft and gentle, like the spirit of the deer.

I needed one more sacred tool for my emerging work in space clearing—feathers to fan my sacred herbs in the art of smudging.

A series of synchronicities followed, and I was gifted several Eagle and Hawk feathers by two separate donors. I must point out that no birds were harmed in the process. The feathers were merely collected after they had fallen.

In Native American tradition, Eagle is considered a messenger from God. Eagle feathers are earned through hard work and facing life's trials. Healers are *given* eagle feathers.

Hawk is considered an observer who witnesses the overall view of a situation. Likewise, hawk feathers are earned by the recipient.

I created a fan with my new feathers and embellished it with a turquoise crystal, revered by native cultures for the qualities of protection, and sacred vision or clairvoyance.

I added smudging and drumming to my space clearing rituals; I promoted my new skills and once again clients *flowed*. I enjoyed helping them create lighter energies in their homes or workplaces, an increase in their own energy and wellbeing, and quite dramatic improvements in their lives.

I was increasingly interested in the ancient art of feng shui, which is often implemented after a space clearing ritual. I learned that focussing on specific areas of the feng shui map or Bagua, and implementing feng shui cures or enhancements could bring about very **specific** life improvements. It felt very similar in principle to my radionic training, using focussed intentions to bring about precise healing.

I sought out more teachers and books, on these and other topics, including a class in sacred geometry facilitated by Gordon Strachan, where we studied the geometry of Chartres Cathedral. Gordon's classes were quite fascinating.

Another favourite author was Stuart Wilde, who wrote in a fun style on an array of esoteric subjects. His books included *The Trick to Money is Having Some* and *Life was Never Meant to be a Struggle*. He had impressed me greatly with his wisdom, and I discovered he was making a rare appearance to an audience in London.

I booked a ticket.

Seats were unreserved but being an early bird, I managed to get a place in the front row. Stuart came onstage to rousing applause, dressed in an Australian hat, complete with dangling corks! I intuited he was *hiding*, although he went on to mesmerise his audience with his customary fun approach. I reckoned Stuart was in an extremely vulnerable place.

I was blessed to get him to autograph two new books, and I hoped he would thrive and continue to write.

Meanwhile, back in Stirling, the Victorian arcade was undergoing an extensive painting and refurbishment project. During this process, many of the other shop units were left vacant and not re let. The arcade was growing quieter, and our regular footfall greatly diminished.

Unfortunately, I had recently expanded into an adjoining shop, to offer a second treatment room, and it was becoming increasingly difficult to balance the accounts. I joined a local business association, and sought help from an enterprise advisor, who devised a plan to see Healthworks through the glitch. A window dresser offered good ideas on maximising the impact of our large window space, and together with other marketing ideas we inched our way forward.

I was now exploring many forms of ancient wisdom, as I was no longer a practising Catholic. A Tibetan Lama from the Bon tradition was living in Scotland, and I went to Glasgow to hear him speak. He seemed very enlightened, and he had great charisma—rather like the Dalai Lama. He offered individual consultations, and I sought his advice on the future of Healthworks.

He told me, "Healthworks will thrive, as long as you focus your energy within it."

Christmas 1998 approached, and money was still incredibly tight. However, at three o'clock on Christmas Eve, I had enough money to pay all the bills. It was that close!

On Boxing Day, I drove to Donegal to celebrate the remainder of the festive season. I looked forward to a great New Year and created a space clearing ceremony, praying for inner peace and happiness for 1999.

Several momentous events followed, not least the ending of a promising new romance!

In hindsight, we were not meant to be, as both of us were nursing broken hearts. Despite this, I left Donegal feeling lighter than I had in years, for my Spirit had called me to start afresh in Ireland!

Many of my Scottish friends thought me somewhat mad and said, "Why would you want to leave Scotland?"

But I knew that I was doing the right thing for **me,** for Donegal had always been close to my Heart.

I still had to overcome feelings of guilt at leaving Healthworks' therapists and class facilitators with less income. However, I worked through these and other issues with a wise counsellor. She helped me realise, I needed to put my own needs first—just like my Egyptian "Dream on the Nile".

I attended one last Native American workshop in the wilds of the Trossachs, on "The Wisdom of the Warrior", facilitated by my wise counsellor. We practised a standing meditation, honouring the Seven Sacred Directions, as taught in Native American traditions. We honoured the North and wisdom, The East and clarity, The South and purification, The West and reflection, The Above and Father Sky, Below and Mother Earth, and finally ending Within and our own inner wisdom.

The meditation was also designed to centre or ground our energies, and was followed by a Sufi whirling meditation where we all spun like dervishes. I surprised myself with the speed of my spinning, and the fact that I remained centred. I was not at all dizzy.

The meditation was a great metaphor for keeping centred, while Life *whirled* around me.

Healthworks finally closed its doors in the summer of 1999, and we held a New Beginnings party to celebrate. I now realised, that all the therapists and tutors would attract fine new beginnings!

Insights from Egypt

- Travel is enriching on all levels!

- Space clearing helps clear away the Past to embrace a brighter Future.

Slowing Down

The Homes of Donegal - summer 1999

"Everything flows and nothing abides, everything gives way and nothing stays fixed."

Heraclitus

My home in Thornhill sold easily, and my furniture and other belongings were soon packed and transported to Donegal. I said some very tearful "goodbyes" to my lovely neighbours and friends, before travelling to Edinburgh to rest awhile with Ann. Toby came too.

Edinburgh felt buoyant with the joys of The Festival. There was a huge menu of world class cultural activities. What to go to? Ann and I booked two tickets for the Japanese Taiko drummers, who sounded my Scottish departure in truly awesome fashion. They were quite spectacular, and I imagined myself in another world, drumming a Taiko drum to the beat of Mother Earth. Of course I quickly had to come back to reality!

Marie and her children Brigid and Annie greeted us on our arrival in Mullaghduff. I was thankful to be in their company for the first part of my new life, and we enjoyed two weeks together in holiday mode, with trips to the beach, delicious dinners, several nights out, and visits to aunts, uncles and cousins. When it was time to say "goodbye", more tears flowed. I knew I would miss my dear sisters, but as they say, "Absence makes the heart grow fonder."

My time at Glasgow University had been desolate without my family, while Ann and Dad's joint departure had sent me into a major depression. However, I felt different this time round. I had spent the last fourteen years studying and practising a variety of natural medicines; thus, I was stronger, and I was also discovering my true self.

Mullaghduff is a small village with wonderful views around every corner. Some inhabitants have views over the Atlantic Ocean, while others look onto two large, scenic lakes. There are two pubs, Neddie's and Bonner's, each vying for regular customers from the small rural community. Neddie's used to house a small store, but it has long since closed. In 1999, one small shop remained, called Maurice's. The town of Dungloe, perhaps eight miles away, housed two supermarkets—much needed for an economical weekly shop.

A main road snakes through Mullaghduff for around one mile, with lots of narrow side roads spreading over an area of several square miles. I knew a lot of the village inhabitants, for we were all related.

On August 24, 1999, I became a divorced woman. My marriage ended quietly, as though it had never happened. I applied for an Irish passport, complete with my maiden surname of Gallagher, for I felt immensely proud of my family heritage.

I began to form a kind of newbie support group with several cousins who like me, had recently returned to the home of their ancestors. We were all self-employed and shared in the challenge of attracting employment in a small rural community.

The population of Stirling town had been over 80,000, while the population of the 1877 square miles of Donegal was a mere 140,000. Incidentally, in the 1841 census Donegal's population was 296,000. Happily, The Diaspora was slowly returning in 1999, in anticipation of the Celtic Tiger.

I soon discovered there were very few other natural medicine practitioners and only one (new) community project in my locality. I found myself a natural medicines *pioneer* all over again. I had to put all my marketing skills into practice once again.

I found the local press were very happy to promote my work and gave me a number of features in local newspapers. I also spoke on local radio, including a series of slots for Inishowen Community Radio on the topic of feng shui. I wrote several articles for the Inish Times and set up new classes in self-healing. I steadily attracted clients.

I wanted to learn Irish and enrolled on a night class. I attended perhaps six or seven classes in all, yet I could not progress. I gave up on becoming a fluent Irish speaker.

I decided to try out other new hobbies, and I enrolled on a

watercolour painting class in Dungloe. My first artistic attempts were pretty dismal, but I persevered and many more classes have followed over the years. I now dip in and out of art classes, and I have had a number of lovely teachers in a variety of mediums.

Donegal is brimming with creative people. It is home to many artists, writers, playwrights, actors, dancers, singers, musicians...

Enya and Clannad hail from Dore, a few miles north of Mullaghduff, Daniel O'Donnell from Kincasslagh, about three miles south, Mairead Mooney and the band Altan from nearby Gweedore...

There must be some invisible *magic* in the air!

I began to write a book on feng shui, and I christened it *The Heart of Sacred Space*. It would be based on my own experiences, after implementing feng shui cures or enhancements. Feng shui and space clearing had helped me move forward after my father's death, the break up of my marriage, the closing of Healthworks, revamping and selling Garlands Cottage, and moving to Donegal!

There were no books on the INNER healing that clients experienced from feng shui. I felt this was part of my new mission. I set up a website of the same name, to promote my business.

Serendipitously, *Image*, a national magazine wrote a fabulous article on my space clearing work, accompanied by a photograph. It heralded a flow of new contacts, and I was blessed with many lovely clients.

I felt my physical health and energy blossom in my new environment, and I felt it timely, to fulfil another long held dream. In Scotland, I had helped promote a charity called Healing Hands Network, which sent volunteer natural medicine therapists to Sarajevo, in Bosnia. The charity had been formed in 1996, after The Balkans War.

Several of my Scottish friends had already volunteered. In order to go to Sarajevo, I first needed to raise funds for my fare and the charity's expenses. I decided to organise a Natural Medicines Day in nearby Kincasslagh Parish Hall.

I contacted a small number of therapists in my local area, who booked tables to promote their business and perhaps do a talk; I sold my collection of crystals and some books, and the funding flowed. I was ready to fly to Sarajevo in the summer of 2000.

First though I wanted to dance!

I had longed to experience a Five Rhythms dance workshop, a form of movement meditation created by Gabrielle Roth in the late 1970s.

I travelled to County Meath, for a week long workshop in early summer to practise Gabrielle's five free form rhythms of dance, named Flowing, Staccato, Chaos, Lyrical and Stillness (I think their names describe them well). Dancing all five rhythms in sequence was called dancing "The Wave".

I danced very tentatively and shyly at first, concerned at not lasting a full week of high energy, physical activity. However, I need not have worried; I paced myself, and I danced to the Five Rhythms every day.

 Classes were interspersed with creative activities, and we were asked to put on group theatrical sketches. I was sent to the lyrical group as I suspect our teacher felt I needed to lighten up a little and embrace my more playful Inner Child.

She would not be disappointed.

Our group spent most of one afternoon painting green spots on a large sheet of paper to depict giant peas on a boat, for Edward Lear's poem *The Owl and the Pussycat!*

We eventually formed a semblance of a plan for our dramatic performance. I would be the narrator, dressed in a pink cheesecloth skirt, raised up to depict a *fairy like* dress. To complete my new image, I carried a wand complete with a sparkly star. The boat contained said owl and pussycat, while the pig and the turkey stood in waiting for the *marriage cue.*

We were indeed a sight to behold, as I recited:

"The Owl and the Pussy-cat went to sea,
In a beautiful pea-green boat,
They took some honey, and plenty of money,
Wrapped up in a five-pound note.

The Owl looked up to the stars above,
And sang to a small guitar,
"O lovely Pussy! O Pussy, my love,
What a beautiful Pussy you are,
You are,
You are,
What a beautiful Pussy you are!"

I think our teacher was somewhat surprised, or was it shocked at our transformation!

I thoroughly enjoyed this dramatic interlude, and I felt my old drama teacher Mrs McGregor would have enjoyed it too!

Finally, I flew via Dublin and London to Zagreb, the largest city in the republic of Croatia. However, I discovered that the onward connection to Sarajevo was delayed until the following morning. Thankfully, I was now in the company of several other Healing Hands Network therapists including a young massage therapist and a female chiropractor. We passed the time chatting and sharing our life experiences, before being bussed to a hotel for a few hours much needed sleep. Our massage therapist, being both outgoing and attractive, befriended one of a number of UN troops who were also diverted to the hotel overnight. They exchanged phone numbers.

In a 2008 statement to the UN, it was estimated that during the Balkans War, a total of 200,000 people died including 12,000 children. Fifty thousand women are believed to have been raped and 2.2 million people were forced to flee their homes. Sarajevo had been encircled by 13,000 troops in a siege that lasted from April 5, 1992 till February, 29 1996. More than 9,500 people died there during the conflict, including more than 5,000 civilians. The number of people wounded exceeded 13,000.

In the summer of 2000, the city of Sarajevo was still bearing the scars of war. Numerous buildings were pockmarked by shells, and a sea of shimmering white headstones lined the surrounding hillsides. I soon learned that landmines littered the surrounding countryside, and it was incredibly dangerous to go walking on open areas.

Despite its outward appearance, Sarajevo held the most beautiful energy. It felt like angels or other heavenly beings embraced the city.

The HHN clinic in central Sarajevo was simple, containing several treatment rooms, a sitting room cum office, accommodation for visiting therapists, and a small kitchen for cooking. I shared a modest room with the young massage therapist, who was incredibly untidy, but lots of fun. The room was littered with clothes, books and toiletries on one side, and very neat and tidy on the other!

I practised spiritual healing rather than my other healing tools, as we already had an in-house reflexologist, massage therapist and chiropractor. Our clients spoke little English, so we relied on an interpreter to discuss each individual's medical history.

The gratitude of the Bosnian people was overwhelming. Every day, they brought small gifts of food to our clinic, and I for one felt very humbled. We never questioned them on their ethnicity or religion; everyone was treated as equals.

One day a week we journeyed by tram or bus to outlying areas, to visit those who could not travel. On our first outreach visit, we climbed a very long flight of stairs in a battle scarred block of flats, to reach an elderly man who was both paralysed and house bound. There was a very special energy around him, and his eyes shone brightly. Despite his limited existence, I believe he had found some form of inner peace, or perhaps *enlightenment*.

We also visited several landmine victims, who had lost limbs. One young man was wheelchair bound after losing both legs. He showed no signs of bitterness, a true eye opener for me.

Yet another memorable visit was to two middle-aged grandparents, looked after by their young granddaughter. They all shared one large three-in-one room, it was their living room, kitchen and bedroom. The family welcomed us into their modest home, overjoyed at the prospect of our visit.

Our interpreter opened our visit with a few words from the lady of the house, who was busy crocheting a pair of slippers:

"Do you like these slippers?" she asked.

"I do," I replied via our third party.

"They are yours," she answered.

I felt very humbled indeed.

I channelled healing for the three family members, while my massage therapist friend gave each a massage.

By the end of our visit my new slippers were ready!

My story does not end there, for on our return visit the following week, I received a crocheted rug and a thick two-toned, hand-knitted cardigan. My friend was laden with similar gifts.

I consulted our interpreter and asked, "How can I repay their generosity?"

"They would be greatly embarrassed if you offered them money," she suggested. "However, they do not have any wood for the long, cold winter ahead, since prices have increased so much."

I left a donation towards their winter wood fund with the interpreter, who later acted with great diplomacy.

I had several items on my *wish list*, before I left Sarajevo. I longed to meet a traditional healer, and I was introduced to one, while walking through an outlying village! We chatted through our interpreter for a while, and I asked if she might like to swap a treatment back at our clinic. Happily, she agreed. My legs had been particularly uncomfortable after the lengthy flight, and I remember feeling my circulation getting a mighty boost from her treatment. I hope she found my treatment therapeutic too.

We now had a weekend off, and I had made several enquiries about the remaining wish on my list, to travel to Medjugorje, a small town not far from Mostar.

On June 24, 1981, six young visionaries first saw an apparition of The Virgin Mary on a local hillside, now known as Apparition Hill. Three of these young people continued to have daily apparitions, whilst the others have visions once per year. I had heard of Medjugorje from one of my clients, who had found great solace and healing on a pilgrimage.

All my travel enquiries proved unfruitful, as it appeared to be a very difficult journey to make via public transport. However, the

UN came to the rescue, when our massage therapist's contact offered his help and agreed to chauffeur us to Medjugorje. He arrived early on Saturday morning, accompanied by a good friend, who was both tall and handsome with smiling, crinkly eyes. I intuited that he was both a wise and gentle *old soul*.

Shyness overtook me for most of the initial journey, while my comrades chatted animatedly. I gazed out the car window, as we sped though breathtaking scenery, along valleys fringed with tall mountains, forests, lakes and villages, not unlike Scotland's Glen Coe or the *bonny banks* of Loch Lomond. However, today's scenery was scarred, and many of the homes we passed lay entombed in rubble, or pockmarked by shelling.

We stopped in Mostar, a town that had endured a siege of nine months, to buy some fresh baked bread, to include in a proposed picnic, and then walked along a modern bridge spanning the Neretva River, and looked down on the ancient Stari Most Bridge now damaged by vicious shelling.

The atmosphere was somewhat heavier here, compared to the lightness of Sarajevo. I do not know why. I did not feel at all comfortable, and I was glad to resume the onward journey. Happily, we soon wound our way up a new series of hillsides, and on into Medjugorje, which was filled with an air of great peace.

The boys parked their car, and we alighted for a much needed coffee in a local café directly opposite the twin towers of St James Church. After imbibing our refreshments, I arranged to meet up with my friends in an hour, for I had promised to deliver a bundle of healing petitions for family and friends. I soon located the appropriate receptacle, depositing my letters among a myriad of others before wandering inside the church to say a few prayers to Our Lady.

Hungry now and in need of sustenance, we journeyed on a little further, to a lovely picnic spot by the side of a lake. Our afternoon was spent relaxing in glorious sunshine, swimming, chatting and eating. My shyness dissolved, particularly when I found the boys shared my taste in music. The journey home passed in a whirl of singing, to music from Dire Straits, Bryan Adams, Simple Minds…

Arriving back in the city, an Italian meal was suggested. I took a welcome shower and transformed myself inside a pretty, pink summer dress—the male response was pretty positive. Leaving the restaurant after a delicious meal, my new UN beau and I walked on past our car, around a corner and back round again in a circle, now lost in each other!

Back at HHN headquarters, we bade our goodnights and arranged another group meal for mid week. This time round, I volunteered to be chef.

The day of my dinner date arrived, and I produced a meal of pasta, salad and garlic bread, followed by poached peaches and ice cream. It was well received. Sadly, it was the last time I saw my UN friend, for he had no further time off.

The rest of the week passed in a flash as our healing work continued. Our team visited a children's orphanage, which captured my heart all over again. We worked with the special needs children, who lay in a series of cots. I can still remember treating a lovely little girl with hydrocephalus, who had beautiful eyes as big as saucers. I prayed that she might get the healing she needed.

Although the people of Sarajevo had been through their own version of hell, many of the people I met there had found some kind of inner peace. Many others I met were still coming to terms with their experiences. I now wondered, what is this mysterious ingredient that helps the human spirit survive such trauma?

I felt truly blessed to have met such inspiring people, and my tears flowed like waterfalls on the day of my departure. I arrived home, determined to return to Sarajevo.

I stayed in touch with my UN beau for several months, but sadly our friendship came to an end for private reasons. However, I often think of him and what might have been.

I remained determined to fundraise for another visit to Sarajevo with Healing Hands Network. The funds flowed, but an alarming health issue arose, which prevented my return.

In the autumn of 2000, I began to pass blood from my bowel. I did not hesitate in seeking medical advice, for I had recently lost an uncle to bowel cancer. Sadly, he had not been diagnosed until it was too late. In fact, it had been a Chinese medicine consultant who had suggested he had cancer, despite numerous medical investigations proving negative.

An urgent colonoscopy was arranged for me, so I booked extra radionic treatment for my nerves on the day of the test. Climbing onto the hospital couch, I felt incredibly relaxed, and the colonoscopy passed in an instant. I waited in the Day Admissions Department for the results.

"You have mild inflammatory bowel disease," said the consultant.

I sighed with relief.

"However, there is a ring of tissue inside your bowel that merits further investigation. I will refer you to Dublin for further tests."

I was referred to another consultant, who arranged for a biopsy of the unusual tissue. I travelled to Dublin for the procedure, which was done under general anaesthetic. Happily, he had a kind demeanour which quickly put me at ease.

I returned to Dublin for my results.

"The tissue is not malignant, but it is of a type that is prone to change," he opened. "We will do a repeat biopsy in a few months, just to be sure."

He then added, "You also have a prolapsed bowel."

I was advised to return for regular reviews, and thankfully the next biopsy was also negative. However, eleven years of further tests and procedures followed. I will spare you the details!

In 2001, Ann and her partner Lawrence decided to move to Donegal, and they found a home to rent, a couple of miles away from me in Braade. Although I now had lots of new friends of my own, no one can match my dear sister. I felt incredibly happy.

A number of my new friends hailed from a shamanic drumming circle, which met monthly in Letterkenny. Each gathering had the same format—we all sat silently together on the floor and drummed—while the rhythm of each drum synchronised, and became as one giant meditative, heartbeat. It felt incredibly powerful and very healing. It was an added bonus to discover so many like-minded people, and I absolutely loved our gatherings; I was now my own version of a Taiko drummer!

I was travelling quite a bit now to see clients, mostly by coach as there are great links to Dublin, Belfast, Sligo and Galway from The Rosses. Bus prices are keen too, so it made good sense to avoid driving. We are also very blessed with a local airport in Carrickfin, a couple of miles from central Mullaghduff, which boasts regular flights to both Dublin and Scotland.

Around this time, I decided to add a new *dish* to my Irish healing *menu*—aura drawings. I had offered these consultations in Healthworks, but was Donegal open to them?

I had witnessed coloured lights around the human body, for more than ten years now, and I was more than familiar with their meaning. In my drawings, I used water colour pencils to preserve each client's image, and then explained the properties of these colours to aid in their personal empowerment. My aura drawings soon attracted a regular following.

"I see you have a beautiful shade of pink around your heart chakra. You are a naturally kind and caring person," I might open.

"Yes, I work with special needs children."

"Pink-hearted people often get taken for granted, as they are often TOO soft hearted.

Remember to take good care of YOU too," I added.

I had learned this from my own experience!

I had also become quite adept at reading the tarot, and I offered my first tarot readings to the public during the famous Mary from Dungloe Festival. Boy was I busy. However, I soon learned that people wanted *predictions* rather than an empowering overview of their natural talents. I stopped offering tarot readings.

One of the students from a local music college offered to teach singing classes, and I joined a group of around eight other women, to learn a number of lovely songs.

I practised at home, in my soprano voice, singing a number of Irish traditional ballads.

Toby was usually my sole audience. He did not appear impressed!

My first book *The Heart of Sacred Space* felt complete, therefore, I sent it to several agents. I received one reply; I was told it needed to be longer. Although I felt somewhat disappointed, I continued to add to my literary *tome*.

I had long held a wish to travel to India to see Sai Baba and I felt a *calling* to go in the spring of 2003. First, I needed to save a fair sum of money for my air fare, food and accommodation for a six-week pilgrimage.

Consultations *magically* increased, and I *manifested* the funds for my dream trip in less than three months!

Insights from the Homes of Donegal

- You are ALWAYS in the right place, at the right time, doing the right thing.

India - spring 2003

"True happiness consists in making others happy."
Hindu proverb

My pilgrimage round southern India started rather badly, for I arrived in Bangalore after two days of travelling via Dublin, London and Sri Lanka, and my baggage was lost! Tired, sweaty and very much in need of a change of clothes, I was in the throes of a very bad mood when I approached the baggage reclaim counter.

"My luggage is missing," I declared, holding back a river of tears, caused by tiredness and frustration.

"Your suitcase is not in Bangalore," I was told after a lengthy wait. "It will arrive on the next flight from London."

I felt utterly powerless now, and my black mood deepened. I reluctantly accepted compensation of 50 US dollars from the airline, to replace my clothes and toiletries.

I had not arranged accommodation in Bangalore, as I had planned to travel directly to Whitefield, an ashram devoted to Sai Baba. Sadly, my bad-tempered demeanour was not a promising start to *enlightenment* in India.

I moved to the hotel reservations counter, to seek comfortable accommodation in the city, while I awaited my *baggage*. I was offered three nights lodgings in a small, central hotel. The cost seemed rather pricey for India. My mood was now black as coal.

Outside the airport terminal, a cheery, middle-aged taxi driver politely asked me, "Where would you like to go, ma'am?"

I gave a very snippy reply.

He began a conversation, despite my obvious dark demeanour, "Is this your first visit to Bangalore, ma'am?"

"Yes."

"What is the purpose of your visit?"

"I am here to see Sai Baba."

"Aaah, he is my guru too..." he continued. "I have a ring that he manifested for me, look. It holds a ruby of very large proportions."

We chatted animatedly for the rest of the journey.

My taxi driver was the very proud owner of an *Ambassador* car, pleasantly filled with the aroma of real leather seats, bringing back memories of my childhood. The scent and the conversation brought an end to my bad mood, and I began to relax.

Bangalore is noisy, busy and home to over eight million inhabitants—more than the whole of the island of Ireland. I gazed out at Bangalore by night, as we passed hundreds of scooters accommodating whole families, including women in beautiful saris, holding tightly onto small babies and children, a multitude of auto rickshaws, with room for three people and their luggage, all blending into a noisy plethora of buses, cars and lorries.

Finally, we stopped outside a small hotel, and I entered the lobby, feeling more than a little disappointed at its somewhat shabby décor. However, I found my room was clean and adequate for my needs. I was now desperate for sleep.

It came in several short bursts, as I succumbed to the mighty throes of jet lag!

However, I greeted the next day, determined to be in better humour, as I set out on a shopping trip with last night's taxi driver.

"I need some new clothes," I told him.

"I get you very good price," he promised.

A couple of hours later, I returned to the hotel armed with a new wardrobe. It included a white silk sari with cotton petticoat (a totally impractical colour), a cotton salwar kameez (a tunic top with matching loose trousers) with two tops in lilac and khaki, and a matching scarf, a pair of stout, plastic, flip-flops, a pair of khaki trousers, and a cotton western style blouse. A bar of soap, a toothbrush and a tube of toothpaste completed my spending spree. The total cost was bang on 50 dollars!

Later, I telephoned the airport. "Has my luggage arrived yet?" I enquired in a much better mood than on arrival.

"It has been traced. You will have it soon—perhaps tomorrow."

I now determined to make the most of my stay in the city and booked an auto rickshaw tour of the most famous sites and temples, including the Lalbagh Botanical Gardens. The gardens were a welcome sight, filled with large open areas of grass, smart flower beds and seats to admire the view. I love people watching and delighted in observing more sari creations; I felt each one was more beautiful than the other. I relaxed more and threw caution and my limited budget to the wind, booking a day trip in last night's luxurious taxi, to the nearby city of Mysore.

I chatted with another western tourist in the hotel lobby.

"I am going to Mysore by taxi tomorrow." I smiled.

"Why go by taxi, the train is less expensive?" he replied.

"The view from the taxi is better," I quipped, and the conversation ended.

Happily, I found sleep came more easily on my second night in India, and I awoke refreshed for my next adventure.

The taxi sped through lots of small villages and towns, while I sat in the front passenger seat, delighting in the view. Indian homes looked very basic by western standards, but the inhabitants smiled back and children waved, making me feel very welcome. The scents of India filled the air—incense, spices and most predominantly DUST.

"Would you like to see my new grandchild?" my companion said.

"That would be an honour," I replied.

Thus, we made our first stop outside a small maternity clinic. Conditions inside were very basic with metal beds, simple striped mattresses, and very few other furnishings. Indeed, the room did not look too clean for a mother and her new baby. However, *mum* looked relaxed and happy, as she proudly showed us her new offspring—a little boy. I was able to hug my first Indian *miracle*.

The second miracle was quite unexpected as we parked outside a small orphanage a few miles outside Mysore called Sri Ranga Patma. It was also home to a modest temple dedicated to Sai Baba and his predecessor Shirdi Sai.

Shirdi Sai had died in 1918, while Sai Baba had entered this world on November 23, 1926. I had already learned that he was believed to be a reincarnation of Shirdi Sai, that he had composed religious songs known as *bhajans*, from the age of seven, was noted for many miraculous healings, and the materialisation of objects such as rings, prayer beads and of course, the sacred ash known as *vibhuti*. Vibhuti tastes of scented flowers and is reputed to heal all manner of ills. I now had a small packet back at home.

Sai Baba and his devotees had raised huge sums of money to help the poor of India, providing free health care in purpose-built hospitals, as well as a number of free educational and other charitable projects.

We were greeted by a rotund Indian at the entrance to Sri Ranga Patma, and he motioned us inside to view the temple—his pride very evident. The walls were covered in pictures of the two avatars each coated in vibhuti. It was a wondrous sight.

Our Indian guide placed two small medals featuring Sai Baba and Shirdi Sai, in the palm of my right hand, and I watched in complete shock as a syrupy liquid began to fill both my palms.

"Please drink, please drink," the guide urged.

I immediately felt a burst of *heavenly* flowers tantalise my tongue. It tasted *divine*. I was even more amazed when my palms simultaneously began to fill yet again with this delicious nectar, which I later learned is called *amritha*. I drank from my hands once more, and then the wonder was repeated for a third and final time, before I handed the two miracle producing medals back to our guide.

"You enjoy?" he enquired.

"It was heavenly," I replied.

He then handed me a plastic bottle filled to the top with amritha. I was more than happy to leave a healthy donation for the orphanage.

I returned to my taxi for a tour of Mysore, yet another veritable feast on the senses. I visited the Amba Vilas Palace with its stunning rooms and gardens, posing in my lilac salwaar kameez for posterity.

"I know a very good place to eat," my driver said.

We lunched at a small hotel, near the palace gates. My

companion joined several other drivers at a separate table, while I dined alone on thali, a delicious collection of small portions of spicy Indian delicacies, including dhal made from spiced lentils (very spicy), vegetable korma (kinder on my tongue), rice and naan bread, all served in individual metal dishes on a small metal tray. I added an order of lassi, a delicious yoghurt drink to soothe my burning tongue.

The journey back to the metropolis of Bangalore was event free, apart from the endless dodging of crazy drivers, cows, dogs and people that lined our route. I reflected on my previous conversation in the lobby. Travelling by train would have been dull, compared to the wonders of my trip by taxi!

I slept more soundly that night, now revelling in the charm that is India.

By day four, my luggage had not returned, and I travelled to my airline's main office in central Bangalore to express my displeasure.

I was told once again, "It will arrive soon."

Increasingly sceptical, I packed my meagre collection of clothes and accessories into a small cardboard box, and travelled fifteen miles or so to Sai Baba's Brindavan Ashram, in Whitefield, where I found more affordable, though shabbier lodgings with a small veranda overlooking a quiet road, lined with deliciously scented flowers. I placed my cardboard box on a small wooden table and took a photograph of my *baggage* for posterity!

I decided I would move again, when better accommodation became available.

Sai Baba was not yet in residence, but was expected to make his annual spring visit in a matter of days—no one knew exactly when. I established a new, quieter pace as rumours began that he would arrive tomorrow, and then another tomorrow....

Meanwhile, I explored the small streets and shops, filled with tantalising and **very** affordable Indian crafts, and clothes, somewhat cheaper than the city centre. It became obvious that my city taxi friend was earning a good income on commission!

I purchased three more sets of white cotton salwaar kameez,

to combat the growing heat. Two sets were embroidered with colourful flowers in shades of turquoise and red, while the other was a pristine white. My sturdy, purple, plastic, flip-flops were perfect for the dusty roads and pavements, and a considerable source of comfort to my now swollen feet.

I was delighted yet again when I discovered a small, local hotel that served my favourite thali, for a very modest price.

I awoke to my birthday on March 8, feeling happy at the prospect of an Indian style celebration. My intuition told me that Sai Baba would arrive today, so I walked to the ashram and waited quietly outside the large metal gates. I did not have long to wait, before a fleet of large cars arrived, escorting the avatar into his ashram. His limousine slid quietly through the gates, and he soon disappeared from sight, just as quickly as he had arrived.

Word soon spread that Sai Baba had finally arrived in Whitefield, and the energy in the surrounding shops, hotels and guesthouses elevated, as everyone became *busy as bees*, preparing for a giant influx of new devotees.

I learned that rooms in the ashram would now be available, but that a selection process was in force that did not necessarily follow western logic. I determined to join the accommodation queue as early as possible. A little later, I stood near the front of a very long queue, witnessing lots of short tempers like my own at Bangalore airport. Many devotees were behaving like extremely naughty, spoilt children. Voices raised and quarrels broke out, but I determined to remain calm. I was now over my jet lag!

The ashram accommodation was eventually allocated. Rooms were given to people in front of me, and some to those behind me. The queue shortened, yet I remained in line!

I began a conversation with a pleasant lady just in front of me.

"Where have you come from?" I asked.

"I'm from Sri Lanka," she replied.

"And you?"

"Ireland..."

I discovered that she was a traditional Sri Lankan dance

teacher, who had visited Whitefield a number of times.

"I know where we might find a pleasant room," she continued, as she escorted me a short distance away, to a well-maintained private house, where they took a small number of paying guests.

We were both delighted when the lady of the house announced, "We have two rooms left."

I was in *holiday heaven*, when we were each allotted clean, homely rooms, with en-suite shower and toilet facilities, for a very modest price. Early in the afternoon, I moved my cardboard box of new clothing and toiletries, before settling into my new lodgings. I telephoned my airline to enquire of my luggage, and was greatly surprised to learn it had finally arrived—a mere five days later than promised!

Returning to central Bangalore by local taxi, to collect my two suitcases—one small, green, soft fabric model filled with a basic wardrobe, inside a large solid case for my prospective Indian purchases—I realised that my new clothing was far better suited for my travels. My western clothes were barely worn on my six-week journey!

Later that afternoon I had my first *darshan* or group blessing from Sai Baba. Darshan means *to see* in Sanskrit, referring to seeing the sacred; it is also purported to bring good fortune, wellbeing and grace.

I queued early with many others outside the ashram. However, another interesting allocation system was in force. I longed to get a good view of Sai Baba near the front of the open temple, known as a *mandir*, but I was allocated a place near the rear!

Meditating quietly, I realised that everything was unfolding quite perfectly.

My meditation was soon serenaded by the crowds around me, singing *bhajans* or devotional songs. The atmosphere became quite peaceful and very serene.

Sai Baba made his first entrance near the front of the mandir, dressed in long saffron robes, topped with his famous mop of black curly hair. He smiled gently, while wandering through the large crowd, now seated in orderly rows upon the hard floor. I put a soft cushion to the top of my shopping list!

Many devotees, including myself, passed envelopes along the rows, with written requests for prayers or healing. Sai Baba took some and declined others. My envelope was happily accepted—another perfect birthday gift.

The proceedings continued with more bhajans, a few words, more blessings on the crowd, and then Sai Baba was gone. We moved out of the mandir in quiet, orderly fashion. It had certainly been a memorable birthday!

Whitefield was soon bustling with visitors and new enterprises abounded. A succession of vacant shops filled with traders selling clothes, books, jewellery in gold, silver, precious and semi precious stones, Tibetan singing bowls, prayer flags...

My budget was modest, and I had no idea of the cost of accommodation elsewhere, so I put thoughts of more purchases to the back of my mind. It would have been very easy to overspend, but I had a total of six weeks planned for my Indian Odyssey.

I adopted a new routine for the next ten days of my trip, attending twice daily darshan, made more comfortable by a new soft cushion!

My body began to release lots of toxins, and my joints began to ache, my breath became smelly, and my eliminatory organs went into overdrive. I rested, drank lots of bottled water, and slept like a baby at night.

I ate in a large canteen where delicious but modest food was prepared by a band of devotees. The menu included new varieties of vegetables like okra (known as ladies' fingers) in spicy sauces, naan and other flatbreads, yoghurt, fruit... It was a healthy diet, but spicy food was becoming increasingly sore on my tongue and my tummy.

Happily, I soon discovered the delights of fresh mango juice—another heavenly drink. I continued to consume my bottle of amritha and felt an explosion of flowers on my tongue twice daily.

I was in awe of the rainbow of colours around me at darshan, for saris shone in many jewel-like hues. It was rare to see two women in identical attire, and I watched them endlessly, falling into my own meditative *sari world.*

I befriended the son of my new landlady, who had just graduated in medicine and was full of fun. We sat on the veranda outside my room and chatted together with my new Sri Lankan friend, often delighting in eating Indian sweetmeats made by his mum. I also enjoyed plenty of quiet time alone, seated in a lovely bamboo swinging chair, silently meditating on a mango tree in the modest garden.

Darshan was becoming increasingly busy, and I felt it was my time to move. A friend back home in Donegal, had recommended visiting the southeastern state of Tamil Nadu, home to a magnificent Hindu temple, dedicated to the goddess Meenakshi and her consort Shiva.

So, I bade fond farewells to my kind hosts and my Sri Lankan companion, before taking an overnight train to the city of Madurai. I left the state of Karnataka, via Bangalore's main train station.

"I take your case, ma'am," a voice called from nowhere. "Please, ma'am."

Hence, I agreed to have my luggage transported atop the head of a very thin but wiry porter, who efficiently escorted me to my allotted compartment, through a sea of bodies, all pushing and shoving to get to waiting trains. I was very glad of his assistance. However, I could see a myriad eyes filled with disappointment at not getting my commission. If only I could have paid them all.

I found my prearranged seat in a modest but clean, open carriage; it was a small window bench, looking onto the side of three tiers of larger benches, akin to bunk beds. My heart melted when a series of small boys with eyes like giant saucers, scurried around my feet, holding cloths to feign cleaning the floors. They held out their hands, begging in a very sad and most humbling sight.

I had already witnessed lots of families living in roadside tents outside Sai Baba's ashram, who begged for food with their children. I bought milk or other foods, rather than give money which might never reach the children's mouths.

The overnight train journey seemed endless, as sleep avoided me once more. The compartment was filled with men, lying back on the rows of lightly cushioned wooden benches. I was obviously a novelty to them; I kept quiet now and avoided meeting their gaze; I did not want to attract the wrong kind of attention.

I arrived in Madurai sleep deprived and grumpy. Outside the station a sea of eager cycle rickshaw drivers greeted me, all anxious for a good fare. One man caught my attention because of a very large, jagged scar across his throat. I felt my heart melt once more, and he was thus hired, much to the disappointment of the others.

"Can you take me to the Meenakshi Temple?" I enquired.

"First I will take you on a city tour, please?" Napoleon replied.

I agreed to his business proposition.

I soon learned Napoleon had a young family to support, and I was glad I had booked the city tour. He pedalled furiously round a series of dusty roads filled with cars, buses, cycle rickshaws, cows, dogs…

He stopped at various historic sites on our journey, and the air filled with lots of tourist information.

"Parking money please, ma'am," he said on several occasions.

I could see no parking meters, and I pondered on how to tackle the situation, in a compassionate fashion.

"I see no parking meters, Napoleon. However, if you are fair and honest with me, I will tip you well," I suggested, as I handed him some rupees in advance.

I was humbled once again, when we made an unscheduled stop outside a little school. He hurried ahead into what I later learned to be his very modest home, and I guessed that my small advance payment was a much needed blessing to his household.

The Hindu temple was indeed awesome with its ten *gopurams* or gateway towers, but it was a small museum dedicated to Mahatma Gandhi that impressed me most. Gandhi was murdered in New Delhi on January 30, 1948 by Natharam Godse, and is still regarded as one of the most inspiring campaigners for peaceful, positive change the world has ever witnessed. I was spellbound by the museum's exhibits, including a small article of blood-stained clothing from Gandhi's premature passing.

I often think of Napoleon and the little boys on the train, and wonder how they are surviving such harsh existences.

I returned to the train station, exhausted after a momentous tour of Madurai. I did not want to stay overnight in Tamil Nadu, as I was eager to reach the quiet backwaters of the state of Kerala, on the southwest coast. I had several hours to wait for my next train, and the station was busy with waiting passengers. I entered the ladies' waiting room, but there were no vacant seats, so I joined the other women lying down on the hard floor, grateful for a rest. My soft cushion was soon put to good use!

The train arrived and very quickly filled to capacity. I was very glad to lie down on my reserved seat, which lay underneath two other tiers of *bunk bed* benches.

However, in the middle of the night an over zealous Indian man called to me, "I lick your feet?"

"No thank you," I replied in my most firm *school matronly* tone!

I arrived in Kayamkulam station, Kerala, sleep deprived once more, having avoided a bout of *tongue reflexology*!

Yet again, I determined to be in a good mood. My plan was to visit another ashram located near the quiet village of Parayakadavu, home to Amma, known as the hugging saint. Mata Amritanandamayi Devi was born on September 27, 1953, near the site of her ashram. She embraces visitors during her darshan, aiming to wipe away their tears, and her hugging sessions can sometimes last for over twenty hours!

I had only recently learned of Amma, and I was intrigued to find out more.

I hired an auto rickshaw and headed in search of an ATM to fund the next few days of accommodation and food. The journey took a long time as ATMs seemed in short supply in the backwaters of Kerala. I remain unsure if this was another ploy to get a better fare!

I was eventually delivered to the ashram, where I booked a

room in a tall tower-like building, with magnificent views of its lush surroundings, and beyond to the Arabian Sea.

I met another western female newbie at the booking office.

"Do you want to meet later, for lunch?" she asked.

"Sure," I replied, glad of some new company.

My new room was small, perhaps fifteen feet by twelve, with a large sink and washing area near a window with a terrific view of the backwaters. It had an en-suite shower and toilet. I hired a mattress along with a light cotton bedcover, to sleep Indian style on the floor.

I learned that lunch would be a large celebratory buffet created by Amma's family, who resided across the adjacent river, so I met my prospective companion in the queue for transportation, in a series of small boats. However, I was feeling a little unwell having succumbed to a chest infection, plus the dreaded Delhi belly.

After waiting together, in line for the buffet lunch, I sat down at a table beside her. Silence followed. She never spoke. Puzzled, I wondered why but I soon realised it was the strange *devotee phenomenon* repeating again, with yet more unusual behaviour!

I returned to my room, flopped down on my bed, and slept.

In late afternoon, I queued on a wooden bench to see a charming, female, Ayurvedic doctor. She prescribed me a cinnamon-like spice, to relieve my chest infection, and a bottle of bitter tasting liquid for my tummy. Both worked like magic; the chest infection was gone in a couple of days, and I had no more problems with my innards in India.

I discovered more about Amma in the coming days.

Since 1981, the Mata Amritanandamayi Math foundation has raised huge sums of money for spiritual and charitable causes worldwide, and Amma has been the recipient of many awards, including an honorary doctorate in humane letters from the State University of New York in May 2010.

I discovered she was on the island of Mauritius, giving darshan to thousands of her devotees, and was not expected back for another week. However, I heard of a quaint seaside town called Varkala, which could provide an interesting interlude, until Amma's return.

I left the ashram on a boat, which passed lots of houseboats rented by tourists, who were obviously enjoying sailing peacefully through Kerala's beautiful backwaters. I put rent houseboat with friends, on my future wish list.

Arriving in the town of Kollam, I found the bustling bus station and the Varkala bus. It soon filled with a small group of western travellers, as I was again asked, "Where are you from?" to my reply of,, "Donegal, Ireland," once again!

"I'm from Cork," a new voice chipped in, from the first Irish person I had encountered on my trip. I was delighted.

The journey passed quickly, as I learned that my fellow passengers were all returning from the north, and a magnificent site called Hampi. The Irishman told me of his travels in nearby Goa, of its heavenly beaches, delicious food and bargain accommodation. It sounded idyllic. I added visit Goa to my future wish list!

Our bus stopped for a new passenger on the edge of Varkala, an enterprising manager of a small group of bungalows, promising great accommodation at very competitive rates. My fellow western passengers and I were seduced by his bargain offer and duly descended the bus. I booked a week in a small bungalow, with en-suite facilities and a lovely veranda. The rent was agreed for just 2.50 euro a night!

A little later, I took a short walk out of the back of my new lodgings, past a communal well, through some trees opening onto a gorgeous sandy beach—perfect.

The front entrance stood at the bottom of a steep hill, topped by an abundance of restaurants, tourist bungalows and shops. They all held magnificent cliff top views of fishermen hauling in the day's catch, while a few crazy westerners sunbathed on the sand below in immense heat!

Varkala's restaurants served continental style breakfasts, with freshly squeezed fruit juices, homemade breads and great coffee. My stomach was very happy! Scattered among the shops and restaurants was an amazing number of yoga schools and Ayurvedic clinics, for many of the people I met came to Varkala to practise their yoga *assanas* and learn new meditation and self-healing skills.

The highlight of my week in Varkala was seeing a traditional Kathakali dancer don his costume and elaborate, scary make up, which took almost two hours to complete. It was part of the theatrics and visitors crowded round him fascinated at this ancient ritual.

I was looking forward to the production, as the room began to fill with a very large audience.

The heat soon became unbearable, and I found it hard to breathe. The ceiling felt like it was coming down on my head; my heart pumped loudly in my chest, and I just had to get outside. I hurried out of the room, gasping for oxygen. I felt so stupid and disappointed at missing the play, and I burst into tears. It was the lowest point on my Indian pilgrimage, and I felt like I needed one of Amma's hugs—right there and then!

The remainder of my days in Varkala passed quickly, as I befriended a lovely Indian family who lived in a one-roomed house, near the communal well in the trees. The man of the household was in his twenties, and a fisherman like many of the villagers. He spoke good English, unlike his wife and family.

"You like to come and meet my family for dinner?" he asked.

I graciously accepted, knowing they would all be disappointed, if I refused.

My dinner included small, freshly caught fish and a mild Keralan curry. It was utterly delicious. No one ate but me and the young man. His lovely wife smiled shyly, while their children ran backwards and forwards, curious to view a western woman visiting their home. We used the universal language of smiles and laughter to communicate.

I had brought my camera to capture these special memories, but the film unexpectedly ran out, and I excused myself to go back to my room for a replacement. On my return the fisherman's wife and children had all dressed in their *Sunday best* for my photographs, the ladies in beautiful saris, and the boys in crisp white shirts and shorts. I felt very honoured and humbled once again. I posted photographs to the family on my return to Ireland, together with writing books and coloured pens for the children.

I returned to Amma's ashram, buoyed with the anticipation of a healing hug. All the rooms were filling now, and I had to share a room with two other travellers. One of my roommates was eager to create some kind of physical boundary between us and painted a trail of ant powder around her belongings, and her designated sleeping area on the floor. I was amused at her behaviour but I was now getting used to witnessing such strange sights!

Once settled, I was asked to perform *seva* or service to the ashram, as part of its practical upkeep. I learned that chopping vegetables, and cleaning showers and toilets were on the list of duties.

I shared my feelings with a fellow traveller after breakfast and said, "I do not want to clean toilets."

Of course that is **exactly** what I was allocated, and I had to relinquish a large dose of pride! My duties turned out to be more than fine and took very little time compared to the vegetable chopping delegation.

I was really missing western food now, as my stomach could not handle too many spices. Happily, the ashram's western café opened, serving a favourite dish of French toast sprinkled with cinnamon, just like Mum used to make me as a child!

I continued to meet other western travellers, including some who had come with friends to discover the treasures of India. Many of these friendships were in difficulty, and I heard a variety of complaints including:

"I came to India with my friend, but she wants to go north, and I want to stay here."

"I need time on my own, we are always arguing."

I was glad I was travelling alone!

One new acquaintance, a German man, regaled us with details of his Ayurvedic treatments. He had been having a series of massages, enemas and cleansing fasts to heal his body, mind and spirit. He was great fun and probably the most *balanced* person I met on my journey.

Amma's return was imminent, and crowds gathered outside the gates to await her homecoming. I stood patiently amidst this throng, as she held her hand out of the door of a large camper van. I was one of many to touch it. Later, she gave a short darshan from her balcony before retiring to rest. I felt a great sense of bliss and very blessed indeed.

I enquired in the ashram office of Amma's plans, and I was told, "She is travelling to Cochin next week, to bless a new temple."

The ashram was now very crowded, and I felt I could wait a little longer for my healing hug, so I decided to travel to Cochin, catch some tourist sights, and include the new temple blessing before travelling onward to the Tibetan community of Bylakuppe, near Mysore. Sadly, my time in India was running short.

Cochin is a large port and the capital of the state of Kerala. It took a daytime train journey of around four hours, followed by a short ferry crossing to arrive at Fort Cochin, where many tourists choose to stay.

I delighted in more conversations with Indian children, before their parents asked me,

"Where are you from?"

"Ireland..."

"Where are you going..."

Coming off the ferry at Fort Cochin, I followed the line of travellers onto a street lined with pleasant accommodation. Fort Cochin is influenced by Portuguese architecture and is very agreeable on the eye. I enquired first in a small hotel, but the rooms were *cell like* and lacked any Indian charm. I followed my intuition to a small guest house a few doors away and booked a very pleasant en-suite room, reached through beautiful gardens. It was yet another Indian *gem*.

The following day, I employed a new auto rickshaw driver who said, "I will show you Cochin, and I give you a very good price!"

He was true to his word and showed me a host of interesting places including my first visit inside a Jewish synagogue.

I stepped inside this holy place, but I was perturbed to find a man talking loudly on his mobile phone. I watched and waited. He was still talking loudly. I went outside and caught some fresh air. I returned inside. He was still on his phone.

I became somewhat *proactive* and approached him, saying, "This is a sacred place. Can you please stop talking on your phone?"

He looked at me as if I had landed from Mars. However, I was now backed up by the ticket collector and a small group of equally perplexed tourists. He was ejected from the synagogue!

Fort Cochin is home to numerous book and craft shops, filled with glorious temptations. I visited a small local art gallery and purchased a delightful painting from a Keralan artist, called Victoria. I filled my case with an array of gifts, including a dozen colourful saris, each one more beautiful than the other. My sisters and friends would be incredibly happy!

The day of the temple inauguration dawned, and I made my way via bus and foot, dressed in my new white, silk sari as a mark of respect. I was watched by a sea of smiling Indian faces. Huge crowds gathered at the temple amidst a sea of tents, filled with stalls selling all kinds of delicious foods, and new ambrosia to add to milk, made from rose essence. I wandered around carrying a cup of this delicious liquid, breathing in the atmosphere of joyful anticipation.

Bhajans soon filled the air, and the temple was duly blessed by Amma. The atmosphere altered, becoming lighter and somewhat *otherworldly*. A group of eagles had appeared overhead, to oversee the ceremony, a sign that something very special was enfolding.

After, the temple inauguration, I entered a huge tent filling with hundreds of devotees, all dressed in their finest attire. I was joined by a small number of westerners, mostly dressed in white. A number of them were preparing a small raised stage, behind Amma's proposed seat and they suggested I join a short queue for western devotees, to await my much anticipated, healing hug.

At last, I witnessed Amma take her seat and very patiently begin the hugging process. She was aided by several assistants, who seemed to grab each devotee as they reached the front of the queue, and then propel them forward towards Amma's lap. Each hug was over in seconds, necessarily so because of the huge crowd.

Although I had watched the unfolding of many other's hugs, I was quite unprepared for Amma's tight embrace, as my head fell into her lap. I rose up quickly, thinking my hug was over, only to be grabbed by her once more as she recited what sounded like, "Doti, doti, doti."

She then signalled to her helpers, that I should join a small group behind her on the raised stage. I tentatively climbed up and sat on the floor, still reeling from two hugs!

I felt a HUGE wave of healing energy surround me as Amma's blessing reached my very core. One single word kept repeating in my mind; I knew that one word was Amma's gift to me. Amma's word remains a very special, spiritual gift, which is my *sacred secret*.

It brought me a great sense of peace, and I felt very thankful I had come for her *darshan*.

Although she has visited Ireland on a number of occasions since my return from India, I have not gone to see her for it has never felt necessary. I got all that I needed from those two healing hugs in Cochin.

The following day, I waited in Cochin central bus station in searing temperatures—it must have been over 40 degrees. I had a very pressing problem with my bladder; I could not pee at all, despite drinking vast quantities of bottled water!

I left Fort Cochin, heading north-east by bus, across the mountain range known as the Western Ghats. The journey onwards was very uncomfortable, as my bladder constantly felt full and irritated; it was relentless. The bus made several toilet stops, but not a lot changed with my waterworks!

I was very relieved to alight in Mysore bus station, in the early hours of morning, but the soft light of dawn did not ease my growing physical discomfort. However, I found the queue for Bylakuppe and waited patiently for a couple of hours, although it felt like an awful lot longer!

The next bus winded through beautiful, undulating, countryside, not unlike parts of Scotland. The weather was milder and gentler, and I nodded on and off to sleep, before finally arriving in a small, rural bus station, a few miles from my intended destination. I hailed another auto rickshaw, which trundled onwards through peaceful roads, surrounded by well-tended crops.

Bylakuppe was founded in 1961 and is the largest Tibetan settlement in India, consisting of twenty villages. It is home to a number of monasteries, nunneries and temples, including the famous Golden Temple, and several Buddhist universities. I found a Tibetan guesthouse (recommended by a friend back home), situated among a sea of green fields, with lovely views. My room was simple and clean, with shower and toilet facilities housed alongside.

Downstairs, a small restaurant served delicious Tibetan *momo* dumplings, with a variety of lightly spiced, meat fillings. The momos were always accompanied by a sea of smiling, Tibetan faces, for the young monks and I smiled and laughed back and forward. I felt very blessed to have such delightful company.

The quiet countryside and the cooler weather eased my body, and my bladder quickly returned to normal function! I spent the next five days in quiet contemplation, walking the tranquil roads nearby, visiting the temples and eating lots of momos. I had lost a considerable amount of weight on my travels, so I really indulged myself!

However, I developed a strange paranoia about snakes crawling under the gap, below my bedroom door, and biting me in my sleep. I took to placing my two (now full) suitcases against the doorway at night, fearful of an early demise like Cleopatra!

Coincidently, I watched a documentary, after my return from India, on the number of fatalities from snakebites, one particular species of which crawls inside homes at night, where their victims die in their sleep from *unknown causes*. Who knows—perhaps my paranoia was justified after all?

I might add that I never saw any snakes in India, much to my relief!

I left the sanctuary of Bylakuppe on a very rickety bus, with thinly padded seats, and I was repeatedly raised into the air on a long series of hair-raising bumps!

Arriving back at the central bus station in Mysore, I smiled when another Indian entrepreneur agreed to carry my heavy suitcases on his head and told me, "I take you to good accommodation."

I visualised a comfortable bed to ease my bruised behind, as he guided me to a small hotel nearby with clean rooms, en-suite facilities and a television. That evening, I delighted in watching several Bollywood films!

My porter was also employed part time at the hotel, to run errands for guests, and he arranged a delicious, western style takeaway meal for my first evening's supper. I soon learned that his wife and children lived some distance away in the countryside, while his modest income was sent home at regular intervals. I was glad I had accepted his offer of *good accommodation.*

I decided to book a coach trip and visit some of Mysore's many delights in one day, including the famous Brindavan Gardens. I stepped onto the coach and was immediately allocated the bumpiest seat at the front of the bus, deemed the best seat for the only honourable western tourist on board!

A sea of smiling faces surrounded me once more, as we hopped on and off the bus, to a series of Tipu Sultan of Mysore sites. My bottom longed for the great water gardens of Brindavan and the Krishnarajasagar Dam, our last stop on a very long tour!

It was nearing dusk, considered the best time to view the garden's showpiece of the great musical fountain. I enjoyed the long walk from the car park, via breathtaking views of the dam, allowing me to stretch my limbs, and finally ease my discomfort!

I passed numerous flower beds, all filled with deliciously scented blooms, laid out in quite formal configuration, like a series of tiers on a wedding cake. A vast array of water features, including narrow rills and ponds, and numerous fountains, all descended towards a small lake, skirting the huge, magical, musical water fountain. I took a boat ride across the lake with a group of others, all eager to see the main feature of the gardens.

A sound and light show followed in the fading, evening light, as the fountain was transformed into a rainbow of exotic colours, accompanied by Bollywood music—all very kitsch, and a delight to my inner child!

The evening's entertainment ended and I made my way back to my *seat of honour* on the coach. Looking out of the window as the last passengers dallied, I was greeted to a sea of saluting backsides— ablutions are often very public in India!

Mysore is host to a kaleidoscope of small shops and street traders, a colourful backdrop to the glorious Amba Vilas Palace. I just had to return and pay homage to the palace and its treasures— reminiscing on my first visit. I was not disappointed for the interior *dazzled* me once more.

I also discovered St Philomena's Church, a gothic cathedral, home to a relic of the third century saint. Saint Philomena was tortured and beheaded for refusing to marry the emperor Diocletian of Rome. I was christened Brigid Philomena Imelda Gallagher, quite a mouthful. Indeed, I did not even believe Philomena or Imelda were real names when I was a child!

I bought a small book on the life of **my** saint in the cathedral shop. It felt like another serendipitous synchronicity.

I now had one remaining day in Mysore and one holiday wish left. I booked a seat on a coach tour to the scenic hill station of Ootacamund, known as Ooty, located in the Nilgiri Hills. The coach would travel through Bandipur National Park, home to TIGERS.

It was a very early morning start, and I was the first passenger onboard. I was of course offered the seat of honour, at the front of the coach once again. I could not refuse! We stopped at several tourist hotels and headed to central Mysore, where two more coaches awaited filled with passengers.

The drivers held a group meeting and decided that three buses could be condensed into two; thus, we were ordered off the original bus, and onto another, where I was allocated a seat right next to the driver. We waited and waited in extreme heat in our new, very cramped seats. A poor man travelling to a funeral in Ooty was ordered to sit between me and the driver, a spot which had no seat pad for the bumpy road ahead!

It was late morning now, and Ooty and the tigers were fading into the realms of a Winnie the Pooh fantasy! I had no choice but to alight, afraid of being stranded in the Nilgiri Hills, far away from my onward flight.

The driver was horrified at my impudence and immediately ordered, "Get back on the bus."

No please ma'am, no would you mind. My hackles went up.

"I will not," I replied firmly.

I was very determined not to be ordered about by any man, much to the delight of two busloads of passengers!

"I would like a refund," I added, determined to win the ongoing battle.

Most reluctantly, my adversary backed down, cheered on by my audience of well wishers!

I wondered how my last day in Mysore could meet dream expectations, when the joy of my first visit to Mysore rose into my consciousness. I hailed an auto rickshaw to Sri Ranga Patma temple and orphanage, for a poignant but fitting, final tribute to my Indian pilgrimage, for it ended where it began.

The following morning, I said my farewells to the staff at the hotel, and my cases were delivered head high, by my porter friend, to the bus station. I decided not to travel by train again and booked one last comfortable, coach journey on a modern coach to Bangalore. The seats were thankfully well cushioned, and I was able to choose my own seat!

The bus station was a good distance from the airport, so I hired one final auto rickshaw— my favourite form of transport. We hurtled through narrow streets barely missing cows, dogs, children, and a busy stream of cars, scooters, auto rickshaws, and lorries. I was filled with a child like JOY!

Insights from India

- Leave your baggage behind, less is more

- Miracles happen…

- Trust your intuition, even though it verges on paranoia

- Buy a soft cushion for bus journeys, train stations and darshan!

Kerrytown – Easter 2003

"Faith is a knowledge within the heart, beyond the reach of proof."
Kahlil Gibran

India had been a great *leveller*, and I had unearthed a new found inner strength. Indeed, I now felt quite BOLD!

On my return to Donegal, I moved home, to a what I expected to be a very serene setting. Once again God had other plans!

Kerrytown is a townland about three miles from the sea, and my former home in Mullaghduff. It embraces a small group of houses, each set several hundred yards apart, and is a peaceful location not least because of its recent history.

In 1938, The Virgin Mary appeared on top of a rocky outcrop, to a young girl and her sisters, as they were preparing some outhouses for guests. The vision of Our Lady was in turn witnessed by others. The Apparition was initially dismissed by the local priest Father McAteer, until a few days later when he too became a visionary!

I regularly prayed to Our Lady at The Kerrytown Shrine, sometimes referred to as *The Rock*.

The Gatehouse in Kerrytown was once part of a gated level crossing, on The Lough Swilly Railway, which terminated at the nearby fishing port of Burtonport. Sadly, the railway closed in July 1953, and the line was dismantled.

A cousin of my mother's owned the Gatehouse and very kindly allowed me to stay for three months until July 2003, when the house was promised to regular summer visitors. Toby and I moved there on Thursday April 17. Ann and Lawrence had kindly cared for him in my absence but he still wanted to show his displeasure at being left alone. He went into a mini sulk!

I travelled to the nearby town of Dungloe the following day— Good Friday—to buy groceries for the week ahead, returning to my new home via the main Dungloe to Loughanure road, where a series of small bog fires now burned. The flames and smoke covered a large expanse of peat bog, a common sight in Donegal as residents often set small fires to reduce heather growth, enabling easier access to the precious peat below. However, if the bog below is dry from lack of rain, the fires can easily get out of control.

Sadly, some fires are set deliberately by arsonists, and huge areas of land, vegetation and helpless wildlife have been destroyed as a result.

Back at the Gatehouse, I looked forward to a quiet night in front of a coal fire with Toby. However, this was not to be, as late in the evening, giant flames lit up the horizon. I gazed anxiously out of my new living room window, while they danced malevolently against the night sky, lighting up all of the houses near the Rock. I watched on in complete disbelief, wondering what might lie ahead!

Venturing outside to assess the situation, I was shocked to see that flames were approaching the Gatehouse from the rear. They were colossal, like the giant waves that surfers search for in the ultimate thrill of surfing inside the wave. I now realised that the fire had already jumped across a series of side roads and was encircling Kerrytown on **three** sides.

I decided to soak the edge of the garden as much as I could, with water from an outside tap, but it seemed like an insurmountable challenge as the flames moved closer. However, I persevered.

All the while, visitors were walking or driving past in their cars, to view the flames.

"The fire brigade will be here soon," they said.

What belongings do you take with you in an emergency evacuation? The answer for me was very little. I went inside and packed my Balinese bells, my deer skin drum, my eagle and hawk feather fan, and some essential legal documents, before carrying them to my car. I took no clothes, jewellery or trinkets. Toby most importantly, was placed in his pet carrier, ready to leave Kerrytown.

Although I was now prepared for a swift escape, I felt compelled to check on my relatives a short walk away. My new landlady lived with her sister and a brother who had only recently returned home from hospital after heart troubles. When I called, her sister and brother were in bed, and they were all oblivious to the flames that were now bordering their garden!

We telephoned the doctor for advice, and an ambulance was arranged as a precaution. Almost simultaneously, the fire brigade arrived and attended to the approaching flames, reassuring me that I would be next in their queue. Satisfied that my relatives were now safe, I returned home.

Finally, my rescuers arrived at my doorstep, and I felt a HUGE sense of relief. Up until that moment, it had seemed like I was participating in a disaster movie and that Armageddon had finally arrived. My body coursed with adrenaline, and I could not sit down and relax for any length of time; I was hopping around rather like a kangaroo!

The flames had now reached trees bordering one side of the garden, and an outhouse filled with Ann and Lawrence's furniture on the other. Thankfully, they were soon drenched with water, and my emergency was over. My heroes and heroines quickly downed much needed cool drinks and hastily moved to the next house needing aid, where a garden was already on fire!

All through the evening and into the night a small long-haired dog stayed with Toby and me, smiling and reassuring us. He seemed to appear from nowhere, and he was most reluctant to leave us alone; I decided to let him stay within the safe confines of the Gatehouse.

Once the fire engine had gone, Toby came out of his basket and I went to bed for a much needed rest. Sleep came in fits and starts for my body was still filled with adrenaline. A few hours later, I awoke with a start, to a crackling sound not unlike heavy rain, alerting me to check outside.

I was alarmed to see a telegraph pole in the neighbouring field smothered in flames, perhaps eight feet or so away from where I stood in my pyjamas!

I phoned the fire brigade, but it had already been notified by a kind neighbour, and was on its way. The flames were extinguished once more, and I settled again into some form of *normality*. Later in the day, I tentatively looked outside, only to witness a neighbour's tree erupt in flames! I went to her aid, and together we doused her remaining trees and shrubs with water.

Yet again, the following day, more flames ignited on the fourth and final border of the garden. This time, I telephoned several of my male cousins and their friends, who mustered down with large shovels to beat out the embers, for the poor firemen and women were now at the point of exhaustion.

A few days later, I checked with all of our neighbours, to see who our faithful canine companion had been, to no avail. I like to think he came as a divine helper or angel in our hour of need!

I had returned from my Indian pilgrimage and *the world* was on fire! What was going on?

Fire is often seen as a cleanser and a forerunner to new growth. I had even walked on fire at Westbank Healing Centre, after the end of my marriage, when I had felt like a phoenix arising from the flames; it had renewed my courage and cleared the way for a new, happier life. I now wondered at the symbolism of the mighty Kerrytown fire?

I prepared to move house again in July, but was unsure if suitable accommodation would become available on time, as lots of houses in Donegal are let for shorter terms over the summer months for higher rentals. However, my dear Auntie Anna whispered in the ear of the postman, and he kept a lookout for suitable places to rent. Sure enough luck prevailed, and a great two-bedroom cottage with stunning views over the Atlantic Ocean, became vacant bang on time.

Auntie Anna, you are an angel!

Sadly, we had very bad news just before my planned move, when Dad's only surviving brother Francie, died suddenly and unexpectedly in hospital. We were all shocked. Francie was a great character and a big fan of the local tradition of marching bands. When Dad was alive he too always wanted to know how the Mullaghduff band had done in the Easter Sunday band competition, and we always telephoned him with news of the results, if we were holidaying in Donegal over Easter.

My removal van was already booked for the afternoon of Uncle Francie's funeral, so I had to hurry back to Kerrytown, immediately after the funeral meal. Marie, Ann and Lawrence helped me move my furniture, before the removal van travelled a few miles to my new home in the townland of Ballymanus.

It was a very sombre flitting.

Insights from Kerrytown

- In times of extreme stress, take a day or even an hour at a time

- A Higher Power **always** watches over us

- Fire is a great cleanser and paves the way for new growth

Stopping the World

Ballymanus – summer 2003

"In the middle of the road of my life, I awoke in the dark wood where the true way was wholly lost."

Dante Alighieri

My new home in Ballymanus sat astride a hilltop, exposed to wild Atlantic winds. Stepping out of my car with bags of groceries on a breezy day became a new challenge. However, this minor grumble was more than compensated by the house's stunning views.

Ballymanus was well known as the former home of a mystic called Miseog, who lived in the early part of the nineteenth century. Among her many predictions was that a great ball of fire would fall on lower Braade, and many lives would be lost.

Sadly, on May 10, 1943 at 9.50pm, nineteen young men lost their lives when a mine exploded on rocks, adjacent to Braade. The dead included my uncle Eddie and could have included my father, for earlier in the evening, he and Uncle Francie had been amongst the crowds of onlookers as the mine had approached the shore. Luckily, they had both decided to head home before the mine exploded.

Dad once told me of his experiences during the Ballymanus Mine Disaster. However, we never discussed it again, as it had affected him very deeply.

In early August, I began to suffer an ache in the upper muscles of my left arm, and I knew something was definitely out of sync. I became somewhat vigilant, fearing a blood clot.

My fears were heightened, when I awoke in the early hours of one morning, suffering severe shortness of breath, accompanied by a heavy pressure on my chest, akin to someone sitting on it! Although I could perhaps have been suffering a heart attack, I remained remarkably calm and lay quietly in bed praying. I did not phone for medical assistance. Instead, I waited till daylight, to drive to my GP's surgery in nearby Burtonport.

I wonder now at my *madness*—please do not follow my stoic example!

The doctor was alarmed, and I could see panic rise in his face. He told me that I needed an immediate investigation, while he simultaneously wrote a note for the Accident and Emergency Department. He added that it could indeed be some kind of arterial or venous blockage. In hindsight, he must have assumed that I had been driven to the surgery, as he did not call for an ambulance. I did not confess to my solitary predicament, for I was now somewhat shocked and dazed. Finally, I burst into a torrent of tears outside the surgery.

I drove back to Mullaghduff and stopped off at Auntie Anna's for some much needed solace. It was one of many times in my life when I wished my mum was still alive!

Auntie Anna and Uncle James kindly drove me to hospital.

The Accident and Emergency Department was thankfully quiet, and a kindly nurse quickly took my details and some samples of my blood for analysis. I was given an ECG, sent for a chest X-ray and waited tentatively for the results. It was a considerable wait. Auntie Anna and Uncle James sat patiently beside me, on the hard waiting room seats, before I was ushered back to see a doctor and told, "We have checked your blood results twice. The results are negative for clots."

A nurse stood nearby, as he continued, "Please raise your left arm."

It felt very painful to lift it now and would not budge above ninety degrees. I felt frightened, frustrated and near to tears once again.

"Your pain is muscular," the doctor finally said.

I did not believe him and questioned his diagnosis. The nurse and doctor told me quite emphatically that the diagnosis was correct; I was given a prescription for anti-inflammatory medication and advised to go home; I was not a happy person.

I returned to my GP the following morning and recounted my tale of woe. He was in agreement with me that my pain was probably not muscular and wondered if I might possibly have an inflammatory condition called costochondritis.

A few days later, I developed swollen lymph glands in my left armpit, and I could feel a sensation in my neck, like tiny droplets breaking away and travelling round my body— strange I know, but as you have already learned, I am highly sensitive!

Other symptoms soon followed: my eyes began to ache and the whites became a cloudy, greyish blue colour; all my joints became incredibly painful, and I felt sensations like hot knives burning through them; I found it difficult to lift my left arm at all; the three middle fingers of my left hand became noticeably swollen; I found it hard to stay warm and slept wearing a long fleece dressing gown, topped with two duvets on my bed, yet I still felt incredibly cold; I was short of breath most of the time and had to prop myself up on pillows to allow some kind of restful sleep; I experienced a constant dull ache behind my left shoulder, that I felt emanated from my left lung, and finally, I developed a sharp intermittent pain over my left kidney!

Terrible insomnia joined my long list of symptoms, and I could not concentrate at all well as my mind had become incredibly foggy. I took to resting, almost twenty-four hours a day, sitting up on the settee, or in my bed.

I reflected on the months prior to my visit to India, I had lost around two stone in weight without dieting and another stone while travelling. I wondered what on earth was happening to my body, for it appeared to be having some sort of major meltdown. All work had long since ceased, and I now felt as though I was in a long dark tunnel, with no light in sight!

I was eventually diagnosed as having a frozen shoulder, and I awaited an appointment with a physiotherapist. I kept regular appointments with my GP, who was incredibly supportive, and prescribed a variety of anti-inflammatory and analgesic medicines, but my myriad of symptoms persisted. Repeated blood tests had shown my inflammatory markers were slightly elevated, but not remarkably so; thus, I still had no overall definitive diagnosis.

I got an appointment with a female physiotherapist who reckoned all my symptoms were due to the menopause and quite common in women of my years; I could not think of an apt reply to her diagnosis!

However, the exercises she suggested did bring some relief from my left shoulder and arm pain. They were done *religiously*; I did not let her down on my homework!

In early 2004, I was prescribed new medication, but unfortunately I began to haemorrhage internally.

There is a well-known saying, "Healer heal thyself."

This new episode of heavy bleeding was my wake-up call. I felt very disillusioned by conventional medicine; thus, I determined to take charge of my health and no longer rely on medication.

My new self-healing regime included several dietary refinements, including eating organic meat, vegetables and bread delivered to my front door by a local farm. The highlight of my week became eating fresh spelt and blackcurrant muffins (spelt is an ancient grain that can replace wheat flour for baking).

Although I was now reliant on social welfare benefits, I decided that this food luxury was *medicinal.*

I continued with my intuitive *prescriptions* and cooked with lots of garlic, beetroot and parsley, all natural blood thinners or purifiers; I then added another prescription of high doses of fish oils—a natural anti-inflammatory. I realised I was deficient in the mineral magnesium, when chocolate became a craving. My magnesium levels were prone to fluctuation, and I often took regular supplements, it was a lot cheaper and healthier than chocolate!

I also returned to a great massage therapist, who realised that my symptoms could be part of a condition called fibromyalgia. She gave me a very thick tome to read on the condition, but it was beyond my comprehension in my distressed and foggy mindset.

In Chinese medicine, lung and colon problems are often considered a sign of unresolved grief. Yes, I had a tendency to bury my feelings and could be described as *somewhat stoic*! In the past, I had channelled my emotional pain into *busyness*—an inherited family trait; I knew I needed to change....

My new home was very close to a beautiful beach and although

I was still somewhat short of breath, I began to walk there as often as the Donegal weather permitted.

I had purchased a board game called The Transformation Game, when I was a buyer for Healthworks. The game was created by The Findhorn Foundation as a means of understanding and transforming the key issues we all face on *Life's Journey*. Choosing a focus or intention for healing before playing the game, allows each player to gain illumination on a possible way forward, whether on a physical, emotional, mental or spiritual level. Players then collect *angel cards* to support them as well as gaining other useful insights. I used the game regularly, as a tool to unveil my healing issues. I then chose Bach flower essences to help clear away my old hurts and emotional wounds.

I found additional insights from watching the television show *Dr Phil*. I had first seen Dr Phil on the famous show *Oprah*, but he now had a show of his own. He utilises his years of clinical experience, peppered with humour and wisdom, to diffuse and heal a myriad of complicated issues. I had lots of new light bulb moments watching his show!

Nature continued to be a valuable ally, on these long dark nights of the soul.

I was surrounded by a small group of cows and their calves, owned by a near neighbour, who loves his animals. The cows reminded me of long distant summer holidays spent with Mum and Grandja.

"How are you today?" I asked my neighbour one morning.

"Grand, I have a cow waiting to calve," he replied.

"Can I watch?" I asked excitedly.

"Of course, but cows like to be alone sometimes."

I saw the first glimpses of the calf's birth through my kitchen window, and the remainder of these miracle proceedings, standing just inside my garden gate. I then walked very gently towards the new mother and her offspring, while my companion checked that both were well. A short time later, still in awe, I watched the newborn stand up, fall down and finally stand up successfully, on shaky, spindly legs. The new arrival gave me another great healing boost.

I remained immensely grateful for simple pleasures, and I kept a daily note of these blessings in a journal.

Although, I no longer went to mass, I returned to Kerrytown on a regular basis, and prayed to Our Lady at the Rock.

I found further peace during meditations at home, sometimes using the healing power of colour, when I regularly used the following technique, which I had passed onto many of my students:

- Lie down comfortably without any distractions
- Close your eyes, and concentrate on your breathing
- Imagine a bright coloured ball of healing light above your head
- Soak in the first colour that comes into your mind; the colour of the light is perfect for your healing needs
- Allow the light to travel downwards, through your head, your neck, your shoulders, your arms and hands, your chest and abdomen, back, hips, legs and feet
- Imagine the light travelling on, into the earth
- Feel your feet fill with energy from the earth now, grounding and balancing you
- Imagine the coloured light and the energy from the earth mixing together and travelling outwards, to fill a huge bubble of energy around you
- Soak in this healing energy, for as long as you need
- Slowly open your eyes when you feel ready
- Take a yawn and a stretch
- Have a glass of water
- Take some time out to review your healing experience

Each colour has significance:

- Red brings courage and inner strength
- Orange aids digestion and promotes more joy
- Yellow aids concentration and optimism
- Green brings balance and welcomes new beginnings
- Blues aid relaxation and enhance creativity

- Purples boost the spirit and help ease painful conditions
- Pastel colours bring gentleness and peace
- Pink encourages self-esteem
- Silver brings more self-awareness
- Gold enhances spiritual wisdom
- White contains all the colours of the rainbow and is great for a multitude of health conditions

I accepted that moving home, losing my health, and relying on benefits, were all contributing to a sense of loss of an old identity and I had a significant dream one night, of rebuilding a house with new stronger foundations. It symbolised a more solid, new beginning.

In spring 2004, I was called back to hospital as a precaution, because of the chest pain on my initial visit. I was given another ECG and a further appointment for an exercise ECG, during which I became quite breathless.

I received an appointment to review my test results.

"Have you ever suffered from depression?" the registrar asked me, while his eyes remained focussed on my notes.

"Yes," I replied.

He did not let me elaborate.

"I will refer you to a psychiatrist," he continued, still avoiding eye contact.

I was angry now and stated quite emphatically, "My shortness of breath and other symptoms are most **definitely** not in my head!"

He relented a little and ordered a lung function test to placate me. However, I remained less than impressed with his bedside manner!

I returned for my lung function tests, and a kindly technician used a spirometer to measure the volume of air inspired and expired from my lungs. She noted my left lung was limited in its breathing capacity, and thus did some further tests. The results showed my lungs were functioning at 70 per cent of normal capacity, and my left lung was not inflating properly. She explained that two conditions presented with these types of findings—lupus and sarcoidosis.

The results were forwarded to my registrar, and I sent out a wish for a little more kindness on my return!

"I will refer you to a respiratory specialist," was his brief response.

My next waiting list was somewhat lengthy, so I wrote a letter of complaint to the hospital, and finally saw a respiratory specialist in November 2004—fifteen months into my illness. She immediately ordered an MRI scan, but the results showed no evidence of sarcoidosis. However, I was subsequently kept under regular review by the Respiratory Department.

Meanwhile, my GP was now advising me to **tell** the hospital that I most probably had connective tissue disease. Systemic lupus erythematosus (Lupus or SLE for short), rheumatoid arthritis, scleroderma and Sjogren's syndrome are some of a myriad of complex connective tissue diseases that are often difficult to diagnose.

I was soon referred to the Orthopaedic Department by my physiotherapist, who thought I might need a manipulation of my left shoulder under anaesthetic. Happily, the orthopaedic consultant deferred on manipulating my shoulder, as he felt it was improving on its own.

I remember thinking it crazy that I had now been under observation by **four** separate hospital departments—General Medicine, Respiratory, Gastrointestinal and Orthopaedic!

Although my finances were still incredibly tight, I continued my own holistic healing programme and booked an appointment with a great reflexologist called Róisín Bonner. My feet felt incredibly painful as she worked on them; it felt as though I had hundreds of nails digging into my skin. I continued with weekly treatments, and my health slowly began to improve; the pains in my joints began to ease, and I could at long last, sleep lying down!

I acknowledged that I needed to address my old grief issues at a deeper level and serendipitously discovered an organisation aptly named GROW.

GROW's philosophy embraces Twelve Steps to Recovery, which include:

Step One – We admitted we had lost our way and needed direction.

Step Two – We took our courage in our hands and asked for help...

During weekly meetings, I learned to take my focus away from the **problems** I was facing, to simple **solutions** that were both manageable and practical.

I also learned of a creative writing course starting locally, where I would perhaps heal more of my pain.

I was somewhat nervous driving to the first class, but I was soon put at ease by a room full of friendly, female faces. A lively series of introductions followed before our tutor laid a series of black and white photographs of women and girls, on a large central table.

"Please choose the photograph which appeals to you most," she suggested. "Then write in silence for twenty minutes, on your chosen image."

I picked a photograph of a girl walking along a path that rose into the distance. The sky fell downwards, making the path seem to disappear into the clouds. The photograph reminded me of my beach walks at Ballymanus. Words *poured* from my pen, and time *flew* past, when I heard, "You can stop now, and read your work to the class, if you wish."

Everyone read their first passage of creative writing, as our small group listened on attentively, gaining insights from one another on our lives, our hopes and our dreams...

This class soon became the highlight of my week, and fresh insights emerged from my psyche. My spirit told me it had become tired of caring for others, and cried out, "What about ME?"

I realised that the loss of my mother at such a tender age, meant that I was not always gentle with myself, and I often put others' needs before my own. These insights reiterated the message from "My Dream on the Nile".

However, I was soon the recipient of an overwhelming show of love from my family, who produced an early fiftieth birthday present—a ticket to see my all-time favourite band Thin Lizzy, in Galway, with bed and breakfast accommodation and a balcony view of the Atlantic Ocean.

The night of the concert was one of the best nights of my life. Thin Lizzy minus Phil Lynott were still amazing, although the crowd of fans was surprisingly small. The band serenaded us once more with "Whisky In The Jar" and many other favourites.

Amidst lots of very joyful dancing, it was wonderful therapy!

The early birthday celebrations did not end there, for the following evening we gathered on our balcony, to witness a fast approaching white stretch limousine. It passed the end of the road then disappeared, returning soon after, to reverse along the narrow street below. Marie produced a plastic, motorised, flying pig and announced, "If pigs might fly…"

My eyes welled up with tears, while *ride in a stretch limo* was ticked off my *wish list*!

Marie, her daughter Annie, Ann, Lawrence and I stepped into our luxurious carriage for a glorious night of hilarity. Our Queens' Guide motto had been "be prepared", and a giant holdall soon revealed a series of delectable delicacies, including smoked salmon and champagne. I felt overwhelmed by my family's generosity and thoughtfulness!

Our driver transported us along the promenade towards Connemara, before stopping to have our photographs taken for posterity. The booking was extended by popular demand, and we returned to *pose* in our carriage around the streets of Galway. A short toilet stop in central Eyre Square brought remarks from onlookers, "Is that yon pop star?" as they watched Annie alight to go to a nearby *convenience*. She is indeed a very striking, blonde, six foot beauty and these remarks only added to the occasion!

Later, we ate a delicious dinner at a bijou Mexican restaurant, buoyed with joy and sisterly love.

The actual birthday paled in comparison, but was nonetheless a great day. I dressed in my white silk sari and produced a small Indian banquet for family and friends.

Insights from Ballymanus

- Seek medical help **immediately** for chest pain, **do not** delay

- Keep a note of your symptoms, and take your list to your GP

- Take some responsibility for your health, and be as proactive as circumstances allow

- Natural medicines and conventional medicine treatments can co-exist

- Accept support from friends and family

- Keep a gratitude diary.

Chelsea - May 2005

"A tree begins with a seed."

Arabic proverb

I was visiting the beautiful gardens of Glenveagh National Park in the spring of 2005, when I shared my thoughts with a fellow gardening enthusiast.

"One of my dreams is to visit Chelsea Flower Show," I said.

"Well let's go then," she replied.

So we did.

On May 26, 2005, we arrived in the grounds of The Royal Hospital, Chelsea to visit the world's most famous flower show—a gardening institution for more than 160 years. On entering the gates, my excitement and nervousness reached epic levels, and my camera went on strike. I do not know why? Perhaps it was nervous too!

I felt extremely frustrated at not being able to photograph the ocean of horticultural delights. However, I was determined to enjoy this special day.

Chelsea is HUGE, so we prioritised our *wish list*, putting *visit the show gardens* at number one. Irish garden designer Diarmuid Gavin was among the exhibitors. I had watched him regularly on television as he revolutionised many of my ideas on garden design. He was a champion of change!

Standing before a sea of lavender and box outside Diarmuid's "Hanover Quay Garden", which had won a silver-gilt medal, I searched for my Irish gardening hero. Sadly, he was nowhere to be found, and I felt somewhat disappointed.

This small glitch was more than compensated for by a wealth of other glorious horticultural exhibits. "The Chelsea Pensioner's Garden" created by veteran designer Julian Dowle, was one of my personal favourites. I loved its simple cottage style design filled with a profusion of roses and poppies, interspersed with vegetables, depicting The Dig for Victory wartime campaign.

A cloud of rambling roses brought back happy memories of my childhood home Beech Cottage, with its rose hedge in three shades of pink and red—a backdrop to lots of joyful photographs, which had always included our dear cat Sooty.

I also admired "The Cumbrian Fellside Garden", another gold medal winner, designed by ex pop singer Kim Wilde and Richard Lucas. This gardening duo recreated scenery from another of my idols—writer Beatrix Potter—with great attention to detail. The rear backdrop was a dry stone wall topped with a line of barbed wire with beads of sheep's wool. A living willow arbour sat centre stage, but the star of this beautiful landscape was a snail, basking on the slate steps at the entrance to the garden. Did he realise he was a gold medal winner, I wondered!

Later, we chatted to a Scottish designer, David McQueen from the Isle of Bute, who deservedly won a silver-gilt medal for his first entry at Chelsea in the *chic garden* category. David kindly copied a poem for me, from his winning design. The words of this poem resonated with me and reaffirmed the way forward.

Just as we had made the decision to wander back to our hotel, we caught sight of Andy Sturgeon, another gold medal winner and a television gardening celebrity. Andy posed in a hammock and spoke to a television presenter as we watched on in AWE. Chelsea was all I had dreamed of and more!

The trip to Chelsea buoyed me somewhat, and I tentatively returned to work part time as a natural medicines therapist.

Although these past two years had been extremely tough on many levels, not least because I did not yet know what ailed my being, I had learned such an awful lot on the journey. I had been literally stopped in my tracks, to reflect on my very busy past, and to tend to my painful wounds. I could not have survived those years without the support of my GP, my family and friends, and the skilled therapists who crossed my path.

I had also transformed one of my deepest fears—being unable to work—and yes I had managed to survive. Indeed, Chelsea had been visited on a financial *wing and a prayer*. I had desperately wanted to go, and the money just appeared. It was one of many of my experiences of the power of manifestation—if you can visualise yourself overcoming life's obstacles, they **will** disappear.

A short time later, the last of my late father's estate was sold and divided, allowing me to book a much needed holiday in the sun. I pondered on where to go? My mind travelled back to Bosnia and the summer of 2000, when I visited Sarajevo in the aftermath of The Balkans War. My heart called me back to Medjugorje and the healing arms of Our Lady.

Thus, I booked a flight to Dubrovnik for September 2005, for a two-week holiday to Croatia. I also organised self-catering accommodation for two nights in the small harbour town of Cavtat; I would then source a small hotel for the remainder of my stay; I visualised a quiet retreat, for my body, mind and spirit.

I walked around Cavtat harbour on the second day of my vacation, before continuing through a number of quiet lanes in search of simple lodgings. There were several signs showing "Rooms to Let".

I intuitively pressed the buzzer of a peaceful, gated residence.

"I am looking for accommodation," I began.

"Please come inside, I have several rooms available," said a smiling, middle-aged man in perfect English. "First, come and enjoy a cold drink with myself and my wife."

I immediately felt at home.

The room was actually a small studio apartment, one of several belonging to the couple, whom I now knew as the harbour master and his lovely wife. The apartment led out into a private garden with a small swimming pool. I later discovered that a pool was a rare luxury in the town. I booked the apartment and moved in.

Fresh fish is my passion when on holiday, and I relished eating fresh squid and other marine delicacies, on my nightly jaunts to the town centre. I relaxed by the small pool during the afternoons, reading an odd book or two, and dozing on and off in the warm sun.

My sleep pattern remained very poor. I might sleep well for one night, struggle to sleep at all for three or four nights, and then

I would fall into yet another slumber of complete exhaustion. This pattern had been repeating over and over, since the onset of my illness, and I found it incredibly debilitating.

Unfortunately, a new symptom had sneaked onto my list, when my muscles felt sore as though I had been in a fight, and kicked or punched all over my body. In 2005, I did not yet realise that my insomnia and muscle pain were inextricably linked.

However, I was determined to enjoy my first holiday abroad, since my trip to India, and I learned a few new words, "dobro jutro" was good morning, "dobro dan" was good afternoon and "hvala" was thank you.

I practised these few words in the local shops and restaurants, where I was greeted with lots of smiles of gratitude.

I took several short boat trips to nearby Dubrovnik, learning of its recent history, and the war that had divided the former regions of Yugoslavia. It felt so very sad that such lovely people had witnessed so many of the horrors of war.

I booked a day trip to Montenegro and a return visit to Medjugorje.

Montenegro was filled with breathtaking scenery; the tour bus skirted a giant fjord that still remains vivid in my memory. The whole region was filled with natural beauty, all largely unspoiled.

My next bus tour meandered through yet more stunning landscapes, as I gazed excitedly out of the window, anticipating another appointment with Our Lady. My last visit to Medjugorje had been too short, and I now wanted to climb Apparition Mountain, the site of Our Lady's first vision. I made it number one on a small *wish list*.

The steep climb presented a major challenge for my lungs in their still fragile state. However, upon reaching the summit, I was rewarded with the most beautiful gift—the scent of exotic flowers not unlike the scent of the sacred ash *vibhuti!*

Incidentally, I had also witnessed this divine fragrance during the funeral of a lovely lady from the village of Mullaghduff, who was also devoted to The Virgin Mary. During communion at her funeral mass, I smelt it around her coffin.

Now on top of this small mountain in Bosnia, I gave thanks again to Our Lady for all the blessings on my journey. I thanked her for the means to have a much needed holiday, for all the support I had received from all the doctors, my family and friends, therapists...

I included the doctors with a poor bedside manner for I knew they were only human. Indeed, they might have been having a very bad day at work!

I descended into the village and deposited a number of healing petitions from myself, friends and family. Although I was still a non-practising Roman Catholic, I attended mass inside St James's Church. It was filled with pilgrims from around the world.

My return to Medjugorje heralded yet more healing.

******

I had first seen emotional freedom technique known as EFT, or *tapping*, demonstrated on Richard Madeley and Judy's Finnegan's television show *This Morning*. I had watched in awe, witnessing many people with phobias improve with one single treatment session!

In October 2005, Ann and I attended my last natural medicine's training weekend, in this simple yet profound therapy. The technique was invented by Gary Craig and consists of a very specific sequence of simple tapping movements, performed on acupuncture points. The tapping is accompanied by reciting a series of positive statements akin to *affirmations*.

"Even though I have this shortness of breath, I love and accept myself completely..." I recited as I tapped.

I *tapped* on this and my myriad of other symptoms, on past painful events, including Mum's death, Dad's death, my miscarriage, the ending of my marriage, the Kerrytown fire...

The benefits of EFT soon became apparent, when my bouts of shortness of breath lessened, and I began to feel more upbeat and optimistic for my future.

Gary Craig has since made learning EFT freely available to everyone, via his website www.emofree.com.

My career as a therapist had now spanned twenty years from

its beginnings at Westbank Healing Centre in 1985. I had studied colour healing, crystal and electro-crystal healing, reflexology, aromatherapy, nutritional medicine, counselling skills, spiritual healing, radionics, space clearing and the ancient art of feng shui. I reckon I had attained the equivalent of a master's degree in natural medicines!

Although my health was slowly improving, I felt much too fragile to channel healing energy for others and my intuition told me it was time for yet more change. Sadly, I realised I could no longer wear my *therapist's hat*.

In late 2005, I relinquished my old career.

I believe that the healing I received from Our Lady in Medjugorje, and my introduction to EFT, were both instrumental in this decision. Although, I did not have a clue how to fill the gap left behind, I knew it would all work out perfectly.

I planned a return trip to Scotland for Christmas, with my sister Marie and her family, who had moved back to Edinburgh after Dad's death. Ann and Lawrence planned to travel too. Unfortunately, the week before Christmas I took a nasty chest infection, and was confined to bed. The infection worsened, and I developed a tight, painful band around my ribs; I was prescribed steroids. Reluctantly, I cancelled my holiday. However, dear Marie searched the internet and arranged a new flight for me for New Year's Eve.

Still feeling somewhat unwell, I took a tentative bus journey to Belfast Airport, and boarded the plane for Edinburgh. As I stepped off in Bonnie Scotland, my depressed demeanour vanished, as Marie and Ann met me wearing Christmas antlers on their heads. Group hugs and gales of laughter followed—Patch Adams, eat your heart out!

Marie very kindly drove us home via the lovely festive lights and Christmas markets on Princes Street. It reminded me of many a childhood Christmas back in Kippen, when Mum and Dad would take us all to Glasgow, to see the lights of George Square, which seemed quite *magical*. They remain one of my fondest childhood memories.

On New Year's Day, we wrapped up warmly and travelled to Holyrood Park, to view the traditional husky sledge racing, where we "oohed and ahhed", at the huskies. *My Inner Child* felt incredibly happy!

Sleep evaded me for the whole of my visit to Scotland, for the steroids made my mind race, and I stayed awake almost continuously. Although somewhat physically exhausted, I returned to Donegal feeling very uplifted. My family's TLC and the power of laughter were perhaps the greatest therapy of all!

A new serendipitous synchronicity followed, when I discovered that my gardening hero Diarmuid Gavin was coming to Alcorn's Garden Centre in nearby Letterkenny.

The great day arrived, and Ann and I delighted in procuring two seats in the second row, of a room full of Diarmuid's admiring fans, who were predominately women. All eyes expectantly watched the stage before his arrival!

Diarmuid was a very enchanting speaker and provided a fabulous slide show of gardens from around the globe, before patiently answering a number of horticultural questions.

Afterwards he kindly posed for endless photographs and signed autographs. I stood patiently in a somewhat lengthy queue, before proudly telling him, "I'm from the Rosses, near Kincasslagh."

Diarmuid smiled back and replied, "I have visited Daniel O'Donnell's home on Cruit Island. You are lucky to live in such a beautiful area."

I beamed back with dare I say it pride!

He then autographed the only slip of paper I could find—a prize draw form for the garden centre.

"To Brigid, Lots of love Diarmuid Gavin xxx," is now framed for posterity!

On the way home, I marvelled again that fate had brought Diarmuid to my doorstep in Donegal!

Back on planet Earth, I had been awaiting a permanent local authority home, in the nearby village of Annagry, and I watched expectantly as several new houses were completed on an existing small estate. However, I learned that I did not have enough points to merit a house, but I soon discovered God had other plans!

My second cousin and her family were allocated one of the new houses, and thus the house she had been renting became available. It was a pretty, detached cottage that was well sheltered from the elements, lying in a little hollow. It also had a large garden, with lovely views of a lake, home to a number of elegant swans. I visualised the plants I had gathered over several years (now in temporary accommodation in old tyres), finally finding a proper permanent home. The large garden was the deciding factor!

I left Ballymanus in April 2006 and looked forward to yet another fresh start.

I discovered that my new home had once belonged to a man called John Mór, an avid gardener, who grew tomatoes in his own greenhouse—a rarity in the windswept landscape of Donegal.

John Mór's spirit soon inspired me to follow a new career path....

Insights from Chelsea

- The way forward is always signposted

- The best things in life are often right on your doorstep!

Life in the Slow Lane

John Mór's - April 2006

"All plants are our brothers and sisters. They talk to us and if we listen, we can hear them."

Arapaho proverb

Toby and I moved into our new home in early April, amid a sea of golden daffodils just like Tennyson's poem. The garden was overflowing with their vibrant, yellow blooms; it seemed like they were greeting us and saying, "Welcome."

Several helpers eased our flitting, and we settled into our comfortable, new abode. Toby enjoyed exploring different surroundings; he was now aged thirteen, and a middle-aged gentleman. However, he was soon interrupted from his idyll, when we attracted new feline company.

I was outside planting my flowers in their new homes, when I heard a distant cry. I thought at first it was a bird. I moved to the front of the cottage, walked around towards the driveway and listened.

Silence.

I was about to return to my gardening, when I heard the sound again. This time it was clearly coming from our new turf shed, which had an open front.

I ventured inside, waiting for another audible signal. A very weak "miaow" soon sounded from behind an old door. I looked behind the door, and there he was—a tiny ginger-haired kitten, with one eye completely closed and badly swollen, squealing for help. My heart melted, as I took him inside. Later on that same day, my vet examined our new kitten, and he was given medication for his sore eye. I christened him "Ginger".

Over the following days, I called on my new neighbours but no one claimed him. He must have been dumped at the side of the road. I am very sad to say that kittens, puppies, dogs, cats and other animals are abandoned each and every day. This is such a poor reflection on humanity and a huge burden on the resources of many wonderful animal charities.

Ginger and Toby settled into an uneasy friendship, for they were both toms and each one vied to be the boss. It was both interesting and uplifting to watch their antics. We soon had lots of extra visitors, all eager to see the new arrival. Ginger loved the attention.

In 2002, I had worked through a life coaching book, and one of the exercises suggested asking friends and family, "What career(s) do you think would suit my talents?"

My sister Margaret had replied, "Gardening," while she had admired yet another of my garden makeovers!

I was living in John Mór's for several weeks, when I tentatively enquired about professional training in organic horticulture, in nearby Gortahork, and I was most surprised to learn that a course was beginning soon—in mid-June. It was certificated, it was part-time, and I would earn a small wage. Perfect!

I enrolled.

I had absolutely no notion of retraining in horticulture, before the house move; I think John Mór's spirit was willing me to go for it.

Since my childhood in Scotland, I have had an on / off love affair with gardening. My childhood home, Beech Cottage, had a HUGE garden that needed LOTS of tending and I was regularly roped into weeding from an early age; it was not exactly what I wanted to do, for I would much rather have been outside playing.

Our garden was full of old-fashioned cottage flowers and shrubs that remain my favourites today: rambling roses, sweet William, snapdragons, peony roses, lupins, lilac, honesty, flowering currant...

We also grew a large variety of fruit and vegetables, including carrots, beetroot, spuds, onions, lettuce, blackcurrants and gooseberries. I often reminisce on the joy of fresh cooked beetroot, placed in a dish with sugar and vinegar, of home-grown spuds dipped in butter and salt, fresh lettuce and spring onions, known as *syboes* and freshly made jam. All our garden produce was both organic and delicious.

I recall having a small flower bed of my own as a child and having limited success growing flowers from seed. The gardening *bug* slowly grew inside me, until it blossomed around the same time as my training in natural medicines. My home in Alderbank Terrace had a small cottage garden filled with poppies, lupins and my other old-fashioned favourites. I pottered there, but did not become truly hooked, till my move back to Stirlingshire. I then became a *gardening addict*, transforming the garden in Bannockburn, Garlands Cottage...

On the first day of my new job, I arrived outside a very large glasshouse, flanked by a series of polytunnels and other buildings. I was somewhat nervous, not knowing what lay ahead. Happily, I was quickly introduced to the horticultural team who were all old hands, and very warm and friendly. I learned that a number of them were extremely musical and had once been students of the local music college, studying alongside my old singing teacher!

I was joined by two other newbies who both shared many of my more esoteric interests. The remainder of the team included a group of friendly farmers and fishermen, who worked at the centre on alternate weeks, to supplement their incomes.

My new work attire was in no way feminine, due to health and safety regulations, and my feet were soon clothed in very unbecoming, steel toecap, safety boots softened by thick woolly socks!

Unfortunately, the temperature inside the glasshouse and polytunnels was akin to a sauna, and became somewhat of a challenge to me. Following instructions, I practised a series of yoga-like manoeuvres, planting and picking vegetables, herbs and fruit destined for local restaurants and shops. I was somewhat out of condition; my muscles ached, and I constantly felt like I had been in a major fight. I was very glad that the course was part time, for I could not have endured any more of a physical commitment. In hindsight, I realise that the warmth and exercise were perfect therapy for fibromyalgia.

One weekly physical reprieve was the sowing of seeds, on

Tuesday mornings, when we lined up in front of a potting bench, to gently tease hundreds of seeds onto trays filled with compost. It was a very precise procedure, and any sowing mistakes would soon be noticed, for we all had to put our names on the labels, complete with the date and the name of the seed. The trays of seeds were then transferred onto a row of heated benches to germinate. Germination rates were subsequently recorded on charts, to tie in with our learning.

We eventually planted the mature seedlings, using the principles of crop rotation, whereby no crop could be planted in the same spot twice in succession, avoiding the build up of pests and disease. I soon considered the soil another **living** entity, full of beneficial microbes and fungi, which we fed regularly with rotted cow manure, pellets of chicken manure, and our own organic compost.

We sowed and planted a variety of salad crops that I had never even heard of before— mibuna, mizuna, amaranth, New Zealand spinach… It took me a while to learn which was which, as a brain *fog* hampered my memory cells. We also grew several varieties of tomatoes, lettuce, aubergines, peppers, chillies, spinach, carrots, leeks, potatoes, garlic, rosemary, tarragon, thyme, chives…

The early spuds grown in the glasshouse were always a hit in the local shops, and local people snapped them up, almost as soon as they hit the shelves. The varieties we grew were Duke of York and British Queens. I delighted in cooking them at home. Yum!

I loved all this new learning, and although my physical body was struggling, I was increasingly upbeat. It was a joy to get out of bed in the morning, to work alongside a great team, where every day was filled with lots of fun banter, with the added bonus of a small wage. Once again, I felt very blessed.

Unfortunately, my lower back had been incredibly sore since my house move, and my pelvis now felt inflamed; I found it hard to sit down at all. On a check-up at the Gastro Intestinal Department, I mentioned my new symptoms to the consultant, and he immediately put my name on the urgent list, for exploration of my bowel. He also advised that I should have my gall bladder removed, after ongoing test results. I agreed to a double op.

My surgical appointment was arranged quickly, and I arrived at the hospital mentally ready for surgery. I changed into a hospital gown and accompanied a nurse to the lift to take me to theatre. However, we passed my prospective anaesthetist who told the nurse,

"I need to speak to my patient."

A series of questions on my medical history followed:

"Are you on any medication?"

"Are you seeing any other consultants?"

I gave him a brief description of my recent experiences.

"I carry a marker for blood clots, inherited from my mother called Factor V Leiden," I added.

The anaesthetist was perturbed. "I will need advice from our Haematology Department on possible prophylaxis. You cannot have surgery until then," he said.

My operation was cancelled; I was not amused!

However, I was a different person from the woman who had attended the Accident and Emergency Department in August 2003. Three years had passed, and I was not afraid to voice my opinion to medical professionals. I complained verbally to both the surgical team and the Complaints Department. As a result, I received an urgent appointment with a haematologist. A number of weeks later, armed with an anticoagulant, I had my gallbladder removed and my bowel checked. Thankfully, there was no sign of malignancy.

Although my surgery was keyhole, it completely floored me. My oxygen stats seemed very low postoperatively, and I was wheeled to the X-ray Department for a chest X-ray. The results showed no abnormality, but I remained an inpatient for an extra night as a precaution.

I was very glad to return home to be with my kitties, and they seemed to miss me as much as I missed them. A couple of days later, I was talking to a friend on the telephone, when I felt my abdomen itchy. I sneaked a look and found it was covered in red welts! Alarmed, I ended the phone call and immediately dialled the out of hours' doctor as it was now evening.

"Come right away," I was told.

Ann accompanied me to Gweedore, where I was ushered into the surgery and a warm, friendly doctor examined me. The welts now covered most of my body, including my eyelids. I could even feel them in my throat!

"You appear to be having a severe allergic reaction," the doctor said as he quickly prepared a syringe of medication.

I then had to swallow a tablet.

"What have you been eating?" he gently asked.

"Nothing unusual," I replied.

"I will send an immediate written report to your GP," he added.

I left the surgery armed with a supply of steroid tablets and antihistamines, in case of another allergic reaction. Still somewhat shocked, and extremely shaken, I was very thankful to have Ann's support.

In the following days, I visited my GP, who felt I had an infection of some kind after my operation. Happily, I never had similar welts on my skin again.

I was unable to work for over six weeks. When I returned for a couple of days, I became rather unwell, took another week off, and then worked half days, until I was able to resume normal working hours, anxious not to fall behind with my studies.

I found the next part of the course extremely challenging, as it involved time in the classroom and LOTS of new information, with regular exams, as well as continuous practical assessments. Although my memory was extremely sluggish from my illness, I persevered and received credits for all of my tests.

Commuting, working and study had taken over my life. There were regular party invites from my new friends, but I was unable to go, for I literally did not have an ounce of spare energy!

Christmas 2006 heralded very sad news. I learned that my ex-husband's middle son Dennis John had died aged just thirty-five from cancer. More grim news followed, when I learned that his oldest son Mark was in the final stages of motor neurone disease, another cruel illness. Mark especially, had been very kind to me after the end of my marriage. He was just forty-one, when he died in March 2007. Dennis had now lost all three of his sons and sadly, three little boys were now left without their dads.

How did I feel?

I guess a mixture of shock, disbelief and sadness—words cannot truly describe feelings in these situations. I did though wonder what kind of loving God could allow this to happen. It was hard to make sense of such a terrible, triple tragedy.

I still cannot comprehend why these things happen....

While I pondered more recently, on Mark and Dennis John's passings, a most beautiful book spoke to me—*It's Not Yet Dark* by Simon Fitzmaurice. It is a very poignant but uplifting account of Simon's journey with motor neurone disease. His words will touch your heart for Simon is very much ALIVE despite this terrible disease. I urge you to read it.

But back to the Past. I had learned that a month long work experience was part of my course syllabus, and I could fulfil another *dream*, to work in the gardens of Glenveagh Castle, which I had visited annually for many years. I did not know how I could manage four weeks of full-time employment but I had a plan in mind; I would take two weeks' annual leave before my placement and have time off in lieu immediately afterwards!

I telephoned my local travel agent, looking for a last minute holiday package that would suit my needs. I longed for sunshine, rest and a bit of culture; I booked a two-week holiday to Malta, an island that I had visited briefly during my marriage.

On the plane journey, I read the airline's magazine and spotted an article on the megalithic temples of Malta, understood to be the oldest free-standing structures on Earth. One of the temples, Mnajdra, would be open at dawn on the spring equinox, when the sun's rays light up the principal doorway and the innermost central niche. It was a ticketed event, and I felt I just had to go.

I rose early on the morning of the equinox and stood in the darkness at Mnajdra with a small group of others. Slowly at first, the rays of the sun slid silently through the temple walls, before finally filling the central chamber. Oh what a wondrous sight! My thoughts stood still in time, and I have since filed this experience among my list of AWESOME life events.

My hotel was busy, with lots of British and Irish pensioners who spent whole winters in Malta's mild climate. I befriended a lovely English lady who was widowed, and we booked a trip together to see a live performance of the *Rocky Horror Picture Show*. However, having never seen the film version, I did not quite know what to expect!

On our arrival, men dressed in black stockings and suspenders showed us to our seats, then regaled us with their on stage dramatic performance. Later, we threw rice, we danced, and we all participated in singing a series of very surreal songs.

It was truly great fun and a real tonic!

I enjoyed yet another unique experience in Malta's capital city of Valletta, when I learned of a small exhibition of the famous Chinese Terracotta Warriors. Eleven life-size soldiers, each one different in appearance and rank, stood among two life-size terracotta horses and other antiquities. I was most surprised to see how tall they all were and marvelled again at the synchronicity of yet another wonderful cultural miracle.

I returned from Malta refreshed. However, I noted yet again that the insomnia that had troubled me for three years was unrelenting on holiday. It was to be another four years before it lost its mighty grip!

I began my work experience at Glenveagh, and I was living out a dream. The castle and gardens are located in the heart of the Derryveagh Mountains, and are reached via bus through spectacular scenery. Mrs Cornelia Adair facilitated the creation of the Pleasure Gardens and Walled Garden in the 1880s. The gardens now cover 32 acres and host a magnificent collection of exotic plants from around the globe. My favourite place is the Walled Garden which has its own microclimate and a wonderful collection of perennials, interwoven with vegetables and fruit.

I joined another student from Dublin, under the watchful eye of one of four gardeners. Our first task was to prune the roses in the Rose Garden. I was more than happy to be standing among so very many beautifully scented flowers!

I continued to learn a HUGE amount about practical horticulture. I was particularly lucky to participate in the joint planting of a Wollemi pine, one of the oldest and rarest trees on the planet. I also spent a lot of time in the glasshouse, sowing and thinning young plants with another student who was a natural comic and great fun.

One further highlight of my work experience at Glenveagh was the launch of the Donegal Garden Trail, heralding a visit from a group of experienced amateur gardeners, who all planned to open their gardens to the public for charity. The group gathered in the castle drawing room, while I stood in the sidelines, listening to their speeches before feasting on some very delicious cakes—I mentally put becoming a member of Donegal Garden Trail on my *wish list*!

My four weeks at Glenveagh flew past, and I created a joyful journal filled with my horticultural experiences, which was presented for assessment, along with my written and practical tests.

Exhausted but happy, I took some time out in lieu, to revive my energy levels.

Good news soon followed; I had passed all my exams with credits. Happily, my horticultural companions all got credits too.

It was summer again, and it was HOT. It was also hectic. *Everyone* wanted large amounts of our great produce. On Thursday mornings, we started work at seven to avoid the sun wilting the delicate salad leaves. I hated getting up so early, but the bonus was an early finish, and I could sit or potter in my own garden. The plants I had brought with me from Ballymanus were thriving now in a large herbaceous border, which had become my pride and joy, so I decided to plant a vegetable plot and grew a good variety of crops that second summer.

The last few years had seen me change dramatically; there was a new person greeting me as I looked into the mirror! *The Heart of*

Sacred Space literary tome no longer resonated with my being, so I put it to good use in my new organic compost bin. It eventually became more refined, and I used it to nourish my new garden!

There was an option to stay on for another year of study in Gortahork—garden design and growing flowers from seed were two of the new study modules. I enrolled along with two other female workmates.

I knew that horticulture was helping me to heal on an emotional, mental and spiritual level, but my physical body continued to feel exhausted, my eyes ached, my muscles still felt like I had been in a fight, and I had major trouble sleeping.

Although I still had no definitive diagnosis, I remained proactive, and continued with my natural medicines treatments, replacing reflexology treatments with radionics, as I seemed to have reached a healing *plateau*.

My diet was much healthier, as I was now eating **copious** amounts of organic vegetables and herbs, all full of vitamins and minerals. I was also eliminating foods that angered my joints. I found red meat, dairy produce, alcohol, sugar and the deadly nightshade family of vegetables, which includes tomatoes and potatoes, all exacerbated my symptoms.

But back to my studies and our new module's practical assignments, which included creating two small gardens for the training centre. We three girls spent some hours discussing these projects, and we finally decided on two designs. The first would be a recycled garden complete with a pond, a bog garden and a lovely creative feature made from recycled wine bottles.

The other would become a sensory garden featuring a series of raised beds, filled with a rainbow of scented plants, a spiral shaped herb bed that provided both dry and damp conditions for its inhabitants, wind chimes to serenade us, recycled pipes filled with wild flowers for bees and butterflies, and a seating area to bask in the whole experience!

We measured our sites, created scale drawings, priced and sourced our materials, and then began the building of the gardens with the help of our farming and fishing friends.

In autumn 2007, I longed for another boost of sunshine to ease my aching body. But where should I go?

My hairdresser Edward had regularly regaled me with tales of his travels abroad, and I remembered him describing the delights of Morocco, and in particular the ancient seaside resort of Essaouira. Thus inspired, I booked a flight to Agadir via Dublin and three night's accommodation in a central hotel in Agadir. I could travel onwards to Essaouira by bus.

Agadir is a large resort with plenty of interesting tourist attractions. My hotel was perfectly pleasant, but it could have been in any city and lacked any Moroccan charm. I explored Agadir on a small train, which gave me an overview of the main places of interest. I explored these later on foot.

On day four, I travelled by minivan to Essaouira, sitting among a group of tourists who were visiting for a few hours. Their short trip would not do the city any justice.

Essaouira is a beautiful traditional Moroccan fishing port, complete with a long sandy beach and the old town or *medina*, filled with a stunning maze of side streets, akin to a labyrinth. I quickly located a traditional lodging known as a *riad*, which consisted of a series of rooms on several floors, based around a central garden open to the sky. Breakfast was served on a quaint rooftop terrace with views over the city and onto the wild Atlantic Ocean. The rooftop included an enclosed seating area for windy weather.

At breakfast, on my first morning, I got talking to a friendly Canadian solo traveller, who became my dinner companion for two evenings. Sadly, I soon learned that he had an addiction to smoking marijuana and was not quite *on this planet*; thus, I decided to dine alone for the remainder of my stay!

I was not short of other male admirers, for I was asked out to dinner by a series of young Moroccan men. I declined them all in favour of unattached banter!

Morocco is a shopper's paradise, and I embarked on daily retail therapy. I enjoyed lots of joking and haggling with shopkeepers, who proclaimed that I must have been a Berber in a previous life! I might add that I always haggle in a respectful manner.

I bought tea glasses, pottery, shoes, pashminas, cotton tops, wooden carvings…

Moroccan food is delicious, and Essaouira had an abundance of fine restaurants, to suit all tastes and budgets. I loved the traditional tagine—slow cooked dishes of chicken or fish, vegetables, fruit and nuts bathed in an aromatic sauce, and served in a clay dish with a cone shaped hood. Street food was also abundant, and I enjoyed an array of fresh breads cooked on al fresco grills.

The harbour area was another culinary *heaven*, filled with small outdoor restaurants serving freshly caught grilled fish, accompanied by salads, fresh bread and lemonade. I delighted in several harbour side meals. I also visited the local market or *souk*, piled high with fresh produce, including pyramids of colourful spices. I bought several spice mixes to take home.

I had enjoyed my first *hammam* (the traditional Moroccan equivalent of a Turkish bath), back in Agadir. It had been an incredibly relaxing, pampering *tourist* experience, but I wanted to try a more traditional hammam. The public hammam in Essaouira was recommended to me by a European lady, who was now a Moroccan resident.

I entered the building wondering what lay ahead, when I was met by a lady in traditional dress, surrounded by a sea of young faces, all newly scrubbed clean and smiling, dressed in fresh pyjamas. Around the walls, a plethora of new pyjamas were hanging for sale.

I stood nervously and said my best "hello", for my Moroccan was rather sparse.

The lady described the forthcoming ritual, using a series of hand gesticulations accompanied by lots of laughter from our audience. I then relieved myself of my clothes and moved shyly to the communal bathing area. A group of Moroccan ladies greeted me with more smiles, before I was scrubbed with a very abrasive mitten to remove my numerous dead skin cells, sloshed with buckets of water, washed in traditional black mud soap, rinsed again, had my hair massaged, washed and rinsed as I dissolved beneath my therapists' mighty hands into a ball of *putty*. My clean and **very** relaxed body eventually departed the hammam. I slept incredibly well that night!

In 2007, argan oil was one of Morocco's beauty secrets. It is very well known now, as I write. The oil is extracted from nuts, which have been digested by goats that have clambered in delight over the argan tree. Visitors can capture this vision of the climbing goats, on many roadsides between Moroccan towns and villages. The oil is then added to face creams and lotions that cost very little in Morocco. I purchased LOTS of pots of argan face cream, to ease any early signs of aging!

I returned to Agadir after seven delightful days, with a recommendation for a very quaint traditional hotel. It was both bijou and lovely, and served excellent traditional home-cooked meals. They were so delicious, that I dined there for the remainder of my stay. It also had a great swimming pool, and I languished in the sunshine, enjoying LOTS of refreshing swims.

Before returning home, I booked a trip to the ancient city of Taroudant, where I caught more new vistas, including women grinding argan nuts, another traditional souk and the stately Hotel Palais Salam, which was once a palace. The trip continued into the Atlas Mountains, where we lunched on yet another excellent tagine.

I felt glad I had sampled the *real* Morocco, and my holiday was later discussed at great length with anyone who would listen!

The winter flew past, and spring arrived once again, heralding a plant sale in Gortahork. It was traditional to grow lots of vegetables for the sale, but this year we added flowers as part of our new learning modules. We sowed pansies, primulas, petunias, poppies, nasturtiums…

They germinated at various rates on the heated benches, and every surface was soon covered in flowering plants. I was in horticultural heaven, tending to their every need and marvelling at these small miracles of nature. The day of our plant sale was exceptionally busy and deemed a big success. Soon after, we planted our two show gardens with many of our *babies*, and a grand opening was arranged.

However, an even more important date loomed—my sisters, Marie and Ann's fiftieth birthday. How did they want to celebrate? Much discussion followed and they decided on a family holiday to celebrate. Where to go? Malta and Morocco were top favourites after my glowing reports.

Morocco was eventually chosen, and I was more than happy to return.

Our week in Morocco was a glorious retreat, filled with sisterly love and laughter. We stayed in Agadir, but booked a private tour to Taroudant for the great day, when we all delighted in watching goats scramble the argan trees, views of the Atlas Mountains, visiting the Palais Salam, the traditional souk and dining in a top rated restaurant.

The holiday was deemed a resounding success!

Back in Donegal, it was time for our show gardens' official opening. Everyone mucked in with the final round of finishing touches, and we were all **very** proud of our achievements. The day coincided with interviews for summer gardening posts at Glenveagh, which was now at number one on my *wish list*. I managed to get the first interview spot and sat before a panel of three, to answer a series of questions with enthusiasm.

I remember being asked, "How would you deal with the problem of invasive rhododendron ponticum in Glenveagh?"

"I do not know," I answered.

Still, I got the job!

I felt incredibly sad leaving all my good friends behind, but I was looking forward to my return to Glenveagh, where I would work part time for the summer. My horticultural *dream* had come true for a second time; this time I worked in my favourite Walled Garden.

Once again, I felt I was in *Heaven on Earth*, as I weeded among an ocean of lupins in a range of colours, a profusion of peony roses, HUGE drifts of luminous blue aconites, geraniums in shades of blue, pink and cerise...

I planted crisp lettuces in precise rows, to create a tapestry of colour among cheery annuals; I stood among tall lattices of soft, scented sweet peas and breathed in their divine essence; I placed smiling calendulas among rows of *sprightly* dark Italian cabbages. They were indeed a perfect match!

One very small insect blighted these halcyon summer days—the mighty Glenveagh midge. It was a torture. Although I wore a special anti midge net over my face and neck, it still found umpteen ways to bite me, and I succumbed to red blotches each time they found a route to my skin. Thankfully, I found a good antihistamine cream that eased the pain and inflammation.

The summer sped by, and it was time to face an uncertain future. However, I now had much more clarity on a possible new career path, for I realised that I wanted to share my horticultural knowledge with others, and in particular children. The way forward was soon signposted. In the autumn, I learned of a formal training in adult tutoring, located in Letterkenny, and I enrolled.

Most of the other course participants had many years of experience in adult teaching roles, and my own experiences teaching natural medicines, seemed to pale in significance. However, I rose to the challenge and found the syllabus incredibly interesting. A range of new topics filled my days, and I created a diary of articles on the History of Adult Education. It was indeed a mighty tome!

Part of our assessment was *on camera*, and I dreaded being filmed. I was not the only one. I chose to demonstrate the planting of spring bulbs in pots, for my *movie premiere*. I reduced my anxiety with a colour visualisation and breathed a huge sigh of relief afterwards.

I completed my training and gained a pass with distinction—the only one awarded in my group.

I had now been living in John Mór's for three years. My health was still far from perfect, but I had a new enthusiasm for LIFE. The dream I had back in Ballymanus of rebuilding a house from its foundations upwards was well under way.

My next trip abroad would help me heal at a deeper and more profound level....

Insights from John Mór's

- Honouring your creative talents, often paves the way for new career opportunities

- Physical exercise, sunshine and warmth play a vital part in healing

- Being part of a fun, supportive team all add to this outcome!

Rome – March 2009

"To get lost is to learn the way."

African proverb

London, Paris, New York, Rome…

I had visited the first three of these cities in my distant past, and I loved them all. In March 2009 it was time to visit Rome.

I prepared for a week long Roman holiday to include my birthday on March 8, by researching the internet for *must-see* visitor attractions, best restaurants, accommodation and transport…

I then booked a flight from Dublin and arranged comfortable lodgings in a boutique hotel, near Rome's university, where I hoped to experience *real* Italian life, away from the main tourist sites. Sadly, I discovered my flight arrived a little too late to avail of the pope's weekly papal audience. However, my birthday was on a Sunday—I could have a world famous Sunday papal blessing while standing in St Peter's Square.

Hoping to add to my horticultural education, I pre-booked a tour of The Vatican Gardens for Saturday March 7. My ticket included entrance to the Vatican Museums, the Sistine Chapel, St Peter's Basilica and the crypt below—home to many famous papal tombs. I was well prepared, as always, thanks to Kippen Girl Guides!

I set off on my dream vacation, full of romantic Piscean anticipation, after reading Elizabeth Gilbert's fabulous book *Eat, Pray, Love*. Elizabeth had healed her broken heart after a bitter divorce by travelling to Rome, India and Bali, meeting her future husband en route.

I arrived in Rome, eager to view the city's many historical sites, and travelled from Fiumicino Airport by express train, to the central Termini station. I gazed out at my new surroundings and was saddened to see a sea of graffiti on many of the city's beautiful buildings—such a crime. Unsure of the best route from the city centre, I took a taxi for the remainder of my journey.

I hoped my hotel would meet my *idealistic* expectations.

Happily, it was perfect. I marvelled at its antique furnishings, the exquisitely tiled modern bathroom and the highlight for me—a painting of angels above my bed!

I unpacked my belongings and went in search of a good, reasonably priced restaurant. I found a small friendly, neighbourhood *trattoria*, where I dined on gnocchi (small potato dumplings) in a delicious sauce, tiramisu (an Italian version of our trifle) and a small glass of Italian vino. The cost was less than I had anticipated; I was more than happy.

I planned to visit central Rome on my second day in the city, when I could travel in comfort by tram, and later discover some of Rome's main visitor attractions on foot. My hotel was directly opposite a tram stop, ideal for my planned itinerary. However, the following morning was beset by rain, and I had to buy an umbrella. Of course the rain soon stopped, and it remained sunny for the rest of the week!

I began my walking tour at the Spanish Steps, marvelling at the view over Piazza di Spagna and its handsome fountain. I asked a group of tourists to take my photograph for posterity. I now imagined myself on a film set for *Roman Holiday*, with Audrey Hepburn and Gregory Peck!

A short walk away I found the famous Trevi Fountain, a fine example of Baroque architecture. I placed a coin in the fountain and made a wish. I spoke to a small group of Japanese tourists on their first visit to Rome. They were as excited as I was.

I was hungry now and wondered where to dine? I walked on through some quieter side streets, where I spotted a local *osteria*. I tentatively ventured inside and was welcomed with "buongiorno" and a sea of smiling faces all nodding in my direction. I knew I had chosen well. I dined on spaghetti marinara, a beautiful salad and fresh baked bread. Once again, the food was incredibly delicious, and the bill was more than affordable. My tour ended at an ice cream parlour, described in guidebooks as the best in the city. It was only a short distance away, and the ice cream was indeed *bellissimo*.

However, these Italian culinary delights had an adverse

reaction on my bones, which now ached considerably. Was it caused by getting damp in the rain, last night's glass of wine, the gnocchi, tiramisu, spaghetti marinara or indeed the ice cream?

I hobbled to the nearest tram stop and returned to my hotel for a much needed rest.

Although beset by pain, I continued to explore Rome's numerous attractions over the following days. The Colosseum, the world's largest amphitheatre, was quite stunning. It was hard to believe it had been built around 70AD. I imagined gladiators within its walls, emulating Russell Crowe in the iconic film *Gladiator*.

A short distance away stood the remains of the Roman Forum, with an abundance of temples dedicated to Saturn, Vespasian and Titus (creators of the Colosseum), Caesar, Castor and Pollux, Vesta…

I stood in wonder as yet more Roman *history* unfolded before me.

My mind took me back to St Modan's High School, where I had studied Latin. Mensa (table) and mensae (tables) reverberated in my brain. It was my least favourite subject (apart from PE), and I left Latin classes after one year!

Next on my wish list were the gardens of The Villa d'Este and its Renaissance water features and fountains. It is located in a small town called Tivoli, just outside Rome.

I caught an early morning tram to a central bus station, where I found an onward (non tourist) bus. We left the city and traversed a landscape dotted with quarries, all digging for the famous Travertine marble. I visualised paths and patios, buildings, and floors all clad in their sparkling Travertine marble *suits*. All too soon, we ascended a steep hill and arrived in Tivoli, where I alighted in a quaint tree-lined square and walked excitedly, to the great water gardens.

I entered the ticket office.

"The gardens are dry today. There is no water," the guide declared.

I was shocked. I would not witness the legendary water fountains!

"Are the gardens still open?" I ventured.

"Yes, you can still visit if you wish," was the reply.

My time in Italy was nearing its end, so I decided to buy a ticket.

I relaxed outside with a coffee from the gardens' café and breathed in the view of several acres of formal Italian gardens, lined with numerous **dry** water features, including fountains, ponds and troughs. The gardens were almost deserted and seemed bathed in an *otherworldly* peace. I walked down to the legendary Cento Fontane, now devoid of water; the long line of famous fountains lay silent. They were still a breathtaking spectacle, although I would rather have seen them in full flow!

The garden descended via several terraces, intersected with formally sculpted hedges, and a series of straight paths and stone walls. Trees and shrubs softened these hard edges, while banks of *smiling* daffodils provided a sunny backdrop. In the absence of water, the gardens were still quite beautiful. A small group of teenage students eventually broke the silence.

An hour or so later, I returned to the town's main square and found a trattoria. I enjoyed one of my favourite Italian dishes—seafood risotto. It was another culinary sensation.

Saturday the seventh finally arrived, and I looked forward to seeing The Vatican Gardens. I arrived early and people watched from a small, expensive café facing the entrance to The Vatican Museums, before I joined a group of around thirty other international tourists, inside the museum.

The garden tour began.

We were greeted by a patchwork of formal lawns lined with large terracotta pots, all filled with mature olive trees. It was immaculately presented. Our tour guide pointed to the pope's favourite arboretum, a peaceful haven where trees and statues intertwined. I could see why he loved it. We were indeed privileged.

Our group strolled past a number of Marian shrines, including a replica of the Lourdes Grotto and a shrine to Madonna della Guardia. There was also a shrine to St Thérèse of Lisieux, one of my favourite saints. We enjoyed seeing several **flowing** fountains, including Fontana dell'Aquilone resplendent with a colony of ducks. I wondered did they know they were swimming in The Vatican Gardens!

Many more statues saluted us, including a monument to St Peter. I delighted in seeing the pope's helipad and wondered would he make a flying visit?

In the Gardens of Palazzina di Leone XIII, I stood amongst formal rose gardens, not yet in bloom, but flanked by a number of formal topiary arches. These gardens overlooked St Peter's Basilica and provided yet more photo opportunities. The tour ended, and I felt very happy to have witnessed such a great Italian horticultural *feast.*

I lunched in a very busy restaurant in The Vatican Museums, before strolling through the museums' endless treasures.

Huge tapestries lined a number of walls, each more exquisite than the other. Other walls were laden with exquisitely painted Madonna, angels and cherubs. It was an overwhelming sight and would take several days to truly marvel over every exhibit. However, I was not blessed with unlimited time. I wondered though at such a vast display of wealth, when millions of people around the world live in abject poverty?

Still, my tour continued, as I witnessed the wonders of The Sistine Chapel and St Peter's Basilica. The ceilings and architecture of both buildings were magnificent. Finally, I descended the steps below St Peter's to see the papal crypts. I found the tomb of John Paul II and stopped to pray. On June 1, 1982, I had seen him *live* in Glasgow's Bellahouston Park among a three hundred thousand strong crowd. It had been a momentous day.

I left the Vatican City, tired yet happy, not realising that more *miraculous* highlights were to come....

The following morning, I returned and entered St Peter's Square via a series of lengthy security checks. Sunday morning traffic had been lighter than I had expected, and I pondered how to pass an hour or so before my birthday blessing. I decided to revisit the papal crypts.

Somehow, I joined the wrong queue and mistakenly entered the main part of St Peter's Basilica, where mass was now being said. I ventured towards the front of the building, after spotting a small crowd of people standing behind a line of pews. They were being closely monitored by several stern security guards. I approached them and asked, "Is it possible to get a better view of the mass?"

I was ushered through to the front of St Peter's, where I found a small space near a large pillar, among a group of other latecomers. I could see the choir to the left of the main altar, but little else. I looked for a better vantage point, and good luck prevailed. I could now view the celebrant, who was dressed completely in white. Is that the pope saying mass, I wondered? No, I thought, he doesn't look like himself, for this man appeared thinner and somewhat severe. Besides, would the pope saying mass not be *advertised*!

It was time for Holy Communion, and I dutifully queued before the priest. He was now joined by a man in a suit, who looked like a member of Special Branch (I had witnessed SB before on my political jaunts—they all look alike, grim-faced and suited with *don't mess with me* looks).

More *ridiculous* thoughts surfaced. Could this indeed be the pope?

I received communion and delighted in finding a vacant seat near the altar. Mass ended and I *floated* outside, in anticipation of my papal birthday blessing. I still wondered about the man in white, so spying two handsome young priests, I enquired of the celebrant's credentials:

"Do you know if the pope said mass just now?" I enquired.

"Yes, I believe he did," was the unexpected reply.

I was shocked and more than a little overjoyed. I had actually received Holy Communion from the pope on my birthday!

I continued to converse with both priests. "It's my birthday today," I blurted.

"Many congratulations. Where are you from?"

"Donegal in Ireland," I replied.

"We are both from Iowa in the United States," they smiled.

The conversation continued with one other surprise:

"My grandparents hailed from Ballintra in Donegal, and my surname is Gallagher," said the priest on my right, as I marvelled once again at *serendipity*!

I said my goodbyes and moved to the central part of St Peter's Square, where I hoped to get a good view of the papal balcony. I was still in awe when the pope appeared a short time later, smiling and waving to the crowds. Thus, I received my second birthday blessing, alongside hundreds of others from around the globe.

Later, I lunched al fresco on the upper floor of nearby Castel Sant'Angelo, looking across the city, towards St Peter's Basilica. I looked down on the bridge below; it was covered in statues of angels.

I felt amazed at how, as a somewhat lapsed Catholic, I had been given such a special birthday gift!

Insights from Rome

- Special blessings come on birthdays!

St Crona's - spring 2009

"Before enlightenment, I chopped wood and carried water. After enlightenment, I chopped wood and carried water."
Zen Saying

My visit to Rome heralded a new turning point in my healing. Just before my holiday I had felt compelled to return to my GP's surgery, noting all my current symptoms on a sheet of paper.

I included:
- Fatigue
- Aching muscles and joints
- Sore eyes with whites that were often blue-grey
- Insomnia
- Recurrent chest infections and aching over my left lung and kidney
- Poor memory and concentration
- Intermittent bleeding from my bowel.

I handed my list to a locum GP, and I was told, "Please come back for a blood test. If the results show an inflammatory condition, I will refer you to a rheumatologist."

My blood test proved positive, and I nervously awaited a Rheumatology Department appointment, wondering if I would finally get a definitive diagnosis.

Meanwhile, I was given a fabulous gift—a voucher for three months membership of a local swimming pool, gym and spa facilities, located a mere five miles from my home. Although I used to love swimming in the Atlantic Ocean or Mullaghderg Lake, I had not entered Donegal's very chilly outside waters in recent years.

I plunged into this new luxurious swimming pond and only managed to swim a paltry two lengths. I determined to improve upon my poor start, and a couple of months later, I could swim for a full fifteen minutes.

I enrolled as a full member for a further year, aiming to further increase my fitness levels. However, I took two steps forward and one step back for some time to come, when I succumbed to yet more chest infections.

On a more positive note, I accepted my first school gardening post in the spring of 2009, with a small local school, blessed with an enthusiastic head teacher. Together we created a vegetable plot with raised beds, to accommodate a variety of vegetable plants and good old spuds. The school also invested in lots of window boxes, which we filled with a rainbow of flowers.

My new career had now left the starting post, and the way forward was soon signposted.

Soon after, I learned of the Heritage in Schools Scheme, a national project funded by the Heritage Council which supports education in Irish primary schools on a variety of subjects related to conserving Irish heritage. Schools can book *Heritage Specialists* in archaeology, crafts skills, nature and wildlife conservation…

I applied for a post but discovered that interviews were scheduled for early 2010. I would need to find alternative employment for at least a year.

I did not remain unemployed for long as I spotted an advert in the local paper for a community employment scheme starting in September 2009. There were several vacancies, and one included working outside with flowers and garden maintenance. Naturally, I applied.

The day of my interview arrived.

"I would like to be part of the gardening team," I declared.

However, the interview panel had another plan in mind when I was offered a placement as caretaker of the church of St Crona!

I was somewhat surprised to be offered this post; it was not at all what I had expected. However, I needed an additional income, and thus I accepted.

I enquired about my new duties, and I was told they would include cleaning the church and working with the gardening team in spring to grow flowers from seed. I relished the horticultural aspect of my new job, for Dungloe has been participating in the national Tidy Towns scheme for a number of years and always produces a lovely show of flowers.

Sadly, I began my first day of employment with a heavy heart.

Ginger, Toby and I had acquired a new feline friend whom I had christened Snowie due to his lovely, white coat; he also had the most stunningly beautiful, turquoise eyes.

Snowie had appeared at John Mór's in the spring, bedraggled and malnourished with a large sore on his leg. I fed him daily, but he remained outside. He snarled if I approached him, and I was unable to take him to the vet. I compromised and sent him distance healing, visualising a soft blue light surrounding his painful limb. Snowie soon mended and became quite approachable when his leg healed. He then proceeded to make himself even more comfortable, sneaking inside at night through my open bathroom window. However, he would discreetly leave the same way in the early hours of morning. He was transforming into a big, softie and Toby and Ginger were intensely jealous!

My dear friend Gina visited us in early summer and said, "Snowie is a cat with attitude," as he swept *nonchalantly* past her, while fawning for her attention!

Sadly, a few days before I began my new job, he became quite debilitated, and he would not eat. I took him to the vet, who thought he might have been poisoned. Although he was prescribed medication, he did not respond and deteriorated rapidly. He died in the veterinary hospital, a few days after my fresh start at St Crona's.

I felt incredibly sad and remained on the verge of tears, for several weeks.

But back to my first day in St Crona's...

The church's sacristan welcomed me and showed me around the church. It is a modern building with a large, central spire of glass that fills the altar with an ethereal light. Rows of seats embrace the altar in a semicircle, allowing visitors to get a good view of the mass. Inside the two main sets of doors lie more large windows—a natural attraction for small children's sticky fingers!

I learned that Saint Crona was a sixth century saint and a cousin of Saint Colmcille. The ruins of a church built by him are sited in Termon, near the village of Maghery a few miles from Dungloe.

He installed a healing stone which still exists on the site, that has reputedly healed a wide variety of health issues.

The priests used the sacristy to the rear of the chapel to prepare for mass, while a small room to its side was used for families with young children. It became my sanctuary for the earliest part of my working days.

After my guided tour, I was shown a huge, metal cross, in need of a clean and polish. I retired out of sight as a few parishioners arrived early to recite the rosary.

I cleaned and polished the cross, while I listened to, "Hail Mary, full of grace. The Lord is with thee…"

I joined in the prayers, "Holy Mary Mother of God…"

The cross gleamed at the end of the rosary.

It was time for morning mass and I was told I could join the congregation, as I could not work while the parishioners worshipped. Feeling rather low and tearful because of Snowie's poor health, I was glad of some unexpected gentle healing from the mass.

Once the chapel emptied after mass, my duties resumed. If the carpet needed cleaning that came first. If there was dust to polish away, a spell of dusting could follow. If I found sticky finger marks on the glass windows, I could produce my glass cleaner…

The year flew past in a simple routine of polishing chalices, crosses, statues, monstrances and other religious items, reciting the rosary, joining the congregation at mass, and then cleaning the church.

My toilet cleaning lessons from Amma's ashram resurfaced, alongside memories of the film *The Karate Kid*, who was apprenticed to a master hoping to become fluent in martial arts. *The Kid* began his training by doing menial tasks. I felt a bit like an apprentice Karate Kid myself!

I recognised that I became a victim of my own failings if I overdid anything—often succumbing to those old familiar *beat up* feelings in my muscles and joints. I resolved to literally stop beating myself up!

I was also forced to heal another old issue—my fear of

funerals. I had avoided attending them since my father's death in October 1995. I attended a good many funerals in my year at St Crona's, and I gradually released my old fears. However, it was still quite a challenge, for I often felt very tearful from my own losses. Fortunately, there were also lots of joyful weddings in the parish.

I carried out my wedding duties as needed, ensuring the church sparkled on each occasion. Although it was a pleasure to watch each couple make their marriage vows, I wondered would they all find lasting happiness?

We had regular visits from local schools when children were preparing for their First Communion, Christmas or Easter celebrations. The children *lit up* the church with their excitement. My cleaning duties would then halt, as I discreetly disappeared inside my little room at the rear.

Ann, Marie and I enjoyed a trip to London in the autumn of 2009, for a healing workshop facilitated by author Doreen Virtue. Doreen has published lots of books on angels and other esoteric subjects, and I had purchased a number of her works. Our weekend away was filled with laughter, healing meditations, and lots of inspiring stories. I returned home replenished with sisterly love and angelic healing.

The community employment scheme encouraged all participants to enhance their existing skills and qualifications, so I enrolled on a daytime writing class in the local library.

The Artist's Way by Julia Cameron was taken down from my bookshelf, and I worked through its creative exercises for a second time. I soon unearthed my old joy in writing prose.

One dreary autumn day, our writing tutor asked us to stand by the library window, silently looking out on the surrounding graveyard.

"Write for ten minutes, on what you observe," she suggested.

I wrote the following short piece, entitled "A Grey Day":

"Under a grey sky, the chimneys spout out smoke as people huddle by their warm turf fires. Outside the library there are hundreds of 'In Loving Memories', the one before me embraced in a heart.

The bell raised on its platform is surrounded by puddles of water today, as the rain lashes down on an autumn Donegal day."

Sadly, the writing class soon came to an end, and I left my name with the local library for any future literary classes.

I still missed dear Snowie and decided to adopt another cat. I visited a local pet charity and fell in love with a lovely white cat, whose eyes were inflamed and sore; I discovered he was recovering from cat flu. When he was well enough, I took him home and christened him Angel.

Approaching the festive season, I decorated my Christmas tree with an assortment of bells and tinsel. Angel could not resist this new *toy*. I cherish a lovely photograph of him playing among the branches.

Although he was another boy, he was a very gentle, more feminine soul and Ginger and Toby soon accepted him as a new member of the household. Indeed, I felt he was a truly healing pussycat, for when he sat near me, I could feel lots of loving energy emanating from his soul.

December 2009 was the start of the worst winter in almost fifty years, when I finally received my first appointment with a rheumatologist. Ann and I travelled by bus to Letterkenny, amongst a scene reminiscent of Lapland!

I entered the consulting rooms, hoping for answers to my disease. As per usual, I had come prepared with a list of questions, written down on paper. I was met with a kind, gentle rheumatologist who was not in any hurry, and took prolific notes on my medical history.

"Please lie down on the treatment couch," he continued. "I will apply pressure to some points on your body, which might help my diagnosis."

"Ouch," they were very painful to the touch.

"I think you may have fibromyalgia," he offered. "However, I will take some more blood tests, and I will arrange a further appointment for you."

I was relieved to finally have a possible diagnosis; it had been a long difficult journey, to put it mildly.

In early *Arctic* January, I received a letter from the Heritage in Schools scheme, and travelled to Dublin for a short interview. I was soon accepted onto their list of heritage specialists. I felt excited for the future and sent out a silent: "Thank You."

The cold icy winter continued.

I drove to St Crona's for my early morning starts, praying that my car would not skid off the road. Thankfully, the car and I remained intact.

My body was now in great need of a rest, and I craved another holiday in the sun. I had long wanted to visit Madeira and its famous spring Festival of Flowers. I booked flights from a budget airline via Belfast then Stansted airports, through my local travel agent. I then arranged comfortable accommodation at a small boutique hotel in Funchal.

In early April, I was in holiday mood, when I received my follow-up appointment with the rheumatologist.

"You appear to have fibromyalgia," he said. "I shall prescribe you some steroids."

My mind filled with memories from my childhood and a friend's mother beset with rheumatoid arthritis. She had been prescribed steroid medication and always looked bloated with fluid. I did not wish to gain any excess weight.

"I would rather not take steroids," I replied.

"Very well, then I can offer you an alternative called Amitriptyline. It is a tricyclic antidepressant that has helped some fibromyalgia patients," he added.

Although I was still loath to take any form of medication, I accepted a low dosage prescription. I was also given a referral letter for physiotherapy.

I researched fibromyalgia symptoms on the internet and discovered they can include:

- Widespread pain or pain in individual areas e.g. the neck
- Sensitivity to pain
- Sensitivity to foodstuffs, bright light, moulds etc.

- Stiffness
- Fatigue
- Poor quality sleep
- Cognitive problems—learning difficulties, inability to concentrate, slow or confused speech—sometimes referred to as *Fibro Fog*.
- Headaches
- Bowel changes and irritable bowel syndrome
- Anxiety
- Depression…

I had suffered every one of these symptoms, except headaches, at the outset of my condition.

I also learned that the exact cause of fibromyalgia remains unknown, but several *triggers* have been noted among sufferers, including physical or psychological trauma, from car accidents, falls or other events. Viral infections are another possible trigger. The disease may also be secondary to other inflammatory or auto immune conditions.

I embarked on my much anticipated holiday on the evening of April 14 and arrived at Stansted Airport, in time for an early morning departure to Madeira. I had booked a room in an airport hotel, but I did not sleep at all well. However, I rose in good time for my very early flight and joined a lengthy queue at the allotted check-in. I glanced upwards at the departure boards. Surprisingly, they were now announcing the cancellation of a considerable number of flights. It was the morning after the volcanic eruption in Iceland!

My queue was redirected to another much longer queue for the Customer Care Centre. I remained shocked, weepy and lacking in sleep, when *The CCC* closed its doors shortly before I reached the front!

A number of airport staff handed out sheets of paper listing our passenger rights under European Law. It was a somewhat confusing list.

They *sang* in unison, "Please go home and await news on our website."

It was the *mantra* of the morning.

I had no home to go to, and I was becoming increasingly upset. I waited several hours for my travel agent to open. Still shocked and in tears, I recounted my tale of woe.

"I am stranded at Gatwick," I opened, choking back loud sobs, amidst rivers of tears. I'm sure the poor girl did not quite know what to make of me!

However, she remained calm and arranged accommodation for me in a local hotel. I trundled through the airport with my suitcase and overnight bag and queued for a taxi. I was greatly relieved to finally get *checked* in for some much needed rest. However, sleep continued to evade me, and the stress of my predicament persisted. Neither meditation nor flower essences nor aromatherapy oils brought me any relief!

Meanwhile, the ash cloud continued to disrupt air traffic.

The following morning, I spoke to my travel agent minus tears, and discovered that I would have to move yet again, as my hotel was now fully booked!

Thankfully, she arranged a good alternative for me. Two nights in another hotel followed, where I continued to keep regular contact with her, whilst keeping abreast with any new *Ash Cloud News* on television. Unfortunately, the ash was not for moving, and my holiday in Madeira was not meant to be.

Reluctantly, I decided to travel home to Donegal and the following morning, I caught a train to central London, and then travelled north to Glasgow. The Scottish train filled with other weary travellers.

"Where have you come from?" was today's mantra.

"Gatwick, Heathrow, Spain, France..." echoed round the compartment.

I counted myself incredibly lucky for I soon learned that many of my fellow travellers had returned from afar and had to pay for alternative travel home. Despite these unforeseen challenges they were a very happy bunch of people, and their lively banter shortened my passage homeward.

Alighting in Glasgow, I boarded a new train for Stranraer. I gazed out on the Ayrshire coast as we hurtled south. It was a poignant journey, filled with memories of travelling with my family to Donegal.

Comfortable bed and breakfast accommodation awaited me in Stranraer, and I fell asleep quickly, relieved to be almost home. It was yet another logistical nightmare to get a ticket on **any** ferry crossing to Ireland, for bookings were now at a premium with *Ash Cloud Travellers*. Thankfully, my travel agent angel had procured me a place on the ferry to Belfast, for the following morning.

Back on terra firma, I caught a bus to the city centre, another to the airport where I retrieved my car, and then I drove onwards. I had a lot of stops along the way, but I got home in the end. My heart burst with delight at returning to *The Homes of Donegal.*

Getting any kind of refund for my cancelled holiday was a marathon affair. My insurance company, like many others did not compensate travellers for ash clouds. I eventually received some refunds from the airline, and an accommodation voucher for my hotel booking, but several months later the booking company went bust. I lost a considerable amount of money.

Disappointingly, my Amitriptyline prescription was producing a number of adverse side effects. My ability to concentrate was now greatly diminished, I felt unsafe driving and my weight had ballooned. I felt very despondent.

I returned to my GP and sought his advice. He suggested an alternative drug called Lyrica, which had been successful in treating a number of fibromyalgia patients. I learned it had originally been used in the treatment of pain from shingles and diabetic neuropathy. It seemed worth trying. Lyrica very quickly spirited me into a more restful pattern of sleep. I felt incredibly relieved for I had been suffering from insomnia for almost seven years!

I reported back to my GP that I was progressing well on medication. Sadly, this did not last long as new symptoms soon emerged—my body began to swell with fluid, and my bowels went on strike—not a good idea for me with my history of internal bleeding.

Reluctantly, I stopped taking Lyrica. My GP then announced that I was incredibly sensitive to drugs, and that acceptance of my condition was my only path to healing. I felt angry at what I felt was his lack of empathy. I now know he was probably right.

It was back to yet another drawing board, and determined to find other means for healing my disease, I searched the local library for books on fibromyalgia. However, there was little written on the condition. I only discovered one slim book written by a recovered sufferer, who praised the value of exercise.

I had been swimming regularly for a year by then, and my fitness levels were certainly improving. However, I kept falling sick with chest infections and it was a case of swim regularly, until I succumbed to another chest infection, rest, return to more swimming …

Sadly, this cycle kept repeating.

Once I stopped taking Lyrica, my insomnia returned. I wondered if I would ever be free from the grips of fibromyalgia. Thankfully, I got an unexpected boost, from another source. I received a telephone call from Dungloe library:

"Would you like to join a new writers' group?"

The answer was in the affirmative.

On April 27, 2010, I tentatively entered Dungloe Library and joined a group of ladies round a small table. Everyone had an interesting life story to share, each one interspersed with lively banter and gales of laughter. I immediately felt at home. Rosses Writers have been sharing and laughing ever since. We also do a little writing.

One of my first creative efforts was based on two roses that one of our ladies brought to class. One rose was fresh and full of life, while the other was dying. I wrote:

"A crimson hue of velvet petals nestles close to create a delicious bloom. Gentle leaves embrace a fine green stem, each one veined with tiny lines. A little three-leaved branch sits quietly in a bend waiting to mature.

Alongside these luscious leaves lies a large rosebud, embalmed in death. Its petals have paled into mottled hues of dark red, pink and orange.

The cycle completed, the two roses rest side by side—a testament to each other's beauty."

I began to draw on my own past and wrote of Mum and Dad's death, my marriage and divorce, the Kerrytown fire and other major life events. I found it great therapy, but I had absolutely no plans to write another book!

On May 24, 2010, my dear companion Toby joined Snowie in heaven after a very short illness. I was only alerted to his deteriorating condition when he hid silently under a hedge; I eventually found him, took him inside, and called the vet. Toby passed away in my arms, a mere mile from home, as Ann drove us to our appointment.

He had been my loyal companion for nearly seventeen years, living in a total of six different homes and accompanying me through many of life's challenges. I buried him in the garden, near one of his favourite spots. Ginger, Angel and I missed him terribly.

I was given a much needed boost when I received my first booking through the Heritage in Schools scheme.

A sea of small, happy faces met me on my first day.

"Miss, can I plant please?"

"Can I dig now?"

"Look, there's a lady bird!"

Children have boundless energy and enthusiasm, and they all wanted to talk to me at once!

They renewed my passion for organic horticulture, and we soon created vegetable beds, filled with carrots, lettuce, cabbage, onions...

We sowed a small wild flower meadow and built a number of *bug hotels* (homes for a variety of insects in structures assembled from wood, sticks and foliage).

I thrived.

It was also time to join the Dungloe Tidy Towns Gardening Team, growing flowers from seed. The male banter was *magic* and provided yet another great remedy for me after Toby's passing. My year at St Crona's was almost over and I now had the option to continue for another year.

Should I take it?

I decided to take a huge leap of faith instead and concentrate on teaching with the Heritage in Schools scheme. My intuition also compelled me to ask the local secondary school for employment. I found I had chosen **exactly** the right time to enquire, and I was contracted to teach the sixteen-year-old pupils organic horticulture, from September 2010.

I planned a holiday in Scotland, before the start of the new school year and booked flights for mid-August. Unfortunately, my dear friend Angel became ill with pneumonia, in early August. My vet began treating him with antibiotic injections.

"I think I can help him," he said on our first visit.

However, Angel peacefully passed away on August 11, 2010, a mere eight months after joining my feline family. I had now lost three dear pussy cats in less than a year— Snowie in September, Toby in May and now Angel in August. Angel died mere days before my holiday. I felt his gentle soul wanted me to go to Scotland.

Poor little Ginger was now my sole companion.

Insights from St Crona's

- Having a medical diagnosis helps enormously

- Keep on praying

- Our dear feline friends are only passing through

- When one door closes, yet another opens.

A Permanent Home – September 2010

"As you teach, you learn."

Jewish proverb

My holiday in Scotland included a *pilgrimage* to Stirling, my first visit since the summer of 1999. As I tentatively made my way to the Victorian arcade where Healthworks once resided, I wondered what had become of the building. Perhaps it had become a hairdressing salon, a tea room, a dress shop…

I was both amazed and delighted when I looked through the windows, to discover that Healthworks was once again a healing centre and shop. My astonishment continued when a familiar face greeted me—a lovely lady who had once attended some of my first self-healing classes!

We chatted animatedly for some time, reliving old memories until she announced, "Would you like to see our healing room?"

I could not refuse.

I ventured upstairs, where I was shown a large new therapy room, once home to our workshops and classes (the former treatment room was not a part of this new business).

"Would you like some time here on your own?" she added.

I accepted her kind offer and sat down in a chair, soaking in the surroundings, as I reflected on my past. Memories surfaced of all the people who came through our doors to learn chi gung, belly dancing, yoga and so much more, the students from the Scottish School of Holistic Healing, the clients who had come in the hope of healing their disease…

Healthworks had been such a huge healing project for me and others, and it had helped fill the void in my heart, after Dad's death and the subsequent break up of my marriage. I felt happy that the healing was continuing….

I quietly went downstairs, bought a few purchases for good luck, and left with a fresh smile on my face.

My next stop was Callander, to visit Peggy, a cousin of my

mum's. She has been a lifelong friend to me, and I always enjoy her company for she exudes similar warmth to Mum. Marie too remains so much like her, full of fun and infectious laughter.

My holiday flew past and on the day of my departure Marie handed me a little package containing memorial cards for my dear deceased pussycats. I was incredibly touched by her thoughtfulness.

The holiday was a real tonic and I returned home feeling somewhat revitalised from yet more sisterly love.

Good news soon followed, when I was allocated a permanent home among the new houses built by the local council. Although I had not merited enough points for a key in 2006, I was now topping the waiting list.

I remained thankful for the intervening years spent in John Mór's, in the townland of Bunaman, on the edge of Annagry. I would now be moving into the heart of the village. Annagry is somewhat bigger than Mullaghduff and boasts two pubs, a hotel, two takeaways, a café, post office, chemist and a branch of The Cope supermarket. It is also home to Danny Minnie's, which has metamorphosed into a very fine, award-winning restaurant. It is my favourite place for family celebrations.

I collected my keys and opened a new front door, to a lovely two-bedroom, end terraced house in a group of three. I was filled with both joy and gratitude.

The following weeks were filled with packing and moving my belongings, plus filling and unloading a small trailer, with a vast collection of flowering plants and shrubs. I left behind a healthy collection of plants for John Mór's next tenant.

Each home I had lived in had helped me to heal.

My home in Ballymanus had stunning views, but it was open to the elements and the fierce Atlantic winds. In that home my old issues were literally *blown away*, while my foundations were rebuilt, as portrayed in my dream.

John Mór's lay in a sheltered hollow, with beautiful views of a lake with swans.

I had studied and learned a LOT in that home. I had met

Diarmuid Gavin, studied organic horticulture for two years in Gortahork, worked at Glenveagh, gained my adult tutoring diploma, and just before I left Bunaman, I finished the Introduction to the Environment module with the Open University!

My new home was in the centre of the village, sheltered from the elements, with strong fences, and good, kindly neighbours. I felt very blessed when one new neighbour and her two little girls visited with a warm welcome, and a bottle of wine.

I could not wait to put my own stamp on a permanent interior and garden. I hired a very efficient female painter, and every room bar my new bathroom was painted in brilliant white, to provide a *blank canvas* for my colourful soft furnishings and my collection of paintings, gathered from around the globe. Sadly, I could no longer paint, as it provoked substantial pain in my muscles and joints, from the repetitive actions and the chemical fumes.

The house has an open-plan kitchen and living area, with the benefit of the morning sun through the living room, and the evening sun through the kitchen. I placed a lovely crystal above my kitchen window to reflect lots of evening rainbows across both rooms. This spectacle continues to feel quite magical, and I still smile inwardly at such a simple pleasure.

I have used a small SAD lamp for many years now and realise I needed LOTS of natural daylight as part of my self-healing regime.

SAD or seasonal affective disorder affects many people worldwide, most notably in countries furthest away from the Equator. Lack of natural daylight can induce a number of symptoms, mostly in winter, but in some sufferers all year round, including:

- Lethargy
- Insomnia
- Irritability
- Sleeping much more than usual
- Depression
- Anxiety
- Cravings for carbohydrates
- Difficulty in concentrating
- Decreased libido…

I use my SAD lamp at various intervals throughout the year, beginning a treatment programme with an hour or so early in the day, then adjusting as needed. I find it best to use the lamp in the morning, otherwise I feel too wide awake at bedtime!

The most exciting part of my house move was having my own garden. It was very sheltered, sunny and just the right size for easy maintenance. It was also covered in long grass, so it provided me with yet another *blank canvas*. I immediately embarked on designing a garden layout, measuring the site and laying out a grid system with string and canes for my new flower beds, a pond, gravel paths, a fenced area to hide my bins…

I based my design on the principles of feng shui.

Once I was well settled in my new home, I pursued a dream from my days at Glenveagh, to be featured in the Donegal Garden Trail.

I enlisted some much needed help, and some of the rows of canes and string in my sea of grass metamorphosed into raised wooden beds, created at a diagonal to the house walls—producing a much more interesting perspective, as visitors enter the garden. It also makes the garden appear larger.

I then constructed a small wildlife pond, using a butyl liner, for I missed my lakeside views from John Mór's. Indeed, this was the third pond I had constructed, the first being in Bannockburn and the second in Thornhill. I had then been gifted with views over Mullaghduff Lake, the Atlantic Ocean, and finally John Mór's lake and swans. I believe my love of water features is a true Piscean trait.

I ordered a small lorry full of good quality topsoil, and the raised planting beds were duly filled, by a strong man, giving my plants a long awaited permanent home.

My house move coincided with starting to teach at the local secondary school, where I would be working with a group of transition year students, who were all boys. In autumn 2010, the mighty outdoors became their organic horticulture classroom, and they designed, and then built a wildlife pond, near the school's entrance. They were all enthusiastic gardeners and a very joyful team to teach!

Working there kept me financially solvent, gave me time to recharge my batteries, and continue on my self-healing quest.

I returned to St Crona's church for mass each Thursday, before attending the Rosses Writers. I also started going to Sunday mass at Our Lady Star of the Sea church in Annagry, where Mum and Dad had been laid to rest. I felt compelled to have my new home blessed by St Crona's parish priest, and I invited close family and friends to share in the blessing, the mass and a home-cooked meal.

In the preceding months, one therapist's name had repeatedly cropped up in conversations—a medical herbalist called David Foley. I had first met David back in 1999, when I had sought sponsorship for my trip to Bosnia. He'd supported me by taking a table at the Natural Medicine Fair in Kincasslagh. I felt guided to book an appointment with David. However, he had a long waiting list.

Meantime, I received my first physiotherapy appointment, after recommendation from the rheumatologist. I did not know what to expect especially after my previous physio's diagnosis of my symptoms being due to the menopause!

However, I was delighted to meet a lovely girl with a Scottish accent, who knew LOTS about my disease. She was also trained in acupuncture, and after recommending a series of exercises to ease my discomfort, she gave me a short acupuncture treatment to see how I would respond. On my next visit, she extended the treatment time, and I soon felt the benefits. I began to fall into a healthier sleep pattern—the first time in more than seven years, apart from my short time on Lyrica. I felt like I had just won the lottery!

I continued with weekly treatments until early 2011, when my physiotherapist recommended I continue privately, with another acupuncturist. Unfortunately, my finances were rather low after the house move, but I did top up with private acupuncture treatments later that year.

During the winter of 2010, I learned through the grapevine that Dennis had recently published a memoir called *Let the People Decide*. I have always admired Dennis's political career, for he has always in my view been a campaigner for positive change.

I felt compelled to read his memoir.

The book was full of stories from his early life, of his vocation, his family, his first marriage, his current relationship, and his young son Adam. However, it appeared I did not exist, for he never mentioned me or our marriage!

How very sad, that he denied ten years of his life…

In early 2011, I was asked to teach organic horticulture, in several schools.

Every school was different; I visited some with established school gardens and some with just a bare schoolyard. I liaised with teachers and pupils on possible development of the sites, relishing each new challenge.

My GP had recommended that I work part-time hours, which was really as much as I could manage, for my energy levels remained low, and I knew I would suffer the consequences, if I overdid anything. My physiotherapist advocated avoiding repetitive movements and rotating tasks as needed. I followed her advice and delegated as much as possible. The children were more than happy to dig soil, plant seeds and weed…

In 2011, I also wanted to celebrate my first birthday in my new home!

On March 8, 2011, I envisaged a small party for a few friends. However, the house move had finally caught up with me, and I suffered a bout of severe pain and inflammation in my lower bowel.

I had no option but to seek the support of my GP, who prescribed a course of strong antibiotics. Although I had avoided antibiotics in recent years, I knew I had to take this course, as I could feel the inflammation move into the lymph glands in my groin. Thankfully, the pain soon receded. However, again I felt it necessary to see my gastrointestinal consultant, back in Dublin.

I duly returned to the capital city, where it was suggested that I have yet another biopsy on my bowel. This would be my fifth or perhaps sixth biopsy, I remain uncertain. Since the internal bleeding began in 2000, I had also endured two colonoscopies and two proctograms—don't ask me for descriptions as they were not at all pleasant. I again felt increasingly stressed, as I awaited yet another appointment in Dublin.

In the meantime, I had another series of medical appointments, for the Haematology Department. A new genetic marker had been discovered in my blood, called Prothrombin Gene Mutation. Combined with the Factor V Leiden marker, it appeared that I was around ten times more likely to suffer a deep vein thrombosis or DVT, than the general population. Again, it was suggested that I take anticoagulants, for long periods of travel or inactivity.

I believe there is some discussion on whether sticky blood is one of several predisposing factors to developing fibromyalgia. Who knows? Time and scientific research will tell.

Happily, I received my first appointment with David Foley, who took my lengthy medical history, examined my tongue, took a note of my pulse, checked my nails, and told me I would probably need to take herbal medicine for two years. It seemed like such a long time back then, but I am so very glad I followed his advice. Several months into my herbal treatment, I began to notice small improvements. The blight of repeated lung infections finally lost its grip, and the bouts of bleeding from my bowels abated, for the first time in eleven years!

I had always connected the reoccurrence of these ailments to stressful events in my life. I was very grateful for a reprieve.

Sadly, one event in early May 2011 sent my stress levels **soaring**—a HUGE bog fire erupted between Dungloe and the village of Lettermacaward. Memories of the Kerrytown fire resurfaced once again, and I could not settle nor sleep. I can still remember driving uphill from my home during the night, to check on the vicious flames that scarred the night sky. I remained shocked, powerless, and full of disbelief.

Twelve units of the fire service bravely battled those horrific fires, and an Air Corps helicopter had to drop 1200 litre buckets of water on the flames, before they were finally extinguished. Bog fires continue to be an annual blight on this beautiful landscape. When will it all end?

Around this time, I discovered a leaflet designed for asthma sufferers in my local chemist. Although I had never been diagnosed as asthmatic, I wanted to conquer my intermittent bouts of shortness of breath, which often appeared for no apparent reason. I also wanted to stop using an inhaler.

Following the leaflet's advice, I introduced a new cleaning regime. As I no longer had carpets, I steam cleaned my floors, I wet dusted my furniture, and I continued to avoid harsh chemicals, using only environmentally friendly cleaning products. I eventually changed all my bedding to hypoallergenic and aired it regularly as advised. I also invested in super comfortable pillows and a very soft mattress topper.

The night time bouts of shortness of breath all but disappeared. Over time, I pinpointed one more *culprit*; if I had any contact with moulds the breathing difficulties returned. I stopped swimming in indoor pools.

Acupuncture had helped get me off the terrible cycle of insomnia, but I now recognise that keeping to a regular bedtime and indeed rising time in the morning, aids good quality sleep, and helps to minimise my fibromyalgia symptoms. If I sit up late or linger in bed a little longer, the old insomnia pattern begins to creep back on board.

But back to 2011!

By summer 2011, each school had an organic vegetable patch filled with produce, as well as plans for improving the gardens, year on year. Once the schools closed for their summer break, I rewarded myself with a real treat—a trip to Dublin, to see Neil Diamond. On a "Hot Summer's Night" on June 25, 2011, I danced the night away to "Sweet Caroline", "Solitary Man", "I am I said", "Crackling Rosie"...

Chatting to the ecstatic crowds in the Aviva Stadium, Neil quipped that he was single and longed for a nice woman to keep his feet warm at night. If he had been auditioning, I would have applied!

On the plane home, Daniel O'Donnell and his wife Majella, joined myself and a small group of other travellers, who had been at Neil's concert. Daniel wanted to know all the *craic* about our legendary night out!

In August 2011, I received a follow-up appointment to see a new female rheumatologist at Manorhamilton, in County Leitrim. Unfortunately, the hospital is not on a regular bus route, and it was a considerable distance for me to drive, so I broke the journey into bite-sized pieces and stayed overnight in Leitrim, creating another mini break. The following morning, I sat before a new doctor who was incredibly kind and supportive, like her predecessor. She took her time reviewing my medical history, and my experiences with Amitriptyline and Lyrica.

"I cannot rule out a diagnosis of rheumatoid arthritis in addition to fibromyalgia," she said.

Since I had experienced bouts of multiple joint pains, since my early thirties, this seemed a credible diagnosis as fibromyalgia can co-exist with other autoimmune disorders.

"We have tried all the major drug routes. However, you are extremely proactive and you are doing everything I would recommend," she concluded.

Indeed, I later discovered that I was following all the advice given on Arthritis Ireland's fibromyalgia information leaflet, which I took home to read. I departed Manorhamilton with the assurance that if I needed the hospital's support, I could telephone for assistance. It was a great relief to have another supportive team to call on. However, I continued to question the significance of my lung problems and wondered if I could still perhaps be suffering from lupus.

Nearing the end of 2011, I received an appointment for another bowel biopsy, but I told the doctors, "No more."

I was tired of biopsies, and I was tired of repeated trips to Dublin, for each biopsy had entailed three visits, one to see my consultant, one overnight trip accompanied by a friend for the procedure, and then another one for the results. It had been a HUGE strain on both my physical energy and my limited financial resources. Although my decision could be described as foolhardy, I am happy to report that as I write, I have not experienced any internal bleeding or bowel infections for over five years!

Another rejuvenating holiday was much needed, and I finally visited the lovely island of Madeira in the autumn of 2011. It has a breathtaking landscape, but I would not like to drive on its roads, particularly in the more rugged north. I took a day trip there, which included travelling to the island's highest point. I was afraid to look out of the window, as we were surrounded by vertiginous drops!

I did though, enjoy two weeks of swimming in an outdoor pool, languishing on a sun lounger, eating beautiful food, and discovering Madeira's many horticultural delights. However, my first holiday priority was a boat trip to see the island's dolphins. I was full of anticipation as I sped out to sea, to witness these beautiful creatures, playing in the mighty Atlantic. I would just love to swim with dolphins in the wild; I have placed this dream on my *wish list*.

I must add that although I have travelled extensively, every time I fly home via Donegal Airport, I am blown away by the views of my own native county. No other place I have seen compares.

Rosses Writers were ready to publish our first book—a collection of short stories, poems, photographs and artwork. My two creative pieces, "Two Roses" and "A Grey Day" were included, as well as "Heavenly Delights" about my love of ice cream, and "A Special Birthday Present", the story of getting communion from the pope.

Our labour of love was named *Patchwork* after a quilt which one of our members had created, as therapy after the death of her husband. Our book was launched to a lovely audience of family, friends and local residents. All proceeds went to charity.

The winter of 2011/12 saw me let go of much more *baggage* from my past, as I continued to space clear. I released everything that made me feel sad, angry, lonely…

As a result of these efforts, I feel I am at long last, much better at asking for help. I counted all the people who have supported me since my house move, and they exceeded ONE HUNDRED!

Life was certainly settling into a much healthier, fulfilling place.

However, in late January I sensed something was wrong with dear Ginger, for he was lying under the settee and seemed to have difficulty breathing. I rushed him to the vet, who guessed that he might have a tumour in his chest. He gave him an injection, but suggested he would need an X-ray to confirm his suspicions. My darling Ginger was soon diagnosed with feline leukaemia, and a tumour on his thymus gland.

I telephoned a dear friend for therapeutic support with radionics, and Ginger rallied round for two or three days, which he spent at home. However, he was no longer able to jump onto fences or walls and could only sit quietly, surveying his favourite places. Sadly, his reprieve was short lived, and his breathing began to labour once more. Ann accompanied us to the vet, where Ginger joined Snowie, Toby, and Angel in Heaven. He was barely six years old.

I planted a witch hazel tree in my front garden in his memory. It is the first shrub to flower every spring near the date of his passing, and its orange flowers remind me of his lovely coat. I no longer keep any pets, for I am not yet ready to endure another loss. I do though feed an amazing collection of beautiful birds that I can view through my kitchen window.

In April 2012, I attended a Natural Medicines Day in Dungloe in aid of charity, where I received a beautiful healing from local resident Máire Gallagher (no relation). I booked a private appointment with her at her home in Annagry and have since made many more appointments to benefit from her healing hands.

My Heritage in Schools work continued, and I added new schools, to my list of clients. I always learn so very much from the children and the teachers. Indeed, my education never stops!

Another great blessing is seeing lots of smiling children wave to me, in and out of school.

I sometimes hear a little voice calling, "Brigid, Brigid."

I then hear the latest news from the school or family garden:

"The bug hotel has lots of ladybirds and some woodlice."

"There are snails eating our lettuce."

"The school pond has tadpoles…"

These conversations continue to gladden my heart.

In the summer of 2012, I wanted to say a big "Thank You" for these and other blessings.

I had prayed to Our Lady throughout the good times and the bad. I felt it only fitting that my next trip abroad should be to Lourdes....

Insights from a Permanent Home

- The healing journey may be slow, but there are *nuggets of gold* on every corner!

Lourdes – June 2012

"Nature does not hurry, yet everything is accomplished."
Lao Tzu

It was late evening, when I arrived at a chic boutique hotel near the Rue de la Grotte—the route to Our Lady's Grotto, and the site where young Bernadette Soubirou had her first of eighteen visions of the Virgin Mary, more than a century ago.

I checked into my room for a three-night stay, and then sought out the grotto, hoping to take part in the nightly candlelight procession. The grotto eluded me. I was jet lagged and could not follow the simple directions from the hotel manager. Instead, I ate a delicious supper in a local tapas restaurant of Spanish omelette and chocolate fondant with white chocolate sauce—a snip at 10 euro. Soon afterwards, I climbed into my antique double bed and fell sound asleep.

I awoke at dawn, rose quietly, dressed and went outside to greet the day. It was too early to avail of breakfast or *le petit déjeuner*. However, the signpost that had eluded me last night now stood in plain view!

Following its instructions, I strode out in gentle light, through streets that were all but deserted. It was still only six fifteen.

I walked past the Basilica of Our Lady of the Rosary, to the location of Bernadette's first vision on February 11, 1858, where I stood silent and still, among a handful of early morning pilgrims, soaking in the peaceful energy. I then posted my bundle of petitions from friends and family, before buying two giant candles to say "Thank you," to Our Lady.

Several of my friends who had already visited, warned me of possible lengthy queues, outside Lourdes' famous healing baths. Happily, I joined a short queue forming on a series of wooden benches, one line for men, one for ladies, all sitting quietly together under an open shelter, while a gentle rain fell outside, bringing an unexpected gift of clouds of delicate perfume, from the adjacent linden trees. I soon discovered that I was surrounded by a group of pilgrims from Portugal. I cannot speak a word of Portuguese, so I simply smiled at my new neighbours.

Time passed quietly, until a nun took charge of a microphone, and we prayed the rosary together. Two ladies later approached said nun and were deemed fit to hold the microphone for the next round of prayers. They began their recitation, and the mike was immediately grabbed back—I do not know why. I began to giggle and was joined by several of my new comrades, all chuckling at the absurdity of it all. Laughter has no language barriers!

A series of official Lourdes helpers began to gather, as it approached nine o'clock. They all worked with military precision, to usher us to new benches just outside the doors to the baths—signal, move, signal, move…

I followed their instructions, until I finally arrived next to cubicle number two, which was screened off by a heavy plastic curtain. The walls facing me held a series of written instructions, in several languages, on the protocol for the healing baths. I had a few minutes to digest them before I was shown inside by a smiling lady with a familiar Scottish accent—she was from Stirlingshire!

I immediately felt more at ease.

Following her advice, I hung my clothes on a peg above a chair and wrapped a blue cotton cape around myself for modesty, as my inquisitive eyes noted another five ladies in the room, while one pilgrim was being immersed in the healing spring, now separated from our vision, by a twin plastic curtain.

Suddenly, it was my turn for immersion, and I was guided behind said curtain and down two stone steps, into a bath of **very** cold healing water. I was now advised to hold my bra in my right hand, while two ladies replaced the blue cape with a wet white sheet, before I was led to a statue of Our Lady at the end of the bath, which I kissed as I prayed for healing—as per written instructions.

Meanwhile, my assistants pushed me down into the water and urged me to sit back. Unfortunately, I was now kneeling and unable to move my knees into a sitting position. Before I could protest, I was deftly guided out again, my bra was retied for me, and the sheet replaced with the blue cloak. It all passed in a whirl, and I was back behind the curtain, changing into my clothes in what seemed like seconds—all part of a very efficient operation.

I parted the healing baths saying, "Merci," in my very best French accent.

I walked back to central Lourdes and bought my petit déjeuner at a nearby café, before creeping back to my lovely bed, where I slept again until afternoon. It felt like a very deep, healing sleep, during which I was shedding LOTS of old dead wounds. On waking, I took a gentle walk around town, ate a simple supper, and retired once more, to my very comfortable bed.

The following morning, I awoke late and breakfasted in my hotel. Out of the blue, I felt compelled to return to the healing baths—not what I had originally planned for my final day in Lourdes. I walked back through now familiar streets, past the basilica and the grotto, both already filling with large crowds of pilgrims.

The queue that awaited me was rather large, with perhaps one hundred people, all sitting expectantly on the wooden benches. Happily, my second waiting time was short, due to the continuing, efficient queuing system. By some strange coincidence, I returned to cubicle number two, where I was ushered inside, undressed, and walked through the curtains awaiting my second immersion. I was well prepared this time and sat back in the spring water right up to my neck!

I was standing outside in bright sunshine by nine fifteen.

Reviewing my two healing experiences, the first took several hours patiently spent on a hard bench, interspersed with fun moments, great camaraderie and divine fragrance. The second took little effort and was over quickly. You could compare these to our journey through life—the easiest and quickest route might get you there on time, but you learn more about yourself and others, along the longer, more scenic route!

I now felt compelled to attend confession, and I moved to another, happily small queue for an English speaking priest.

Although I had attended confession a number of times in recent years, this conversation was very relaxed, and I poured out my past.

As I left the confessional the priest told me, "Use the strength you have gained from your experiences, to help others."

I departed Lourdes feeling somewhat lighter, as I journeyed onwards by train, to the historical city of Carcassonne. The Pyrenean Mountains stood proudly in the distance, still topped in snow, as I gazed soporifically out of the windows.

"Les Pyrenees sont couvert de glaces," my brain murmured!

The Pyrenees are covered in ice, or is my school girl French confused? I pondered on whether glaces is ice, or indeed my favourite ice cream!

Travelling to Carcassonne was yet another pilgrimage for me, as I had become fascinated by the history of its Cathar people, after reading the novel *Labyrinth* by Kate Mosse.

Cathars also known as the Albigensians, believed in two Gods—the God of Good and the God of Evil. Cathar priests were known as parfaits, and as women were considered equals, there were also female *parfaits*. Their sole religious sacrament, the *consolamentum*, was believed to remove all sin, and was received as death *came nigh*.

They found killing abhorrent and did not eat meat, or indeed use any other animal products. They also believed in reincarnation. Unfortunately, Pope Innocent III and the Catholic Church, felt threatened by their beliefs. In June 1209, a crusade was ordered against them.

Carcassonne fell under siege from 1 to 15 August 1209, and Viscount Raymond Roger Trencavel of the city's Château Comtal, was captured. He died in prison on November 10, of that same year. Meanwhile, the crusades continued, and many more sieges followed including Lavaur, Minerve, Termes, three sieges of Toulouse…

In November 1229, Pope Gregory IX ordered the notorious Inquisition, under the leadership of the Dominican Order. On March 16, 1244, more than two hundred Cathar men, women and children, who had refused to recant their faith, were burned alive on a pyre, after enduring a siege of the fortress of Montségur, lasting ten months. On the eve of the pyre, it is believed that four people managed to escape, fleeing towards Usson Castle, where they retrieved their churches' treasures, which had been hidden during the siege. There is some speculation over what these treasures included…

The last burning of a Cathar, was in 1321.

It is difficult to estimate the total number of lives lost, during this period. However, it is believed that around one million people, of both Cathar and Catholic faiths, were murdered indiscriminately. Both the crusades and the Inquisition, remain a sad blight on the history of the Catholic Church.

On a happier note, the old *Cité* of Carcassonne has been restored and preserved. It was declared a UNESCO World Heritage Site in 1997. My sister Marie had visited briefly and was smitten by its charm; I knew I would enjoy my visit.

I had pre-booked an apartment, full of period charm, in Rue de la Gaffe, nestled beneath the hilltop home of the old cité and Château Comtal. The cité walls originated in the thirteenth century and still stand proudly, with their fifty-three towers and drawbridge intact. The Pont Vieux (old bridge) spans the River Aude and links the older parts of Carcassonne with the more modern district known as the Bastide Saint-Louis.

A short but steep walk, from the Rue de la Gaffe, took me upwards to the old cité, where I was rewarded with an abundance of quaint shops, all vying for my attention. Numerous gastronomic delights provided a feast on my senses, from a myriad of lovely restaurants, set among tranquil gardens.

I delighted in trying the region's famous dish of cassoulet, a dish of duck and Toulouse sausage, laid on a comforting bed of white haricot beans. I also sampled some wonderfully therapeutic ice cream—café, cassis, citron, chocolat, framboise…

My relaxed demeanour continued throughout my week in Carcassonne, and I did very little apart from walking to the cité and revelling in its charms; I made a pilgrimage up the steep slopes every day that week.

The interior of the Château Comtal seduced me too, as I toured its ancient halls and ramparts, and drank in the views of the River Aude and the Languedoc region below. Despite its somewhat sad history, I felt a great sense of peace within the château's walls.

I stepped back in time, once again, amid the eleventh century Basilica of St. Nazaire and St. Celse, as pigeons flew above a trio of exquisite singers, who seemed oblivious to bird droppings falling from above. I returned for Sunday mass and happily avoided any ornithological hits!

The plans I had envisaged, of visiting Montségur, Lastours... dissipated as the *Lourdes effect* bathed my being. My lasting memory of Carcassonne, is of lying on my antique wrought iron bed, in the Rue de la Gaffe, *mesmerised* by the stars, the cité and the château. I have vowed to return some day....

Insights from Lourdes

- Lourdes heals in unexpected ways…

- Perhaps I have lived in Carcassonne before?

The Lourdes Effect – summer 2012

"Beware the barrenness of a busy life."

Socrates

Between returning from Lourdes, and my Tom Jones concert experience, I ticked off another wish from my list, when my bijou garden was included in the Donegal Garden Trail for 2012. It had taken me five years to fulfil this dream; thus, I felt an immense sense of achievement, and dare I say it—pride!

Let me guide you round my garden as it was at the end of July 2012:

You would be *welcomed* by three slender birch trees, standing amidst a sea of smiling cornflowers, corncockle, poppies, wild campion… This wild flower meadow, which cost less than 5 euro, provides an ongoing haven for bees and butterflies.

To your left is my herb garden, filled with aromatic rosemary, tall fronds of dill and fennel, silver haired sage, and chives topped with purple pompom flower heads. Behind these culinary delights lies my spring bed, filled with speckled lungwort, pink perennial geraniums, purple foxgloves, and several species of aquilegia, also known as columbine or *grannies' bonnet*.

A wildlife pond covered in marginal plants, hides behind a wall of rosa pimpinellifolia, with yellow evening primrose, and majestic acanthus or *bear's breeches*. This *small sea* is surrounded by pale candelabra primula, purple astilbe, fiery mimulus and several varieties of iris. Climbing roses and clematis send out new branches, laden with flowers against the walls behind.

A purple elder shades some Crocosmia Lucifer, brought back from my travels in Madeira. They stand to attention, beside some deep purple scabious, which I rescued from a garden centre, in a state of near death. Happily, they have now made a full recovery!

A whitewashed raised bed, made from reclaimed breeze blocks, is filled with three apple trees, surrounded by an abundance of wild strawberries, sown from seed while I worked at Glenveagh.

Each and every plant in my garden carries a special memory.

I offered my Donegal Garden Trail visitors a guided tour, and their generous donations wound their way to my favourite Donegal animal charities.

In autumn, I resumed my teaching work with the transition year students in Dungloe. This was to be my last winter spent there, as my body reiterated the Lourdes message: "Slow down and rest more."

I began to visualise a trip to sunny climes for the winter of 2013, and wondered about visiting Bali, a long-held dream. I began to research flight and accommodation costs, and reckoned it might just be doable, on my limited income. Sunshine holidays have been a key ingredient in my healing *recipe*, and I am now quite proficient in arranging budget holidays!

Meantime, the *Lourdes effect* continued.

I bought a copy of one of my favourite magazines and discovered they were holding a competition for writing a memoir. The winner would get a publishing contract. Although the competition deadline was October 31, 2012, a mere two months away, I felt I just had to enter. I must add that before reading said magazine, I had absolutely no intention of writing another book!

I took the competition details to the next meeting of the Rosses Writers, and a fellow writer Kate decided to enter too. Kate was already a published author, and I greatly admire her writing style. Thus, we encouraged one another, as our potential manuscripts grew. I was able to submit my first three chapters for the writing competition, before the closing date. Sadly, neither Kate nor I won a prize.

In early 2013, I returned for my annual top-up of acupuncture treatments. I was in much better shape than the previous year.

My physiotherapist noticed immediately, "You look much better, Brigid, your face is no longer grey," she commented.

I had not realised I had looked so off colour before, but sure enough when I look at old photographs, she was spot on—I did look somewhat grey!

People often wonder if acupuncture is painful. Yes, it can be, particularly when the needle is being inserted, but thereafter, I find a sense of calm seeps into my body, and I usually drift into a nice meditative state.

When I embark on a fresh series of treatments, I usually feel somewhat worse before I feel better. My joints can complain ferociously, I might feel extra sleepy, pee a lot…

This is sometimes called a *healing crisis*; thus, I always make sure I have cleared my diary of commitments for a day or two, to allow myself time to rest and restore.

I must add that I have experienced healing crisis during most of my natural medicine treatments, but I always trust that my body is letting go of any pain it no longer needs nor wants, not only on a physical level, but on an emotional, mental and spiritual level, for they are all interconnected. After two or three treatments, my negative symptoms fade, my chi or energy feels renewed, and I move on to the next stage of my healing journey.

Imbolc, is the first day of spring, and a day for new beginnings. It is also my patron saint, St Brigid's Day, who has many patronages, including poets and scholars. February 1, 2013, was therefore felt an auspicious day to launch Rosses Writers' second book.

My contributions included several short stories and one poem, on an eclectic mix of topics, including angels, pollution, Mayan prophecy, ancient Egypt and the Queen and Prince Philip's visit to Ireland!

In anticipation, we increased our print numbers, hoping to raise even more funds for local charities. Our launch was a big success, and few original copies were left unsold.

I will now move on to a more *earthly* topic:

Candida albicans yeast live alongside healthy bacteria in the gut to aid digestion, and the absorption of nutrients from our diet. A normal bowel can contain 4 to 5 lbs of these substances known collectively as *bowel flora*. Health problems can occur when Candida overgrows, due to a diet high in refined sugar and carbohydrates, repeated use of antibiotics, long periods of stress, the contraceptive pill…

Candida then changes into its mycelial form, which can burrow through the bowel wall, giving rise to what is known as a leaky gut. Toxins from the bowel can then seep into the bloodstream, leading to some or all of the following symptoms:

- Cravings for sugar, refined carbohydrates or alcohol
- Fatigue
- Lethargy
- Aching joints
- Sore muscles
- Insomnia
- Poor memory
- Depression
- Allergies
- Fungal infections e.g. Athlete's Foot or Thrush...

Sounds familiar?

Yes, pretty much all fibromyalgia symptoms come under the umbrella of a Candida albicans overgrowth. They also co-exist with some of the symptoms of SAD or seasonal affective disorder which I had already taken to task.

I had seen many clients in my natural medicines practice with Candida symptoms, and my diploma in Nutritional Medicine from Raworth College, helped me advise on diet and nutritional remedies.

In spring 2013, I embarked on an anti-Candida regime, that would last for a full six months. Up until this time, I had gently worked on my diet, reducing or eliminating foods that I could pinpoint as exacerbating my fibromyalgia symptoms. The anti–Candida diet eliminates:

- All sugar, including sweets, cakes, biscuits and fruits high in sugar
- Foods containing yeast
- Fermented products including vinegar and alcohol...
- Food carrying moulds—cheeses, cartons of fruit juice...

I had eliminated alcohol, another Candida no no, from my diet many moons before, as it had just added to my fatigue. I have never missed it.

Garlic is one of a number of supplements which aid in the elimination of Candida and the healthy restoration of the bowel. I already ate plenty of fresh garlic, but I increased my intake for good measure, and yes, I created quite a pong!

Coconut oil has become immensely popular in cooking and skin care. It contains a substance called caprylic acid which pierces the cell walls of Candida, destroying it in the process. I began to consume a tablespoon of raw, organic, coconut oil daily, to this end.

Finally, I added supplements of healthy bacteria in the form of probiotics. These are generally sold in health food stores and need to be kept refrigerated.

Drinking plenty of water is vital, during this period of high detoxification. Gentle exercise and rest also help.

I began to visualise the former overgrowth of Candida albicans starving of sugar, yeast and moulds, being attacked by the opposition army of garlic and caprylic acid, then being overrun with new healthy bacteria from the probiotics. I felt the first rounds of this mighty battle were won after a month or so, but the final defeat took the full six months!

You might wonder why I did not embark on this diet sooner. Purely and simply, this diet is **very** cathartic, and when the yeast is dying off, you feel incredibly poorly. However, once I had passed the initial *die off* period, I found the diet fairly easy to follow. My energy levels eventually began to rise, my head cleared of *fibro fog,* and I lost over a stone in weight.

Since coming off the diet, I have continued to fine-tune my eating habits. My consumption of sugar, yeast and fermented foods remains low; I rarely eat cheese, red meat or highly processed foods, eating organic food where possible; I prefer to drink soya, almond or hazelnut milk instead of cow's milk, and I have reduced my caffeine consumption.

Breakfast for me is the most important meal of the day, where I eat at least one portion of protein, which seems to keep my blood sugar and energy levels more stable. I tend to eat small, regular meals these days for similar reasons.

The more I have refined my diet, the more easily I notice the effects certain foods have on my health. You will be glad to know that ice cream somehow released its addictive grasp in summer 2014, and I no longer get so many cravings!

I continued to attend David Foley for herbal supplementation, and two years from my first appointment, I could definitely feel the benefits. I was no longer suffering from endless chest infections, my bowel was healthy, and I felt an inner strength that I had not felt for many, many years, if at all.

I had done a HUGE amount of inner work on my addiction to busyness, and I feel Our Lady of Lourdes helped me move into a place of gentle self-acceptance. I had finally taken on board the message of my "Dream on the Nile" that compassion begins with oneself.

Donegal's wealth of creative talent continues to restore and uplift me, and on July 13, 2013, I experienced another healing boost that I will never forget.

Clannad, a band famed worldwide, who hail from nearby Dore, were appearing in concert as part of the Earagail Arts Festival. They would be ably supported by other local musical talents, Fidil (a young and energetic traditional group), the Henry Girls (three sisters who create beautiful harmonies), and Altan, another traditional music group of international repute. I just **had** to buy a ticket!

On the evening of the concert, I parked my car near the road to Mullaghderg beach and boarded a park and ride bus, that took me to Carrickfin Airport, the location of the huge concert marquee. Errigal Mountain stood majestically in the background, adding to the occasion. The day had been hot, and the evening was balmy; thus, I was able to dress for summer, in a maxi dress, embellished with what else but colourful flowers!

I looked out of the window, as I passed Auntie Anna and Uncle James's home, my former home in Ballymanus, Auntie Peggy's…

It seemed as though I was seeing the Rosses landscape for the very first time, and I felt somewhat emotional, knowing that I lived in an area of such breathtaking beauty. I alighted to a welcome from the students of the Rosses Community School, followed by many other local people who had volunteered to act as a reception team, helping people to their seats, selling programmes…

Ever the early bird, I found a vacant seat in the front row, and although I had come on my own as none of my close friends managed to procure a ticket, I did not feel at all lonely. Indeed, I was surrounded by lots of familiar, smiling faces, and I passed the time chatting to a number of my new companions.

The concert began, and all three support acts were phenomenal, but I had primarily come to see Clannad, and to hear Moya Brennan's magical, mystical voice. The air was electric with anticipation when they finally took centre stage, to enchant us with the theme tune from *Harry's Game*, "In a Lifetime", "Newgrange", "I Will Find You"…

Each new song added to my growing *euphoria*.

The stage took on an otherworldly air, and the band now seemed to glow. I could see their auras expand and fill with somewhat heavenly colours. I took some photographs from my prime front row seat, and you would swear that Moya Brennan had sprouted wings. Sadly, her wings were the curves of her harp!

Alas, the evening came to a close, and I made my way to the exit. However, standing before me was yet another Rosses music legend, Daniel O'Donnell. Suddenly, I remembered a message I had not passed on to him, the last time he crossed my path, after the Neil Diamond concert.

"Diarmuid Gavin told me he is asking for you and Majella," I interjected, still somewhat *high* from the music.

I was sitting back, on the Mullaghderg bus, before Daniel could reply!

He must have wondered, who on earth I was, but I had finally delivered a promised message, from my gardening hero, whom I had met for a second time in May 2012, at Donegal's North West Garden Show. I had enjoyed a friendly bit of banter and again had told him **very proudly**, that I hailed from the Rosses!

Two weeks after seeing Clannad, my garden opened for a

second time under the Donegal Garden Trail. This time round the garden was bathed in extreme sunshine, during a rare Donegal heatwave!

My trip to Lourdes and Carcassonne, the Tom Jones concert, the night of July 13, 2013, being included in the Donegal Garden Trail, and my two chats with Diarmuid Gavin all remain among my most cherished memories.

Insights from the Lourdes Effect

- Compassion begins with oneself

- Addictions take a HUGE amount of work to heal

- Donegal is ALIVE with creative talent.

Bali "Hi"

"Don't open a shop unless you know how to smile."

Jewish proverb

"Visit Bali," had remained patiently on my *wish list* for nearly twenty years. Finally, in October 2013, I travelled to my dream island.

Bali is the smallest of thirty-four provinces of the Indonesian islands and has suffered more than its share of hardship, with two bombing tragedies, in 2002 and 2005, decimating its tourist industry. The island is now recovering, with a record number of tourists of over 4 million, in 2015. Australians visitors top the poll, followed by Chinese, Malaysian ...

I arrived in Ngurah Rai Airport in the capital of Denpasar, after two long days of travel from Donegal, and was greeted by a kind, smiling face who introduced himself as Nyoman. The temperature outside was now around 30 degrees, so we quickly made our way to his complementary air conditioned taxi, and travelled onwards to the small, friendly, family run establishment that I had booked via the internet.

I planned to stay for nine nights on the south of the island, in the beach resort of Seminyak, before moving to the creative hub of the island, the town of Ubud.

I wanted to know EVERYTHING about the Balinese way of life, and I quizzed Nyoman:

"How long have you been working as a driver?"

"Eighteen years."

"Where do you live?"

"I stay at the hotel, but on Saturdays, I travel home to my village."

"Where is your village?"

"Two hours away, near the town of Tabanan."

Our conversation continued, until we reached my hotel.

"The beach is a short walk down that path," explained Nyoman. We were now at the check-in desk, and I turned round to say "Thank you," and give him a well deserved tip, but he had disappeared!

The girl who greeted me had impeccable manners, was super efficient, and with a radiant smile, handed me a very welcome glass of freshly squeezed fruit juice. Turning round to assess my new surroundings, I glimpsed a swimming pool, amid beautifully manicured gardens, and envisaged jumping into its cool waters VERY soon.

My room was a delight and featured a magnificent king size bed, decked out in white linen, adorned with small, sweetly scented flowers. The furniture was made from dark wood and included a long dressing table, two bedside cabinets, a large wardrobe, coffee table, and two comfortable chairs. The chairs sat next to a huge window that framed the pool and gardens. I entered the bathroom. It was home to a beautifully crafted, dark wood cabinet under a central wash basin, complete with lovely toiletries, and pristine white towels. A huge walk-in shower embraced the whole of one wall.

I knew I would enjoy my stay.

My tired body was soon refreshed with a lovely swim, before I languished by the poolside, people watching. The other residents appeared to be multinational and included a number of families with small children.

Finally, I unpacked before studying a menu of pampering therapies, opting for a reflexology treatment in my room—exactly what I needed. My tiredness soon evaporated as I relaxed atop my bed, with firm, capable hands working on my feet. The bill was a fraction of the price back in Ireland.

That evening, I dined early in the poolside restaurant, on chicken satay (spicy peanut sauce). It sat on its own mini barbeque, all sizzling hot and delicious. Soon after, I retired to my lovely bed, with a dose of homeopathic arnica, to further ease my jet lag.

Next day, I rose late and gazed in anticipation, as the chef poured pancake batter around a pinwheel of banana, before my first Balinese breakfast reached my table. I was not disappointed, for the pancake was truly delicious. I then discovered another new pleasure—Balinese coffee. It is very low in caffeine, and I downed several cups!

I needed to exercise my legs now, as I wanted to avoid blood clots after the lengthy flight. I had taken prophylaxis in the form of Clexane—an anticoagulant, and I had already injected my stomach area four times over the previous four days. I now had one more dose to administer. Although I had recently endured three long flights, my legs were incredibly comfortable. However, they were still swollen; thus, I pored over a local map, before making my way to the beach, for a decent walk. Perhaps, I could reach Kuta, around three miles away?

A few years before, I could not have envisaged such a lengthy walk, for my knees and hips had been very painful, indeed my knees regularly complained on rising or kneeling. Happily, these complaints magically disappeared with my first series of acupuncture treatments!

I wandered down a short path to a lovely beach that stretched way into the distance. Sun loungers spilled around its edges, beside a few, small beach cafés. Unfortunately, the sand was very soft and my feet soon sank, so I resorted to walking on a pavement that edged a quiet road alongside the beach. I was greeted with lots of curious, smiling faces all along my route.

Finally, I reached the outskirts of the city of Kuta, where a large shopping centre greeted me. I went inside. Unfortunately, it was filled with a number of shops that graced high streets back home. Hot, sweaty and once again in dire need of a drink, I found a small café and ordered a large glass of water, before escaping onto a new road lined with traditional Balinese shops and stalls.

Kuta was the site of the first Bali bombing, and I stopped to pray at a memorial for the 202 souls who lost their lives in 2002. I was joined by a small number of other tourists. I learned that a large Peace Park is planned for the site of the bombing, where the Sari Club once stood. This poignant experience was yet another reminder to live every day as though it were your last.

Over the following days, I walked a myriad of roads around Seminyak, lined with hundreds of independent shops, each displaying tempting treasures that would not have been out of place on the Côte d'Azur. Prices were incredibly low, and my purchases included six pieces of colourful, cotton knitwear from a small retailer in "Double Six Road" for around 20 euro!

I could now say a few Balinese greetings:

"Selamat pagi" meaning "Good morning."

"Selamat jalan" meaning "Goodbye,"

And

"Suksma" meaning "Thank you."

The hotel staff and local shopkeepers seemed to appreciate my linguistic efforts and rewarded me once again with lots of lovely smiles!

I took one guided tour from Seminyak, to the most southerly point on the island called Uluwatu, site of a sprawling Hindu temple. The surrounding forests are filled with monkeys, and I was warned to keep sunglasses, food and mobile phones out of their reach. I visualised *Three Wise Monkeys* living in the trees, wearing sunglasses and taking snaps of each other!

Partway through the trip, I alighted at beautiful Padang Padang beach, reached via hundreds of steep steps, through a narrow cave-like entrance. I did not realise at the time that this was the site of a major scene from the film *Eat Pray Love*, where Elizabeth Gilbert played by the lovely Julia Roberts, turns down a midnight swim from a nubile, naked Adonis. At this point in the film, she has a *light-bulb moment* and returns to the more dependable Philippe, who became her husband!

My journey ended with sunset at Jimbaran, a town that witnessed the 2005 Bali bombing tragedy. It is home to a number of five star hotels, and the beach is lined with expensive seafood restaurants.

My driver suggested, "Perhaps you would like to dine on the beach?"

"No, I think I shall explore a little instead," I replied, for I did not fancy dining alone on a beach at sunset, like actress Pauline Collins in the film *Shirley Valentine*!

Instead, I discovered the local fish market, filled with row upon row of benches overflowing with exotic seafood. Local people shopped there with their children, and I was able to capture more memorable photographs.

However, the highlight of my time in Seminyak was seeing my hotel's family perform a ceremony for the full moon. The preparations began in early morning, with everyone gathered in their best attire—the women in jewel coloured, lace tops with contrasting sashes and beautiful sarongs, the men in less colourful sarongs and crisp shirts. There was much busyness for several hours, as a series of baskets were piled high with fruit and flowers, and placed on several altars, as offerings to the Hindu gods.

Finally, they were ready for the official full moon ceremony.

I continued to watch *spellbound* through my bedroom window, as a Balinese priest dressed in brilliant white, began to recite prayers, while holding a bell and ringing it ceremoniously over his heart. I felt very privileged to witness this replica of my own Balinese bell, and I now knew why the hotel had such a beautiful, peaceful ambience.

I was sad leaving Seminyak, but I was excited at the prospect of four weeks in Ubud. My next journey took me northwards, past a succession of beautiful garden centres and shops, selling high-end furniture, wood and stone carvings, that could easily grace the pages of the magazine *House Beautiful.*

I had chosen to stay in new boutique style accommodation in Nyuh Kuning, a village on the edge of Ubud. It was also home to Ketut Liyer, the healer who found fame in both the book and the film of *Eat, Pray, Love.* The village borders the Sacred Monkey Forest, home to approximately 340 long tailed, macaque monkeys that attract thousands of visitors.

My accommodation provided eight delightful rooms for guests, and like many similar Balinese homestays, it is reached through the owner's living quarters. I walked past a series of outdoor family rooms, including the family kitchen, day room and temple, into a beautifully landscaped garden and room complex, complete with a small, stone swimming pool.

After a welcome drink of freshly squeezed fruit juice, I made my way upstairs and was greeted by a very comfortable four poster bed—what a pity to have no one to share it! The room also featured skilfully crafted, fitted wardrobes and an adjoining bathroom that was another five star experience, at a one star price. How lucky was I?

Once again, I felt at home immediately.

Breakfast was served on my own private balcony, as I looked out across the Sacred Monkey Forest and down over the stone pool. I enjoyed more delicious Balinese breakfasts with choices of banana pancakes, scrambled egg, French toast, freshly squeezed fruit juices…washed down with cups of aromatic Bali coffee.

I now spent my mornings swimming and lounging by the pool, reading my holiday novels, and watching the world go by. I felt so relaxed that I often sat on the edge of the pool, just meditating on my feet!

When the temperature had cooled somewhat, I delighted in the antics of the monkeys in the Sacred Monkey Forest, stopping to watch them play, or carry their young, or clean each other's coats…

I took LOTS of photographs.

The streets of Ubud filled with tourists from morning till late afternoon, all anxious to see my monkey friends. They then disappeared to other parts of the island, and Ubud became quiet once more.

"Jalan Monkey Forest" or Monkey Forest Road was home to many tempting boutiques, shops filled with artisan crafts, and a countless number of spas. I carried out lots of spa research and enjoyed more reflexology, several facials and massages…

My favourite spa was located down a quiet lane and had been built over a healing spring. I had long wanted to try a traditional Ayurvedic treatment called shirodhara, where warm, aromatic oil is poured slowly over the forehead for mental clarity and relaxation.

I booked a treatment, followed by a full body massage, and a bath filled with flowers. I emerged from my nirvana, feeling incredibly relaxed, yet the price of this heavenly pampering was only 15 euro!

The Balinese restaurants I visited were surrounded by yet more beautifully landscaped gardens, providing a plethora of photo opportunities. The food was always delicious, beautifully presented and modestly priced. An added bonus was the predominance of organic and raw food restaurants, as well as a regular organic food market, which my body loved. I enjoyed two all-you-can-eat buffets, with traditional Balinese dance entertainment, a few yards away from my accommodation, where I was also serenaded by frogs that lived in the restaurants' splendid ponds, filled with water lilies. I think they were happy to see visitors!

All these very affordable food blessings allowed me to have LOTS of guilt-free retail therapy, and I delighted in buying all my Christmas presents, a little stash of birthday gifts and cards, plus a surfeit of trendy, new clothes. However, many of the highlights of my holiday were unexpected and cost absolutely nothing.

I particularly enjoyed sitting up on my four-poster bed, looking out through a wall of glass, towards the Sacred Monkey Forest. The view was hypnotic, and I watched it for hours on end. I had arrived at the beginning of the rainy season, when it was common to have lightning storms at night. The sky lit up with hot reds, oranges and yellows, as I watched in AWE at the wonders of nature.

"Would you like to make some offerings today?" I was asked one morning.

Of course, I replied in the affirmative.

Later, Iput and Njurah, patiently explained how to make small woven baskets from bamboo leaves, while I followed their instructions. It was quite a precise operation, and I took several attempts to make a decent basket, before Njurah finally announced, "Now, you can fill it with flowers..."You must arrange them like this."

I copied him and gathered a small bundle of red, then orange, pink and purple flowers and laid them in my basket. Finally, I topped them with some green foliage, chopped in delicate strips. All the colours had been dictated by Bali's own version of feng shui called Tri Hita Karana. Eventually, I completed four baskets of offerings and then placed them on four separate altars within the *homestay*, whilst offering up my own private prayers. I placed one before Ganesh, the elephant god, who is associated with good fortune, and often graces Balinese shops. His statue guarded the swimming pool and several of the other shrines.

"How many offerings do you make each day?" I asked.

"Thirty," was the reply!

I had become friends with the shopkeeper next door called Ketut, who sold a beautiful selection of traditional crafts. I wanted to buy something special from her, which might bring both of us good luck, so I purchased a large wooden carving of Ganesh and a Buddha wall plaque. I have placed them both in my garden, welcoming yet more inner peace and good fortune…

A period of mass murder blighted the islands of Indonesia in 1965, when more than 5% of the population of Bali were massacred.

The small village of Petulu, located a few miles north of Ubud, is home to mass graves from this terrible period in the island's history. In the last week of October 1965, the villagers decided to hold a cleansing ceremony, and on November 7, large numbers of herons arrived in Petulu for the first time. A welcome ceremony followed for the herons, during which the officiating priest fell into a trance, and learned that the birds were there to guard the village. It is believed that they are the lost souls of those who died in the massacres.

When I heard the story of Petulu, I put a village visit at the top of my holiday *wish list*. I learned that the herons forage for food (mainly eels), from dawn till dusk, so I hired a local taxi driver—Erick—to collect me in time for their evening return to the village. As we arrived, the trees were filling with birds, many of them nesting. It was a truly wondrous sight.

"There is a warung (café) over there, where you can sit and watch," Erick suggested.

So I tentatively stepped along a little path through the paddy fields and joined half a dozen others watching the heron spectacle. A little later, I gazed in wonder through the lenses of a pair of complementary binoculars and marvelled at such a beautiful miracle, after the atrocities of the past.

Ubud hosts a huge number of daylight cultural activities, which allowed me to further enjoy myself and keep to my strict sleep routine. Most of these artistic blessings are centrally located, facilitating easy access on foot.

Advance research had given me many ideas for my holiday *wish list*, and I was inspired to book a *batik* workshop. A batik *veteran* from Calgary was already embellishing a sarong in browns and ochre, when I arrived in a taxi. After an introductory chat, I opted to create a floral wall hanging and proceeded to choose a suitable pattern, before tracing my picture onto cotton and pouring a thin trickle of molten wax onto my lines—quite a tricky task, which needed a very steady hand. Thankfully, I got some assistance from our teacher Widya, or I would have been waxing for several days!

Finally, I was able to complete my masterpiece, painting a series of tropical flowers in my favourite colourful hues. It was then washed to remove the wax, and I posed for a photograph with the resulting wall hanging, which now adorns my bedroom wall.

I befriended several other travellers—a couple from Switzerland, another from Austria, two ladies from Toronto, and an exuberant woman from Hawaii, who all shared information on favourite restaurants and other places of interest. My Austrian friends were exceptionally fit, and they often explored Ubud at dawn. At their suggestion, I began my one and only very early morning walking jaunt, in streets that were practically deserted. The only traffic I met was parents taking their children to school on scooters. Later, I spotted a sea of youngsters, gathered in orderly groups in the town's sports field, at a little past seven o'clock. I walked on past an array of shops with wares outside, free from the threat of theft, and I photographed rows of stone Hindu warriors silently waiting for their shop to open!

Finally, I arrived at the early morning flower market, now bustling with eager customers, amidst a glorious profusion of heavenly scented blooms, destined for altars all around the island. In a few short hours it would transform into the tourist craft market, filled with day tripping coach parties anxious to purchase Balinese souvenirs.

Ninety-two per cent of the Balinese population are Hindu, 5.7% Moslem while the remainder are a mix of Christian and Buddhist. The Balinese Hindu calendar is 210 days long and the largest of their festivals is Galungan, which fell on October 23 in 2013. Galungan is considered the day when ancestral spirits return to Earth to visit family, returning to Heaven ten days later, in a festival called Kuningan.

I felt incredibly blessed that my holiday had coincided with this Hindu tradition.

The islanders were incredibly busy in the days leading up to the festivals, making extra special offerings to their deities and erecting bamboo poles called *penjors*, that were carefully decorated with small hanging altars, weighed down by offerings of incense, fruit and flowers. Soon, every street was filled with colour, and the festive mood was contagious.

In another Galungan tradition, groups of young boys travelled the streets in dragon-like costumes. The dragon or *Barong*, is usually inhabited by two small boys, rather like a pantomime horse, all accompanied by a *band* playing drums and other noisy musical instruments. I watched the boys dance and cavort comically to crowds of residents, who happily added to the boys' monetary collection boxes. It reminded me of my childhood Halloween activities, when my sisters and I dressed in costumes to perform our singing *masterpieces* for neighbours!

On October 14, a member of the Balinese royal family passed away, giving rise to a special *Palebon Agung* Cremation Ceremony. On November 1, I was once again humbly honoured to witness a rare royal cremation procession. The date of November 1 was considered auspicious, although it was only two weeks after the death of Tjokorda Istri Sri Tjandrawati, wife of Tjokorda Gde Putra Sukawati. Normally, preparations for royal cremations take several months!

In Ubud Palace, I watched many skilled crafts people prepare a huge funeral tower 25 metres high, called a *Bade*, embellished with an array of colourful, scary masks and a cacophony of beautiful patterns. Incidentally, this tower was nine tiers tall—the maximum being eleven tiers, reserved for a ruling king.

I was somewhat apprehensive on the day of the cremation, fearing huge crowds amid 30 degree temperatures. However, my fears dissipated when I found a shady tree to stand under, awaiting the cremation procession. The streets were busy, but there was plenty of space for everyone, including lots of happy family groups. The children's antics kept me amused as I waited.

Earlier in the day, the corpse had been placed in the funeral tower at Ubud Palace, in preparation for the route along the main street to the Dalem Puri Royal Cemetery. I also learned that 2000 pallbearers carried it, changing teams every 100 metres. The Bade was preceded by a magnificent, purple, wooden sarcophagus in the shape of a bull, believed to ensure safe passage to the afterlife. The corpse would then be transferred to the sarcophagus at the cemetery, before being set alight by two large flame throwers.

I did not witness this latter part of the poignant proceedings, nor the cleansing and blessing of the remains, before the ashes were scattered off a beach in Sanur. However, I watched on in awe as the bull and the Bade slowly made their way towards me, preceded by groups of ladies in traditional dress, men playing an assortment of musical instruments, members of the royal family carried in sedan style chairs, together with a colourful procession of multinational residents and tourists.

As the Bade loomed closer, I was overcome with respect for those who had prepared such a vision—it was GIGANTIC. I also witnessed a fire engine spraying welcome water on the pallbearers, who must have been VERY hot!

I enjoyed several other momentous cultural experiences

including a trip to ARMA Art Museum, filled with wonderful Balinese treasures and surrounded by yet more beautiful gardens. It was another mighty feast for the senses.

I also visited Goa Gajah Temple dedicated to Ganesh, located a few miles outside Ubud, where I was met by a local guide, who accompanied me down a series of steps to an unusual cave temple, believed to be of ninth or eleventh century origin.

"Do you wish to bless yourself in our healing spring?" my guide queried, as I descended more steps, towards the temple.

How could I refuse? I was subsequently led to a statue of an ample bosomed lady, for a liquid blessing, where I sent out a few silent prayers to Ganesh, who is also known as the remover of obstacles. Finally, I entered the holy cave, totally devoid of visitors, where I prayed yet again, at an altar recess, before returning to face the World.

The Yoga Barn provided a walk down memory lane, when I booked a place on my first sound medicine class since my sessions with Harriet Buchan. I was unsure what to expect, but it was a lovely surprise when a Balinese priest entered the room, to speak very eloquently to our group, on the importance of sound and sacred ritual in Balinese culture. The class ended with a lovely meditation.

"Please lie down and relax," the priest suggested.

I closed my eyes, as he walked around the room, blessing us all with his sacred bell. I thanked my guardian angels for giving me such a wonderful gift.

I arrived for another sound medicine class, advertised as being on Sufi wisdom. A short talk followed, before we held our left hands high as we turned gently, focussing on our lowered right hands, to whirl in a Sufi meditation. I was transported back to Scotland and my last workshop in the wilds of the Trossachs, on "The Wisdom of The Warrior!"

I attended one more serendipitous, sound medicine class, scheduled to include sacred chanting—another former joy. However, a lovely Australian man was holidaying in Ubud and he had agreed to facilitate a class on shamanic wisdom!

After a series of introductions, he produced an abalone shell filled with dried sage and led our group in a smudging ritual. I took the sacred smoke and wove it around my body to cleanse my aura. A short time later we were led in a meditation, serenaded by a deerskin drum. I walked back to my lodgings, totally amazed that I had received **three** wonderful, sound healings, reminiscent of my past!

I ventured back to the Yoga Barn yet again, for one of its weekly specials, called Sunday Dance—somewhat akin to the Five Rhythms classes I had experienced before I had travelled to Sarajevo. I looked on at a series of lithe bodies in various states of undress; the *hot* young men were mostly topless, while most women showed off their toned bodies in skimpy tops, yoga pants or shorts. I now felt somewhat overdressed in my newly acquired cotton shift dress, which allowed plenty of air to circulate around my older, larger limbs!

However, once the music started, I determined to let go of my inhibitions and release my own inner *yogini*. I gyrated round the room, only stopping for water breaks, on the cool balcony. I finally admitted defeat, covered in a waterfall of sweat and a very red face. A cold shower would have been very useful!

My next exercise foray was somewhat more ambitious for me, and I would never in a month of Sunday Dances have considered it, had I not spoken to a lady, who told me her friend aged seventy had found it lots of fun. So boosted by this singular recommendation, I booked a **Downhill** Eco Bike Tour!

I was collected very early and joined a small group of other tourists, to journey north to Kintamani, a town overlooking Mount Batur, an active volcano rising to 1717m, which last erupted in 2000. The vast lava fields from the eruption of 1968 could be viewed from our breakfast stop in a local restaurant, where I wondered if we would witness a new volcanic eruption. Photographing the stunning mountain and adjacent lake, I questioned my sanity for I had not been on a bicycle for more than fifteen years!

Happily, a short stay of execution followed—a visit to a Luwak coffee plantation, where a poor creature called an Asian palm civet consumes coffee berries, digests and ferments them internally, and then defecates them in a new more aromatic form. Luwak coffee is known as the world's most expensive coffee. Indeed, Jack Nicholson and Morgan Freeman's ashes were placed on either side of a tin of Luwak coffee, atop a Himalayan mountain, in another of my favourite films, *The Bucket List*!

Leaving the coffee plantation behind, we stopped to begin the highlight of our trip—the downward descent!

Our tour guide equipped us with bicycles of the right size, helmets for our safety, and bottles of water to prevent dehydration. Meanwhile, a lovely Australian couple gave me great tips on the intricacies of gear changing, before our little group set off, on tarred roads, free from busy traffic and potholes.

Throughout our bike ride, we encountered only an occasional scooter, but lots of smiling children cheered us all along our route. Thankfully, I had a minder—a second tour guide— who kept a good watch over me and added to my education on gear changing. I soon relaxed and actually began to enjoy myself. However, I remained at the rear of our group for the first half of our trip!

"We will stop here," my minder announced.

We joined the others outside a village house, where the owners welcomed us into a series of buildings, not unlike my base in Nyuh Kuning, though somewhat less affluent. Ketut, one of our guides, pointed to two large round stones, sitting in the main courtyard.

"These stones guard the family members' placentas and will protect everyone throughout their lives," he said!

The rear of the compound held a garden, planted with rows of vegetables and a few flowers. The shade provided a welcome retreat from the sun for a family of chickens complete with chicks. Meanwhile, two suckling pigs looked out over a stone pig pen, with imploring eyes—their fate was sealed. Suckling pig is considered an essential part of traditional ceremonial delicacies, and sadly they lead a short life.

Villagers in rural areas are largely self-sufficient, supplementing home-grown vegetables, chicken and pork with locally grown rice.

The rice paddies were our next bike stop, where we learned of the length of the rice growing season—three in a year—the irrigation system known as *subak*, and the organic method of fertilisation, using ducklings to manure the fallow paddies, whilst fattening them up for the restaurant delights of Balinese smoked duck or crispy duck. Incidentally, everyone who works in the rice paddies shares in the season's crop, although the landowner gets the largest portion.

As we stood amidst the paddies, having stepped over subak streams and slippery clods of earth, to delight in the endless green landscape, I had a burning question and asked Ketut, "Are there many snakes in the rice paddies?"

His reply was brief, "The farmer kills them every morning."

Later, we witnessed a poor, muddy worker plough a flooded paddy field with a large version of a garden rotavator, and we learned that he earned around 7 euro for ploughing a field of ten square metres—considered a small fortune by Balinese standards. I wondered how many snakes he witnessed every day!

Our tour continued, stopping at a village temple filled with beautiful Balinese women, all chatting and laughing, whilst making flower offerings. They presented me with yet another wonderful photo opportunity, dressed in a rainbow of traditional lace tops and sarongs.

I was now wilting from the heat and asked, "Are we there yet?"

Thankfully, *The End* was in sight and we stopped, our guides handed out very welcome iced face flannels, before a group discussion followed, and we were asked, "Do you want to go for lunch now, or do you want to continue onwards for another 8km UPHILL?"

Guess which decision I made?

Six of my travelling companions voted for the lunch NOW option while two younger, energetic models chose the uphill route. Ten minutes later, our group delighted in a feast fit for a king, in a lovely restaurant, complete with its own organic vegetable garden. The *uphill team* joined us later, obviously the worse for wear and regretting their choice!

However, pride comes before a fall, and five days before I departed Bali, I came back down to earth with a thud.

It was early morning and a gentle rain fell, as I walked downstairs onto a set of wet stone steps. I must have still been a little giddy from my bicycle tour, for my feet suddenly slipped, my legs went skywards, and my derrière landed on the stone with a mighty thump. Oh the pain!

However, my first thought was to preserve my dignity and reposition my dress, now askew, in full view of the *homestay* staff. I quickly regained my composure and limped upstairs in searing pain, where I swallowed two homeopathic Arnica tablets, in the hope of a reprieve. It did not come.

Eventually, I managed to clamber onto my bed and lie down, now consumed by torrents of tears of both frustration and agony. I cried for several hours, despairing over my pain and my remaining holiday plans. I had wanted to participate in a day at a celebrated cookery school, and I had booked a whole **four-hour** spa marathon.

The Balinese are generally very reserved and thankfully gave me privacy to weep. I emerged with a hobble at lunchtime to the staff's great concern, and they advised me to seek medical attention. I initially felt reluctant, given my Donegal Accident and Emergency Department experiences, but by evening I saw the wisdom in their advice. I now had grave concerns. Would I be safe to travel home on the plane? Did I have any broken bones?

Next morning, I managed to gingerly board a taxi, accompanied by my accommodation's manager. We arrived at a medical clinic, where I was examined by a kind doctor, who advised, "You will need an X-ray."

I was transported by ambulance to a nearby hospital, shown to a waiting area, had my X- ray within minutes, waited to take it with me, arrived back at the clinic for an assessment of the results, viewed the X-ray with the kind doctor, received a type written report for my own GP, and was taken back to my accommodation in another ambulance. This all happened in less than **two hours** and cost me just 35 euro—HSE take note!

I was told, "You have no broken bones. However, you do have soft tissue damage. There are also a number of arthritic changes in both your lumbar and cervical spine."

I returned to my base in Nyuh Kuning and went to ground for two whole days. I could no longer swim, or walk to visit my monkey friends, but I had plenty of time to reflect. I realised I had taken a bike ride too far, as the message of Lourdes rose into my consciousness once again, "SLOW DOWN!"

On the second last day of my holiday, I made one final short trip, with the aid of a walking stick, to say a sad, "Goodbye" to my friends in the Sacred Monkey Forest. On my final day, I bade another tearful farewell to my lovely Balinese *homestay* friends, who had provided such exceptional hospitality.

Thankfully, I made the journey home, a tentative step at a time, aboard three separate planes and finally, the Donegal bus.

I visited my GP's surgery, with my Balinese X-ray and my written report, and was told, "The damage will take a few months to heal."

I was advised to take short daily walks, to increase the blood circulation to my lower back, and thus aid in its healing. I did **exactly** as I was told, and I could feel my back growing stronger as the weeks progressed. Approximately two months after my return, I was able to walk with ease.

I returned to Bali in autumn 2014, and enjoyed another wonderful, though slower paced, holiday on this beautiful island.

Insights from Bali "Hi"

- The best things in life are often FREE

- SLOW DOWN

- True wealth is good health

- It can take a lifetime to learn to love ourselves!

Epilogue

"Life is a journey, not a destination."
Ralph Waldo Emerson

One Sunday morning, shortly after my first visit to Bali, I stood outside Our Lady Star of the Sea Church, as several members of the choir emerged through the doorway.

"Do you want to join us?" they seemed to *sing* in unison.

I accepted their timely nudge, and I am now a **very** happy member of the choir. Three years later, I can even sing in Irish!

I have embraced the *Lessons of Lourdes* and I no longer visit Donegal schools under the Heritage in Schools scheme; I shed an abundance of tears, bidding farewell to the children and teachers.

On a brighter note, I had a **very** relaxing vacation in 2015 on the Greek islands of Skiathos and Skopelos, made famous by the film *Mamma Mia*. I sang more than usual whilst on holiday!

I continue to visit the Rock at Kerrytown on a regular basis; I take more gentle walks; I no longer open my garden for The Donegal Garden Trail, and I sit more often *watching the daisies...*

Leabharlanna Poibli Chathair Baile Átha Cliath
Dublin City Public Libraries

My Top Ten Tips for Self-Healing

1. Have faith in a Higher Power.
2. Appreciate every day and its gifts, for Life is perfect, right NOW.
3. Become proactive, research support groups and learn from others with your disease.
4. Seek out a sympathetic GP and consultant, and write down a list of questions before each visit.
5. Trust your intuition on what is the right treatment package for YOU; explore natural medicines and conventional medicine options, for both paths have much to offer.
6. Avoid isolation; cultivate mutually supportive relationships with family and friends; ask for help when necessary, and do not hide your true feelings behind a mask.
7. Learn to be gentle with yourself; REST and PACE your activities.
8. Find a JOYFUL form of exercise, and create a programme that nourishes you on all levels. Be prepared for setbacks but remember, "This too shall pass."
9. Eat small regular meals, avoiding highly processed foods. You may find some foods exacerbate your symptoms—seek professional advice, and eliminate any dietary culprits.
10. Nurture creative hobbies and a career path that feeds your Spirit. Serendipity will do the rest!

Contact the Author

Dear Reader,

I hope you enjoyed 'Watching The Daisies'.

As an author I love feedback. We are living in a wonderfully technological age, where you, the reader, have the power to influence discourse and have a say in how future books are written. Please do take the opportunity to let your voice be heard by submitting a review of my book on whatever site you purchased it from. It would be most appreciated.

I can also be contacted via the channels listed below.

Blog: https://www.watchingthedaisies.com
Twitter: @watchingthedai1
Facebook: https://www.Facebook.com/watchingthedaisies

Resources

The following resources have all helped me on my self-healing quest.

Arthritis Ireland www.arthritisireland.ie
Provides a booklet Living with Fibromyalgia.

GROW www.grow.ie
GROW offers a supported programme for growth and personal development to people with mental illness and those people experiencing difficulty in coping with life's challenges.

EFT www.emofree.com
This is the official website of EFT Founder Gary Craig. Free complete EFT tutorial.

Radionics www.radionic.co.uk
Website includes information and a list of radionic practitioners.

Bach Flower Essences www.bachcentre.com
Website provides information on Dr Edward Bach and Bach Flower Essences.

Transformation Game www.findhorn.org/workshops/game/products
Game is available to buy online.

SAD (Seasonal Affective Disorder) www.sada.org.uk
Offers help and support to those suffering SAD or winter blues.

Bibliography

The ISBN – 10 numbers are listed below, together with the years these books were first published.

Bach, Dr Edward. The Twelve Healers And Other Remedies. 158421464. 1933.
Bailey, Alice. Esoteric Healing. 1577331109. 1953.
Bek, Lilla. What Colour Are You? 0855001461. 1981.
Bek, Lilla and Pullar, Philippa. To The Light. 0041310268. 1985.
Bek, Lilla and Pullar, Philippa. The Seven Levels Of Healing. 0712694730. 1986.
Cameron, Julia. The Artist's Way. 1585421464. 1992.
Chopra, Deepak. Creating Health. 0395755158. 1987.
Gimbel, Theo. Form, Sound, Colour And Healing. 0852071868.
Kingston, Karen. Creating Sacred Space With Feng Shui. 0553069160. 1996.
Kingston, Karen. Clear Your Clutter With Feng Shui. 0767903595. 1998.
Kubler – Ross, Dr. Elizabeth. On Death And Dying. 1476775540. 1969.
Linn, Denise. Sacred Space. 10034539769X. 1995.
Page, Dr. Christine. Frontiers Of Health. 1844131076. 1992.
Roth, Gabrielle. Sweat Your Prayers. 0874779596. 1997.
Samms, Jamie and Carlson, David. Medicine Cards. 0312204914. 1988.
Tisserand, Robert. The Art Of Aromatherapy. 085207140X. 1977.
Wall, Vicky. Aura Soma : Self Discovery Through Colour. 1594770654. 1991.
Wilde, Stuart. Life Was Never Meant To Be A Struggle. 1561705357. 1987.
Wilde, Stuart. The Trick To Money Is Having Some. 1561701688. 1989.

Acknowledgements

I could not have written this memoir without the help of a number of people. My family and friends have patiently read my words and given constructive criticism as needed; Rosses Writers have given me support and advice; Sue Leonard gave sound advice on my writing style and structure; Olive O'Brien of Creative Writing Ink has patiently edited my work and Brenda Tobin has given wise counsel on content. I have also been blessed to have the support of Laurence O'Bryan and his team at Books Go Social.

A big thank you also to Orla Kelly Publishing and to Rob Williams for cover design.

Thank you to each and every one of you, for without your support I would never have completed this journey.

Lightning Source UK Ltd.
Milton Keynes UK
UKOW04f1406061217
313972UK00003B/74/P